WARFIELD

ALSO BY W. N. HURLEY, JR.

Available from the publisher: Heritage Books, Inc.

Neikirk-Newkirk-Nikirk, Volume 1
Neikirk-Newkirk-Nikirk, Volume 2
Hurley Families in America, Volume 1
Hurley Families in America, Volume 2
John William Hines 1600, And His Descendants
Maddox, A Southern Maryland Family
Pratt Families of Virginia and Associated Families
Lowder Families in America

Our Maryland Heritage Series:

Book One:	*The Fry Families*
Book Two:	*The Walker Families*
Book Three:	*The Fulks Families*
Book Four:	*The Watkins Families*
Book Five:	*The King Families*
Book Six:	*The Burdette Families*
Book Seven:	*The Soper Families*
Book Eight:	*The Brandenburg Families*
Book Nine:	*The Purdum Families*
Book Ten:	*The Perry Families*
Book Eleven:	*The Stottlemyer Families*
Book Twelve:	*The Browning Families*
Book Thirteen:	*The Miles Families*
Book Fourteen:	*The Lewis Families*

Our Maryland Heritage

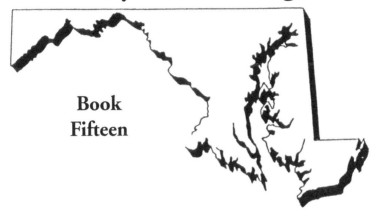

Book
Fifteen

The
Warfield
Families

William N. Hurley, Jr.

HERITAGE BOOKS
2007

HERITAGE BOOKS

AN IMPRINT OF HERITAGE BOOKS, INC.

Books, CDs, and more—Worldwide

For our listing of thousands of titles see our website
at
www.HeritageBooks.com

Published 2007 by
HERITAGE BOOKS, INC.
Publishing Division
65 East Main Street
Westminster, Maryland 21157-5026

International Standard Book Number: 978-0-7884-1211-6

INTRODUCTION

This is the Fifteenth in our series of families having their origins in Maryland, with descendants now found in all parts of the United States. This study of the Warfield families has been limited somewhat to those members of the family having their American origins originally in Anne Arundel County, Maryland, with movement into Montgomery County, and the counties from which it was formed, although others will be mentioned as they are found in other locations.

As will be seen, the Warfield families were among the early settlers of Anne Arundel County, from the humble beginnings of the immigrant indentured servant, to positions of wealth and prominence throughout the Colony, including one who became Governor of Maryland.

As colonists continued to arrive, seven original counties were formed in Maryland under the Colonial Governor: Anne Arundel; Charles; Kent; Somerset; St. Mary's; Calvert; and Talbot. As settlers moved steadily westward, and took up new lands, it was necessary to form new centers of government to serve them and, over time, sixteen new counties were formed from the original seven, as well as the City of Baltimore. The researcher must be familiar with this formation, in order to know the sources of information for any given timeframe. The following tabulation demonstrates the formation of each of the counties of Maryland:

Formation of the Counties of Maryland

Name of County	Formed	Source County or Counties
Allegany	1789	Washington
Anne Arundel	1650	Original County
Baltimore	1660	Anne Arundel
Calvert	1654	Original County
Caroline	1773	Dorchester & Queen Anne's
Carroll	1837	Baltimore & Frederick
Cecil	1674	Baltimore & Kent
Charles	1658	Original County
Dorchester	1669	Somerset & Talbot
Frederick	1748	Prince George's & Baltimore
Garrett	1872	Allegany
Harford	1773	Baltimore
Howard	1851	Anne Arundel
Kent	1642	Original County
Montgomery	1776	Frederick
Prince George's	1695	Calvert & Charles
Queen Anne's	1706	Dorchester, Kent & Talbot
Somerset	1666	Original County
St. Mary's	1637	Original County
Talbot	1662	Original County
Washington	1776	Frederick
Wicomico	1867	Somerset & Worcester
Worcester	1742	Somerset

ORDER OF PRESENTATION

We have divided this study into ten chapters for ease of reading and continuity of thought. We begin the study with a short chapter devoted to the immigrant ancestor, Richard Warfield, born in London c.1646, his marriage to Elinor Brown after his service as an indentured servant in the Maryland Colony, and their children.

Chapter 2 is devoted to the family of John Warfield, born 1673, son of the original immigrant.

Chapter 3 presents the family of Richard Warfield, one of the sons of John Warfield of 1673, and a grandson of the immigrant.

Chapter 4 is devoted to Benjamin Warfield, born 1702, yet another son of John of 1673, and a grandson of the immigrant.

Chapter 5 discusses the descendants of Edward Warfield, whose date of birth is lost in time, but who died in 1810, and was also a son of John Warfield of 1673, and a grandson of the immigrant. One of the sons of Edward was Levin Warfield, who married Anna Hobbs and had children, as discussed in this chapter.

Chapter 6 is devoted to the descendants of yet another Edward Warfield, whose birth is once again unknown, but who died in 1836 and was a son of Levin Warfield mentioned in the previous chapter. He was therefore a great great grandson of the immigrant ancestor, Richard Warfield of 1646.

In Chapter 7, we will discuss the descendants of another of the sons of Richard, the immigrant. This chapter deals with his son and namesake, Richard Warfield, Jr., born c.1677.

Chapter 8 continues the descendants of Richard Warfield, Jr. of 1677, through the lineage of his great grandson, Joseph Warfield born c.1758.

Chapter 9 contains reports of several members of the Warfield family who were found in Frederick County, but have not been identified within the main body of the text.

Chapter 10, in similar fashion, contains references to a number of family members found in records of Montgomery County and other Maryland locations.

The work is followed by a Bibliography of sources searched, and an all-name, every page, index.

A WORD OF CAUTION

The data contained in this report is not intended to be an all-inclusive genealogy of the family under study. It has been prepared from information found in a variety of sources, including records found at the library of the Montgomery County Historical Society, such as: family files, census returns, church and cemetery records, obituary collections, and the published books and abstracts held by the library in their research collection. We have expanded that by correspondence with others interested in the family, and by personal research in the courthouses of Montgomery, Frederick and other counties of the state of Maryland; the Hall of Records in Annapolis; and census records at the National Archives. In addition, rather extensive research has been conducted at the Family History Center of the Mormon Church in Montgomery County. We have not confirmed all of the data by personal examination of contemporary records, and can not, therefore, vouch for its accuracy in all cases. Others are, of course, just as prone to making mistakes as we are, but the information reported is as accurate as we could make it from the records studied.

We recognize that it is virtually impossible to report such an extensive amount of data without an error creeping in some place. Occasionally, we may have reported a date of birth, which is in reality the date of christening, or vice versa. In many cases, we will report dates as approximate, but they should lead you to the general time frame, so that you may distinguish between individuals with the same name. Throughout the text, I have used terms which should caution the reader: such as, apparently; may have been; reportedly; about; possibly; could be; and similar terminology, to indicate that the information given has either not been verified by extant contemporary records, or appears to fit a given set of circumstances which, of themselves, are believed to be correct.

Our goal has been to gather all of the available material into one convenient package, which should be accurate enough to provide the casual reader with an insight into their family history. The serious researcher should verify the material with independent research. Good luck, and please forgive our occasional error.

AND A WORD OF APPRECIATION

As mentioned in the Introduction, this is the fifteenth volume in our series titled generally *Our Maryland Heritage*. None of the books in the series could have been produced without assistance from a number of people; too many to list here individually.

I would, however, like to recognize a few of them who have perhaps contributed the most - and a very belated recognition it is at this point in the work. With apologies, then, for not having done so in the very first volume of the series, let me thank a few very important people.

Jackson Harvey Day very generously has permitted me to use his major study of *James Day of Browningsville and his Descendants* as a reference work for those families associated with the Day ancestry, saving me untold hours of independent research. In the course of time, members of most of the families in our series have intermarried with each other, and the Days have been busily engaged in that effort. Indeed, James Day, the subject of the study mentioned, was himself married to Sarah Warfield as his second wife, who bore him eight of his total of eighteen children from three marriages. Thus, many of the descendants of James Day reported by Jackson Harvey Day share Warfield ancestry.

Throughout the various books, there are references to letters received from various correspondents, each containing valuable personal information. Without attempting to rename them here, we want to recognize that contribution also.

There have been many others, many of whom I do not know, in libraries and courthouses, who have helped along the way, and we are grateful to them, also, for every piece of information shared.

SPECIAL NOTE OF THANKS

Finally, and most importantly, I want to thank Jane Sween, the librarian of the Montgomery County Historical Society, and the volunteers who work with her. Jane has untiringly assisted me with research of the files of the library, with the knowledge that only she possesses. It is also Jane who has guided me toward each new family for study, suggesting which might be the most important for the next effort. Jane is unquestionably the most valuable resource that can be found in the library, and without her, much of the available information would be difficult, if not impossible, to find.

CONTENTS

Chart of Descent
Arrangement of Presentation

Richard Warfield
1646
The Immigrant
Chapter 1
*
*

* *
*   *
*   John Warfield
*   1673
*   Chapter 2
*   *
*   * * * * * * * * * * * * * * * * * *
*   *   *   *
*   Richard Warfield   Benjamin Warfield   Edward Warfield
*   md Marian Caldwell   1702   1710
*   md Sarah Gambrill   md Rebecca Ridgely   md Rachel Riggs
*   Chapter 3   md Ann White   Chapter 5
*   Chapter 4   *
*   *
* * * * * *   Levin Warfield
       *   1753
Richard Warfield, Jr.   md Anna Hobbs
        1677   *
      Chapter 7   *
          *   Edward Warfield
          *   died 1836
Alexander Warfield   married 1805
    married 1723   Eunice Etchison
    Dinah Davidge   Chapter 6
          *
          *
Joshua M. Warfield
md Rachel Howard
          *
          *
    Joseph Warfield
        1758
      Chapter 8

CHAPTER 1

Richard Warfield
1646-1704
The Immigrant

The Warfield family is represented in Maryland (and America) quite early, and prominently. In the Warfield family file folder at the Library of the Montgomery County Historical Society, in Rockville, Maryland, there are numerous papers relating to the family, and its early history. One such paper from the records of Bertha Talbott states that records found in Annapolis show that one Richard Warfield arrived from Berkshire, England, and in 1662 and 1665 purchased the tract of land called *Wayfield* or *Warfield*, for three hundred pounds of tobacco. It appears from other sources that Richard was transported from England to the Colonies as an indentured servant by John Sisson about 1659, who died, and Richard then served part of his indenture under Cornelius Howard. The purchase of land as reported earlier would have been shortly after completion of the normal term of indenture of about four years. The origins of the family in England are apparently yet not proven, with some historians supporting Surrey, or the west end of London.

Yet another report in *The Warfields of Maryland*, 1898, by Professor Joshua Dorsey Warfield, repeat the writings of Edward Warfield in 1828, which is about the closest we will get to a first-hand report. He wrote: "From information obtained from my father, (Edward of John, the 1st), Richard Warfield, our progenitor, came early in the 17th century. He brought with him many implements of husbandry, household furniture and a variety of other articles necessary for planting. He was, thereby, enabled to establish himself very comfortably, and by his industry and steady application, soon secured a handsome estate. He lived to an advanced age and saw all of his children well settled." That account, written that much closer to the period in which Richard, the Immigrant, lived in the Maryland Colony, is perhaps more accurate than others. If, in fact, Richard brought with him the articles described, he was surely not an indentured servant. As noted following, however, one Richard

Warfield was surely transported to the Maryland Colony by John Sisson as an indentured servant; in 1674 he received a grant of land in Anne Arundel County, "for having served his time to Cornelius Howard." It is conceivable that there were two Richard Warfields in the Colony at about the same time.

As stated above, in 1898, Professor Joshua Dorsey Warfield published his book entitled *The Warfields of Maryland*, printed by The Daily Record Company in Baltimore. He was a member of the Historical Society of Maryland, and the book or pamphlet can probably be found in the library of the Society. A copy is available in the library of the Montgomery County Historical Society in Rockville. His study is devoted to the descendants of the immigrant ancestor, Richard Warfield, with the first few pages recounting the early origins of the family. According to Professor Warfield, the family had origins either in Wales, or in Normandy.

Unfortunately, that book contains very few dates, and with the repetition of names, it is rather difficult to follow the generations. We will not attempt to duplicate that study, but will report on that part of the family who are descended from Richard Warfield of 1646, who were later found in Montgomery County, and a few in adjoining counties, as they relate to those principally under study.

This Richard is referred to in *Founders of Anne Arundel and Howard Counties*, by Joshua Dorsey Warfield, stating that he settled west of Crownsville, in Anne Arundel County. This county is the place of origin of many of the families of Maryland, located along the Chesapeake Bay, where ships from England commonly unloaded their passengers and cargo. The Warfields intermarried with many of the other prominent families of Maryland, and later descendants include the surnames Howard, Duvall, Dorsey, Waters, King, and many other well-known families of the state.

From articles appearing in the Maryland Genealogical Society Bulletin, by Richard T. Foose, the family can be well traced to very early origins in England, which is recommended reading for anyone interested in the sixteenth century origins. It appears from those reports that the early immigrant ancestor of the family in Maryland has been well identified as Richard Warfield.

The most complete record of the family in America, and of its ancestry, appears to be set forth in Volume 1 of *Anne Arundel*

Gentry, by the highly respected Henry Wright Newman. His report on the family occupies well over one hundred pages in that volume and is highly recommended reading. Volumes 2 and 3 of the same report contain numerous references to members of the family, as they intermarried with other early families in Maryland. As to the immigrant ancestor of the family, Newman supports the accounts that Richard Warfield was transported to the Maryland Colony by John Sisson as an indentured servant. Newman concludes that little can be found from the published records relative to the assumed English background, and the family is not registered with the College of Arms. A check of *The General Armory of England, Scotland, Ireland and Wales,* by Sir Bernard Burke, does not reveal a single entry under the name Warfield.

The serious researcher of these early members of the family in Anne Arundel County should not overlook *Anne Arundel County Church Records of the 17th and 18th Centuries,* by F. Edward Wright. Valuable as well is *Anne Arundel County, Maryland Marriage Records 1777-1877,* compiled by John W. Powell for the Anne Arundel Genealogical Society. Finally, there is a two volume set of *Cemetery Inscriptions of Anne Arundel County, Maryland,* edited by John Thomas Gurney, III for the Genealogical Society.

The family is discussed in some detail beginning on page 203, in *Ancestral Colonial Families, Genealogy of the Welsh and Hyatt Families of Maryland and Their Kin,* by Luther W. Welsh, Lambert Moon Printing Company, Independence, Missouri, 1928.

We have examined each of these books just referred to, and excerpted some of the information. However, as stated elsewhere, our study here is more directed towards the Warfield families of Montgomery and Frederick Counties, who are in reality somewhat later generations descended primarily from the Anne Arundel lines.

Presumed by some to have been the son of John Warfield (1613) and Rachel Clarke, Richard Warfield was baptized April 27, 1646 at St. Dunstan's West, Fleet Street, London, and transported to the Maryland Colony about 1659 by John Sisson, settling in Anne Arundel County. Richard must have been transported from London, or a nearby port; a check of *The Bristol Registers of Servants Sent to Foreign Plantations 1654-1686,* by Peter Wilson Coldham, does not reveal the name of either Sisson as a Master, or any Warfield sailing from the port of Bristol during that period. About 1670, Richard was married in Anne Arundel County to Elinor Browne, born c.1649, died February 13, 1719 in Anne Arundel, daughter of Captain John Browne, Mariner. Richard died in 1704 in Anne Arundel, leaving a will. He was a planter, Captain of Militia, and a member of the first Vestry at St. Anne's, in Annapolis. He is widely credited with being the progenitor of the Warfield family in America. Anne Arundel County records of November 11, 1662 report the petition of John Sisson for land warrant for transportation of persons to the Colony including Richard Warfield. In all, he received six hundred acres, indicating that a number of others were transported. The will of John Sisson, probated March 16, 1663/4 bequeathed his servant boy Richard Warfield to Cornelius Howard. Richard had completed his indenture by 1669, at which time he and Edward Gardner were granted a tract of land called *Gardner's Warfield.* It was not until February 13, 1674/5 that Richard Warfield of Anne Arundel County proved his rights to fifty acres of land for serving his time to Cornelius Howard.

Over time, Richard extended his land holdings to over 2,000 acres, including the grants known as *Warfield's Right, Warfield's Forrest, Warfield's Plaines, Brandy, The Addition, and Warfield's Range.* The latter tract, located along the Middle River of the Patuxent, is closely identified with the family, being somewhat over fifteen hundred acres, and upon which several of the sons of Richard resided.

Richard reportedly married Elinor Brown, daughter of John, and they had children, born in Anne Arundel County. His will was probated February 11, 1703/4, and can be found at the Hall of Records in Annapolis. There, he mentions several tracts of land, and his children. They will be listed first as a family group, followed by individual listings of the four sons:
1. John Warfield, born c.1673/5, of whom more in Chapter 2.
2. Richard Warfield, Jr., born c.1677, and of whom more in Chapter 7.
3. Alexander Warfield, born c.1678, of whom more as Child 3.
4. Benjamin Warfield, born c.1680, of whom more as Child 4.
5. Mary Warfield, born 1679, died 1700; married to Captain John Howard, Jr., born about 1667, only son of John Howard

and Susannah Norwood. John Howard lived on the tract called *Timber Neck* in Baltimore County, and after the death of Mary about 1703, he was married secondly to Katherine Greenberry Ridgely, daughter of Nicholas Greenberry and the widow of Henry Ridgely. Mary was mother of three children:

a. Benjamin Howard of Baltimore County. Married 1716 to Catherine Buck.

b. Absolute Howard, died young.

c. Rachel Howard, married Colonel Charles Ridgely, son of Charles Ridgely and Deborah Dorsey.

6. Rachel Warfield, born about 1681, married c.1700 to George Yates, Jr., born c.1674, died September 13, 1717 in Baltimore County, Maryland, oldest son of George Yates, the Provincial Surveyor, lawyer and magistrate, and had children:

a. George Yates, III, born c.1701, died about 1742. Married c.1720 in King William County, Virginia, to the daughter of Michael Guinney, and had children, born in Caroline County, Virginia:

   (1) George Yates, IV, born c.1727, died December 11, 1777 in Caroline County. Styled Captain, he was married to Frances Fielding Lewis.

   (2) Michael Yates, born c.1722. A doctor, he married Martha Marshall.

   (3) William Yates.

b. Joshua Yates, born c.1703

c. Samuel Yates, born c.1704, died April 4, 1773. Married about 1725 to Joanna.

d. Benjamin Yates, born c.1707

e. Eleanor Yates, born c.1709

f. Mary Yates, born c.1711

g. Rachel Yates, born c.1713

7. Elinor Warfield, born July 10, 1683 of whom more as Child 7.

CHILD 3

Alexander Warfield
1678-1740

This son of Richard Warfield (1646) and Elinor Brown was born in Anne Arundel County about 1678, and died 1740. He lived south of the present village of Millersville on the tract called *Brandy* and also owned about thirteen hundred acres called *Venison Park*. A surveyor, he married Sarah Pierpont, and had children:

1. Samuel Warfield, married 1727 to Sarah Welsh, born November 26, 1711, daughter of Colonel John Welsh (1672) and his first wife, Thomasin Hopkins. Children:
   a. John Warfield, born about 1730; married in 1761 to Mary Chaney, and had children.
      (1) Richard Warfield, married first to Nancy Benson and second to Elizabeth Lucas. Children were born to both marriages.
          (a) Thomas Benson Warfield, married to Isabel Lucas.
          (b) Benjamin Benson Warfield, married to Ann Woodfield.
          (c) Richard Benson Warfield, married to Ann Marsh.
          (d) Ruth Warfield, born June 10, 1789, married her cousin, Jesse Pumphrey.
          (e) Mary Warfield.
          (f) Nancy Warfield, born 1805, married to her cousin, Thomas Warfield.
          (g) William Lucas Warfield, married Henrietta Yeadhall.
          (h) Rachel Warfield, married John Wellham.
          (i) Jonathan S. Warfield, married his cousin, Sarah Warfield.
          (j) Eleanor Warfield, married Dominick Shillenburg.
          (k) Sarah Warfield.

      (l) Enoch Warfield, born 1821, died 1898. Married first Caroline Hawkins and second September 30, 1852 to Flavilla Duvall of Prince George's County.

      (m) Caleb Warfield, married Margaret Williams of Pennsylvania and had children.

      (n) Joshua Warfield.

  (2) John Warfield, married to Mershaw.

  (3) Samuel Warfield, married to Susanna Donaldson and had children:

      (a) Thomas Warfield, married his cousin, Nancy Warfield, daughter of Richard Warfield and Elizabeth Lucas.

      (b) Allen Warfield, married first Miller and second Disney.

      (c) Sarah Warfield, married her cousin, Jonathan S. Warfield.

      (d) Dennis Warfield, married Elizabeth.

  (4) Benjamin Warfield, married Rebecca Spurrier and had children:

      (a) Allen Warfield, married Sarah Kelly.

      (b) Thomas Beale Warfield, married Elizabeth.

      (c) Launcelot Warfield.

      (d) Tabitha Warfield, married Cromwell.

      (e) Temperance Warfield, married Yeadhall.

      (f) Rebecca Warfield, married Yeadhall.

  (5) Nancy Warfield, married Edward Smith.

  (6) Betsy Warfield, married Charles Carroll.

  (7) Nelly Warfield, married William Westley.

  (8) Polly Warfield, married Thomas Forsythe.

  (9) Rachel Warfield, married David Clarke.

b. Vachel Warfield, married September 23, 1786 to Eleanor Griffith, daughter of Charles Griffith, Jr.

c. Gerard Warfield or Jared Warfield, married to Susanna Ryan and moved to Pennsylvania.

d. Samuel Warfield.

e. Richard Warfield, reportedly married a daughter of Thomas Welsh of South River.

f.   Welsh Warfield, died single.
g.   Mary Warfield, born October 22, 1754, married Green-
     bury Pumphrey. At least one son:
     (1)   Jesse Pumphrey, married to his cousin, Ruth War-
           field, born June 10, 1789, daughter of Richard
           Warfield and Nancy Benson.
2.   Alexander Warfield.
3.   Absolute Warfield, a bachelor. On October 19, 1748, the
     Maryland Gazette announced that Absolute Warfield, at Mrs.
     Sarah Warfield's house near the head of Severn River, has
     land for sale called *Venison Park,* in the fork of Patuxent
     River in Anne Arundel County, about six miles from Mr.
     Snowden's Iron Works.
4.   Richard Warfield, married Sarah Gaither, daughter of John
     Gaither, and had children:
a.   Lancelot Warfield.
b.   Richard Warfield, Jr., married Nancy Gassaway. Lived
     in Frederick County, and had at least one daughter:
     (1)   Sarah Warfield, married to her cousin, Amos
           Warfield, and had children, listed under her hus-
           band's name, which see.
5.   Rachel Warfield, married 1735 to Lancelot Todd.
6.   Sarah Warfield, married John Marriott.
7.   Catherine Warfield.

CHILD 4

Benjamin Warfield
1680-1718

This son of Richard Warfield (1646) and Elinor Brown was
born in Anne Arundel County about 1680 and died 1718, the
youngest son. He patented *Wincopen Neck* on the Savage and
Middle Rivers, and inherited part of *Warfield's Range,* but did not
live there. Married 1705 to Elizabeth Duvall, born August 4, 1687,
daughter of Captain John Duvall and Elizabeth Jones. After the
death of Benjamin, Elizabeth was married second to John Gaither,
II. Children of Benjamin and Elizabeth were:

1. Benjamin Warfield, Jr., died young.
2. Joshua Warfield, died 1779, married Ruth Davis, daughter of Thomas Davis. Children:
   a. Benjamin Warfield.
   b. Joshua Warfield.
   c. Henry Warfield.
   d. Thomas Warfield.
   e. Caleb Warfield.
   f. Mary Warfield.
   g. Elizabeth Warfield.
   h. Elinor Warfield.
3. Elizabeth Warfield, forn March 27, 1706; married October 2, 1722 to Colonel Henry Ridgely, III, son of Henry Ridgely, Jr. (1669) and Katherine Greenberry (1674). Children:
   a. Katherine Ridgely, born November 14, 1723, married Captain Philemon Dorsey (later Colonel), the son of Joshua and Ann Dorsey. At least one daughter:
      (1) Catherine Dorsey, born November 30, 1746, married Captain Benjamin Worthington Warfield of the Revolution, born 1734, died 1788, and are the ancestors of Governor Edwin Warfield (1848). Captain Benjamin was a son of Benjamin Warfield (1702) and his first wife, Rebecca Ridgely. They had several children, and descendants, discussed under their father's name in Chapter 4, which see.
   b. Ann Ridgely, born 1725, married Honorable Brice Thomas Beall Warthen.
   c. Greenberry Ridgely, born 1730, married Lucy Stringer.
   d. Henry Ridgely, born 1728, major, married Ann Dorsey, daughter of Joshua and Ann Dorsey.
   e. Nicholas Ridgely, died young.
   f. Benjamin Ridgely.
   g. Joshua Ridgely.
   h. Charles Greenberry Ridgely, born 1735, married Sarah Macgill.
   i. Elizabeth Ridgely, born 1737, married Colonel Thomas Dorsey, son of Basil Dorsey.
   j. Thomas Ridgely.

k.   Nicholas Ridgely.

l.   Sarah Ridgely, born 1745, married Colonel Charles Greenberry Griffith, son of Orlando Griffith.

CHILD 7

Elinor Warfield
1683-1752

This daughter of Richard Warfield (1646) and Elinor Brown was born July 10, 1683 in Anne Arundel County, and died 1752. Married August 24, 1704 to Caleb Dorsey, born November 11, 1685, son of the Honorable John Dorsey of *Hockley* in Anne Arundel County, and his wife Pleasance Ely. Thirteen children:

1.   Basil Dorsey, a twin, born July 25, 1705. Married Sarah Worthington, daughter of Thomas Worthington.

2.   Achsah Dorsey, a twin, born July 25, 1705. Married first April 3, 1728 to Amos Woodward, and second to Fotterell.

3.   Sophia Dorsey, born March 20, 1707. Married May 23, 1743 to Thomas Gough.

4.   John Dorsey, born October 7, 1708, died 1765. Married to Elizabeth Dorsey, daughter of Joshua Dorsey.

5.   Caleb Dorsey, Jr., born July 18, 1710, died 1772, of *Belmont.* Married 1735 to Priscilla Hill.

6.   Samuel Dorsey, born March 9, 1712, died single.

7.   Richard Dorsey, born June 10, 1714. Married Elizabeth Beale Nicholson, daughter of John Beale and Elizabeth Norwood.

8.   Eleanor Dorsey, born January 4, 1715. Married first Thomas Todd and second William Lynch.

9.   Edward Dorsey, born September 1, 1718, an attorney. Married Henrietta Maria Chew, daughter of Samuel Chew.

10.   Joshua Dorsey, born July 13, 1720, died single.

11.   Deborah Dorsey, born November 25, 1722. Married to Ely Dorsey, son of John Dorsey of Patuxent.

12.   Mary Dorsey, born May 18, 1725. Married John Ridgely.

13.   Thomas Beale Dorsey, born December 18, 1727. Married Ann Worthington, daughter of John Worthington, Jr., and Helen Hammond.

CHAPTER 2

John Warfield
1673/5-1718

This son of Richard Warfield (1646) and Elinor Brown, was born about 1673 to 1675 in Middle Creek Hundred, Anne Arundel County, Maryland, and died 1718. Married February 16, 1696 to Ruth Gaither, born September 8, 1679, oldest daughter of John Gaither (1646) of South River and his wife, Ruth Morley. Children:

1. Richard Warfield, of whom more in Chapter 3.
2. John Warfield, born c.1700, died 1776; married c.1740 to Rachel Dorsey, born July 6, 1717, died December 14, 1775 in Anne Arundel County, daughter of Joshua Dorsey (1686) and Anne Ridgely, and had children. He left a will dated February 8, 1773 and probated March 13, 1776, naming his wife and children. He was a slave holder, mentioning seven of them. Children:
   a. Anne Warfield, born December 6, 1741; married John Wayman and had at least two daughters:
      (1) Mary Wayman.
      (2) Amelia Wayman, married Colonel Lyde Griffith.
   b. John Warfield, born April 29, 1744, died 1776. Inherited the tract called *New Design* under his father's will, and the remainder of the land in the Barrens. He left a will dated November 30, 1775 and probated January 1, 1776, naming members of his family. To his brother Joshua, he left the tract he had earlier purchased from him, called *Warfield's Range,* and his interest in the tract *Resurvey on Harry's Lot.* He was a doctor and apparently single.
   c. Sarah B. Warfield, born November 12, 1746 and married to Colonel Henry Griffith. From the terms of the will of John Warfield, brother of Sarah, they had children:
      (1) Lloyd Griffith.
      (2) Allen Griffith, who received from his uncle the lands called *Warfield's Addition.*

d. Henry Warfield, born January 13, 1748. Not named in his father's will; apparently deceased.

e. Charles Warfield, born February 1, 1752; married Catherine Dorsey, daughter of John Dorsey (1734) and Ann Dorsey (Dorsey) (1740). He received 500 acres of land in the Barrens under the will of his father. He had six sons and six daughters, not one of whom was married.

f. Amelia Warfield, born April 3, 1755, died single.

g. Rachel Warfield, born October 1, 1757; married to Captain Samuel Griffith, born May 7, 1752, son of Henry Griffith (1720) and Ruth Hammond (1782).

h. Joshua Warfield, born April 27, 1761, of whom more.

3. Benjamin Warfield, born 1702, of whom more in Chapter 4.

4. Alexander Warfield, married Thomasine Worthington, born January 9, 1724, daughter of Thomas Worthington (1691) and Elizabeth Ridgely (1696), and had children. His will was dated November 18, 1749 and probated in Anne Arundel County, January 24, 1749. He mentions lands in Frederick County (later Montgomery) called *Warfield's Vineyard, Warfield's Range,* and *Timber Bottom.* After the death of Alexander, Thomasine was married second to Francis Simpson, whom she survived also. Children of Alexander were:

a. Elizabeth Warfield, married first West Burgess, and second John Dickerson.

b. Deborah Warfield, married Caleb Burgess.

c. Thomas Warfield, the eldest son, never married, but received the bulk of his father's land.

d. Alexander Warfield, born c.1737, died December 2, 1812, aged 75 years, 2 months, 27 days, single. Buried with his brother Brice, following.

e. Brice Warfield, born February 3, 1742, died April 30, 1817. Buried in the Warfield family cemetery on part of *Warfield's Delight,* near Johnsville, Frederick County. His wife was Susanna Dickerson, and their son is buried there also. Records indicate also a daughter:

(1) Surratt Dickerson Warfield, Sr., born June 7, 1787, of whom more.

(2)   Deborah Warfield, born February 18, 1792. Married March 29, 1813 to Benjamin Browning, born August 26, 1786, son of Jonathan Browning, Jr. (1750). Benjamin appears as head of household in the 1850 census for Clarksburg District of Montgomery County, with his wife and two male Brownings. The two are apparently a son of Benjamin and Deborah, and his son (their grandson). The two in the census were:
(a)   Alfred Browning, born c.1815, apparently married and widowed, with one son; living in the household of his parents:
1.   Surratt Dickerson Warfield Browning, born May 15, 1834, of whom more.

f.   Ruth Warfield, never married.

g.   John Worthington Warfield, probably born c.1749. Married first Susanna Holland, and second Mary Ridgely. The will of William Holland, dated September 23, 1769 was probated January 22, 1781, and filed in liber B at folio 14 in Montgomery County. The will names the various family members and legatees, one of whom is "Susanna Warfield, wife of John Warfield," which would appear to be the couple here under study. John is apparently the child born after the death of his father, whose will states that his wife is "now big with child." He lived on the Great Seneca in Montgomery County, and was rather prosperous. His will was dated December 14, 1802 and probated March 11, 1811 in Montgomery County, Maryland, filed in liber G at folio 233 and refiled in liber VMB 2 at folio 261, will records of the county. It names several tracts of land that are familiar locally: *Warfield's Vineyard, Mt. Airy, The Gap Filled Up, Mitchell's Range, Gravelly Hill.* He also names his wife as Mary, leaving her the home property, comprising two hundred acres of *Warfield's Vineyard,* (proving that she was his second wife). Children:

(1)   Arnold Warfield, born 1776 at Baltimore, died November 12, 1859 in New York. Married March

21, 1798 in Montgomery County, Maryland, to Margaret Browning, born September 7, 1779, died January 6, 1859 in New York, the daughter of Jonathan Browning, Jr. (1750). He inherited the bulk of his father's holdings under the will, except for the part left to his mother. Arnold moved to property he had inherited from his uncle at Clifton Springs, New York, where they had children. At least eight sons, including:

    (a)   Perry Gould Warfield, born May 10, 1813 in Baltimore, died April 7, 1881 in Ohio. Married June 9, 1844 to Caroline Bell and had six children.

    (b)   Thomas Worthington Warfield, who built a group of houses on the property in New York; single.

    (c)   Lewis Warfield, who had three sons in the Union Army and one in the Confederate Army.

  (2)   Alexander Warfield of Seneca, in Montgomery County. Under his father's will, this son inherited the home property after the death of his mother, and a negro boy named Isaac. Married February 8, 1807 to Mary Harwood, the daughter of Samuel Harwood and Mary Elizabeth Stockett.

  (3)   Araminta Warfield, married Cooper, and apparently widowed by 1811; married second to Benjamin Fitzgerald.

  (4)   Nancy Warfield, married Thomas Stevens.

  (5)   Sarah Warfield, married James Day, and of whom more following.

5.   Elinor Warfield, an infant death.

6.   Ruth Warfield, married September 15, 1719 to Richard Davis and had children:

  a.   Richard Davis, Jr., a captain.

  b.   John Davis.

  c.   Thomas Davis.

  d.   Caleb Davis.

e.   Elizabeth Davis.

f.   Ruth Davis.

7.   Mary Warfield, married January 1, 1729 Augustine Marriott and had children:

   a.   John Marriott, married a daughter of Alexander Warfield.

   b.   Achsah Marriott, married John Hall of *White Hall,* and had children.

   c.   Mary Marriott, married John Sewell of Indian Landing and had children.

8.   Edward Warfield, born August 11, 1710, of whom more in Chapter 5.

9.   Philip Warfield, of whom more following.

Surratt Dickerson Warfield, Sr.
1787-1851

This son of Brice Warfield (1742) and Susanna Dickerson was born June 7, 1787, probably in Frederick County, and died November 6, 1851. Although usually found as Surratt D., his middle name is very probably Dickerson, after his mother's maiden name, and his nephew, Alfred Browning (1815), named his own son Surratt Dickerson Warfield Browning, apparently after his uncle. Surratt was married March 10, 1812 to Matilda Spurrier, born April 22, 1785, died June 7, 1849; buried with her husband at Liberty, as are two of their children. He appears as head of household in the 1850 census for the Eighth Election District of Frederick County, without a wife, having been widowed the previous year, with five children. Surratt D. is also listed as a slave-owner, having five females and three males ranging in age from six months to fifty-three years. In the report on agricultural production in the county for the year ending June 1, 1850, he is listed as owning 150 acres of improved land and 50 acres unimproved, for a total value of six thousand dollars. His machinery and tools are valued at two hundred dollars. He has 8 horses; 7 milch cows; 13 other cattle; 15 sheep; and 30 swine; his livestock being valued at seven hundred and fifty dollars. He has raised 500 bushels of wheat, 100 bushels of rye; 300 bushels of Indian corn; 200 bushels of oats; and 50 bales of ginned cotton. He also has produced 30 bushels of peas and beans, and 1,000 pounds of butter. He put up 20 tons of hay and 15 bushels of clover seed. As can be surmised from these figures, Surratt was an active farmer, and apparently a good one, and rather well-to-do for the times. His children were:

1. Alexander Warfield, born May 2, 1815, died August 17, 1831.
2. Henrietta Warfield, born 1818, married December 14, 1835 John A. Warfield of Frederick County, born 1813. They appear in the 1850 census of Eighth Election District of Frederick County, with four children:
   a. Alexander Warfield, born 1836, but see Alexander S. D. Warfield, following.
   b. William F. Warfield, born 1841
   c. Dennis T. Warfield, born 1843
   d. John A. T. Warfield, born 1846
3. Elizabeth Warfield, born 1818
4. Surratt Dickerson Warfield, Jr., born 1820. This son was not living in his father's household in the 1850 census, having established his own household in the same election district in Frederick County, with a wife, Jane, born c.1820, and six children. She was probably Clarissa Jane Gore, and they were married in Frederick County April 12, 1842. He also owned slaves, having two females and one male listed in the census. He was not quite on the same plane with his father in production of agriculture, but he owned 85 acres of improved land and 40 acres unimproved, valued at three thousand, five hundred dollars. He had 3 horses and four milch cows for his growing family, and raised substantial crops. The names of at least two children are shown as found in the transcribed census, but are believed to have been misspelled by the enumerator, not unusual. His children included:
   a. Norcisa E. Warfield, born 1842 (Narcissa, perhaps)
   b. Anna Warfield, born 1844
   c. Surratt R. Warfield, born 1846
   d. Terecia Warfield, born 1848 (Teresa, perhaps)
   e. Nathan C. Warfield, born 1849
4. Richard D. Warfield, born 1830
5. Ann M. Warfield, born 1832. Married February 11, 1851 to William H. Jones in Frederick County.

6. James H. Warfield, born 1835
7. Rachael C. Warfield, born 1837

Alexander S. D. Warfield
1836-1898

This individual may well be the same Alexander listed as a son of John A. Warfield (1813) and Henrietta (Warfield) Warfield (1818), above. If that be the case, he would then be the fourth great grandson of Richard Warfield (1646), the Immigrant ancestor. In any case, according to the records of Mt. Olivet cemetery in Frederick, he was born October 27, 1836 and died May 5, 1898. Buried with him is his wife, Isabella, born August 9, 1833 and died October 1, 1911. There are also two sons and four daughters buried with them:

1. John Thomas Warfield, born May 25, 1857, died September 1, 1868.
2. Sarah Elizabeth Warfield, born February 28, 1861, and died August 12, 1863
3. Nelly Louisa Warfield, born March 22, 1863, died August 18, 1863.
4. Charles L. Warfield, born February 24, 1875, died August 26, 1875.
5. Lilly Belle Warfield, died December 1, 1876 at 5 months.
6. Molly Warfield, no dates, died at one week.

Surratt Dickerson Warfield Browning
1834-

This son of Alfred Browning (1815) was born May 15, 1834, and died November 2, 1887. Buried at St. Barnabas Episcopal Church cemetery, Sykesville, Carroll County, Maryland. Served as private, Maryland 2nd Regt, Cavalry Co. A, during the Civil War. Married May 5, 1864 to Sarah Elizabeth Thompson, born February 20, 1845, died May 29, 1905, daughter of John Thompson (1817) and Rebekah Shipley (1815). Sarah appears as a widow in the 1900 census for Howard County, with the three youngest children still living at home. Children included:

1. William Ellsworth Browning, born and died July 21, 1864.
2. Mary Elizabeth Browning, born 1866. Married to Charles Hansen, and to Charles Rau. This child has also been reported as Sarah Elizabeth Browning, first married to John Hansen, which may be correct.
3. Maydecker Browning, born 1869. Married first to Elijah Dorsey, born 1865, died 1889; and second to Albert Oswald.
4. John Browning, born December 1, 1871, and died February 10, 1917.
5. Hannorah Browning, born October 19, 1873, died April 14, 1948. Married to Thomas P. Hatfield.
6. Grace Ursula Browning, born September 18, 1877, died January 19, 1943. Married to Emery Dixon.
7. Jacob Marion Browning, born August 6, 1879 at Sykesville, in Howard County, Maryland, died June 23, 1942. Married August 12, 1904 to Elsie Pearl Arrington, born October 6, 1884, died April 5, 1957, the daughter of William Thomas Arrington (1856) and Priscilla Elizabeth Grimes (1862). They had children, probably born in Howard County:
   a. Ethel Browning; married Michael Joseph Vicari, Jr. This is perhaps the same Ethel born January 20, 1906 and died June, 1968 at Aberdeen, Maryland; and Michael born June 8, 1888, died December, 1984 at Aberdeen. There were at least two children:
      (1) Ethel Lorraine Vicari.
      (2) Mary June Vicari.
   b. Thomas Morris Browning, married Mildred Murray, and Angela Haddaway. At least one child each marriage:
      (1) Thomas Morris Browning, Jr.
      (2) Gladys Ann Browning.
   c. Goldie Browning, married William Howard Thomas and Leroy Glass. Two children from the first marriage:
      (1) William Howard Thomas, Jr.
      (2) Ethel A. Thomas.
   d. Dorothy May Browning, married Charles Ely. At least one child:
      (1) Dorothy May Ely.
   e. Jacob Maynard Browning, stillbirth August 30, 1924.

8. Charles Edward Browning, born August 20, 1882; married to Ginny Selby.
9. Laurena Browning, born August 15, 1884. Married Oscar Madiera, and second Charles Hamilton.
10. Susannah Warfield Browning, born November 13, 1886, died March 21, 1926. Married to Thomas Franklin.

Joshua Warfield
1761-

This son of John Warfield and Rachel Dorsey was born April 27, 1761 in Queen Caroline Parish, Anne Arundel County, Maryland. He received 350 acres in the Barrens under his father's will and 50 acres adjoining the home plantation called the *Kirk,* and *New Design*, as well as the dwelling plantation after his mother's death. He was married October 6, 1781 to Elizabeth Dorsey, daughter of Thomas Dorsey and Mary (or Lucy) Warfield. They had one child, and he was married second January 13, 1783 to Mary Ann Jones, daughter of Captain Isaac Jones of South River, and had the remaining ten children:

1. Thomas John Warfield, married Sarah Sellman.
2. Roderick Warfield, married Henrietta Spurrier and second to Ann Stockett, born June 10, 1792, daughter of Dr. Thomas Noble Stockett (1747) and Mary Harwood. Moved to Kentucky and had ten children.
3. Warner Washington Warfield, born c.1787, died 1867; said to be of Charles County. Served in the War of 1812. He bought the tract called *Bagdad* near Sykesville. Married his cousin, Catherine Dorsey Warfield, daughter of Beale Warfield and Amelia Ridgely. Children:
    a. Marcellus Warfield, married Josephine E. Lawrence, daughter of Colonel John Lawrence, Jr. of Linganore, and Martha West of *The Woodyard.* Two daughters.
    b. William Henry Warfield, a merchant in Laurel, married January 4, 1859 at the home of the bride to Charlotte Duvall, born 1835, the daughter of Dr. Mareen Merriken Duvall (1807) and Harriet Evans of Anne Arundel County. No children.

    c.   Manelia E. S. Warfield, married October 27, 1869 to Henry Jenkins. No children.

4.   John Warfield, died 1860, unmarried.

5.   Harriet Warfield, married Ralph Dorsey, son of Benjamin Dorsey. Five sons, three of whom died without children.

6.   Rachel Warfield, unmarried.

7.   Amelia Warfield, unmarried.

8.   Mary Warfield, unmarried.

9.   Anne Warfield, married Thomas Pearce.

10. Sarah Warfield, unmarried.

11. Margaret Gassaway Warfield, unmarried.

Sarah Warfield
d/1821

This daughter of John Worthington Warfield (1749) and his second wife, Mary Holland, was born in Montgomery County, Maryland, and married there November 7, 1795 to James Day, as his second wife. She died December 18, 1821. James was born September 8, 1762 in Frederick County, Maryland, in an area that later became Montgomery, when it was created in 1776, son of John Day (1720). James had first been married to Cassandra Beall, born 1769, daughter of Clement Beall (1734) and Priscilla Perry (1741), and was the father of three children from that first marriage. James was married yet a third time August 30, 1823 to Sarah Mark, born c.1799, by whom he had seven more children, for a total of eighteen children in all. James Day is the principal subject of the book, *James Day of Browningsville and his descendants, A Maryland Family,* by Jackson Harvey Day, 1976, Columbia, Maryland. All of his descendants from his three marriages comprise the body of the work, covering several generations, and the reader is referred to that publication for the details of the family. Suffice to say here that James Day and Sarah Warfield had eight children:

1.   Elizabeth Day, born September 22, 1769

2.   Urban Day, born December 1, 1798

3.   Mary Day, born February 24, 1801

4.   Luther Day, born August 26, 1803

5.   Lorenzo Day, born August 10, 1805

6. Jefferson Day, born November 4, 1807
7. Hester Ann Day, born November 1, 1809
8. Sarah Ann Day, born March 22, 1814

Philip Warfield

This son of John Warfield and Ruth Gaither inherited from his father part of *Venison Park*; purchased the tracts called *Discovery* and *Altogether*. Married Nancy Anne Purdy and had children:

1. Edmond Warfield, married December 22, 1792 to his cousin, Mary Ann Warfield, daughter of Seth Warfield. Children:
   a. Mary Warfield.
   b. Anna Warfield.
2. Philip Warfield, born 1751, married Susannah Hobbs, daughter of William Hobbs. Children:
   a. William Warfield, born c.1778, died July 14, 1810. Married April 12, 1803 to Martha Bye; five children:
      (1) Mary Warfield, born 1805
      (2) Maria Warfield, born 1807. Married first Holloway, and had a son. Married second Joseph Walker, and had children:
         (a) William Holloway.
         (b) Daniel H. Walker.
         (c) Martha W. Walker, married Lindlay Holloway.
         (d) Deborah Walker.
         (e) Lewis Walker.
         (f) Abel Walker, married Hannah Frence.
      (3) John Warfield, married first Lydia E. Smith and had a child. Married second Rebecca A. Wilson, and had two children. Married third Jane Billanger. His children were:
         (a) William Smith Warfield, married to Malvina Howell and had children.
         (b) Lydia Warfield.
         (c) Emma Warfield, married to Volney S. Cooper and had children.
      (4) Andrew Warfield, married Annette Barrie.

21

(5)   Jacob Holloway Warfield, married Mary A. Clarke and had children.

b.   Nathan Warfield, had two sons and moved to Ohio in 1825. Could be the same Nathan who was married December 6, 1819 in Montgomery County to Eliza Hobbs.

c.   Charles Warfield, died in Maryland 1805

d.   Daughter, married to Samuel Leek.

e.   Eleanor Warfield, married January 9, 1804 John Gibbins.

3.   John Warfield, married first December 3, 1788 to Aseneth Hobbs, and second to Nancy Bosley (or Rogers), and moved to Kentucky.

4.   Ephraim Warfield, married March 1, 1794 to Ariana Worthington Watkins, born July 27, 1769, the daughter of Thomas Watkins (1736) of South River, and Elizabeth Jones; and moved to Montgomery County.

5.   William Warfield, married Sallie Watkins, daughter of Nicholas Watkins, and moved to the west.

6.   Richard Warfield, married March 9, 1803 Sarah Ann Watkins daughter of Nicholas Watkins and Sarah Disney.

7.   Ruth Warfield, single.

8.   Sarah Warfield, married Lancelot Dorsey, born July 17, 1747, died March, 1829 in Anne Arundel County, son of Michael Dorsey and Ruth Todd, and had six sons and three daughters.

9.   Lydia Warfield, married a son of William Hobbs, Jr., and had two sons and three daughters.

10. Elizabeth Warfield, married Jeremiah Duvall and had one son.

11. Nancy Warfield, married Joseph Higgins.

12. Amelia Warfield.

13. Rachel Warfield, single.

14. Mary Warfield, moved west with relatives.

CHAPTER 3

Richard Warfield

This son of John Warfield (1673) and Ruth Gaither (1679) was married 1721 to Marian Caldwell, and second to Sarah Gambrill. Four children born to the first marriage; two from the second:

1. John Warfield, born c.1722. Moved to Frederick County. Married Miss Dorsey and had children:
    a. John Warfield, Jr., married Miss Kervick.
    b. Surratt D. Warfield, State Senator of Frederick County, as sometimes reported, although it seem unlikely that he is a son of this family. Surratt D. (probably Dickerson) was born in 1787, at which time John Warfield would have been 65 years old; not impossible, but not likely. We believe that Surratt D. was actually a son of Brice Warfield (1742) and Susanna Dickerson, as reported earlier above.
    c. Nina Clarke Warfield.
    d. Mary Anne Warfield, born October, 1761 of whom more.
2. Seth Warfield, born c.1723, of whom more.
3. Richard Warfield.
4. Luke Warfield, no descendants.
5. Joseph Warfield, never married.
6. Rachel Warfield, married Philip Turner.

Mary Anne Warfield
1761-1820

This daughter of John Warfield (1722) was born in October of 1761, and died March 7, 1820. Married July 25, 1780 to Eli Hyatt, born October 16, 1754, died July 28, 1815 at his home in Frederick County, near Hyattstown. He was a son of Meshach Hyatt, and owned the "Red House" on the north side of Hyattstown, and was said to have weighed nearly four hundred pounds. Eli is believed to have served in the Revolution, enlisted by Richard Talbot. Eli and Mary Anne had eleven children:

1. John Hyatt, born October 15, 1781, died November 15, 1781
2. William Hyatt, born April 25, 1783, died Frederick County. Married 1813 Peggy Kinna, who died in Sandusky, Ohio. Children:
    a. Eli Hyatt, died in Maryland aged 64. Married 1844 to Lydia Michael.
    b. John William Hyatt, died in Ohio, aged 58. Married Sarah Bowlos.
    c. Mary Ann Hyatt, died in Champaign County, Ohio, aged 71. Married John T. Michael.
    d. Rebecca Hyatt, died in Ohio aged 60. Married Alexander Bowlos.
    e. Elizabeth Hyatt, died in Washington County, Indiana, aged 61. Married James Weddle.
    f. Philip Hyatt, died in Springfield, Ohio. Married 1842 in Frederick County, Maryland, to Joanna R. Flook.
    g. James D. Hyatt, died in Tiffin, Ohio. Married Susan Flook, probably in Frederick County.
    h. Margaret Hyatt, married Henry Bowlos.
3. Elizabeth Hyatt, born October 15, 1785, died May 13, 1855. Married 1804 to George Davis, born February 3, 1775, died May 6, 1850, son of Richard Davis of New Market, Frederick County, Maryland. Both buried in the Quaker cemetery near Monrovia. Twelve children.
4. Asa Hyatt, born December 18, 1787. Married May 12, 1812 to Mary Ann Phillips, born November 18, 1796, daughter of Levi and Eleanor Phillips. Children:
    a. Levi Thomas Hyatt, born January 6, 1815. This is perhaps the same Levi T. Hyatt who is head of household in the 1850 census for the Clarksburg District, although his age would be about five years off in that report. We suggest that he is the same individual, however, in that there is a child in the family with a most unusual name, probably named for the brother of Levi; as well as a child named for Levi's father. Levi was a constable, and his wife was Elizabeth, born c.1825. Children:
        (1) Ella Hyatt, born c.1846
        (2) Asa Hyatt, born c.1848

(3) Theophilus Hyatt, born c.1849

b. Eleanor Ann Hyatt, born April 21, 1816. This is probably the Ellen A. Hyatt who is reported as married in Montgomery County on September 12, 1835 to David A. Zeigler. They are found in the 1850 census for the county, living next door to Levi T. Hyatt (above), her brother. David was born c.1813 and is listed as an innkeeper, with six children in 1850. We found the family again in the 1860 census for the Clarksburg District, with seven children. They are next found in the 1870 census with a lengthy list of family members, including some of the seven listed in 1860 who can be identified, as well as a number of others who are apparently grandchildren. We will make some effort here to place them in family groups based on the order in which they appeared in the census. There are at least three individuals not placed in family groups, including: Clarence Zeigler, born c.1869; Airy E. Zeigler, born c.1846, and perhaps the mother of Eda M. Zeigler, born c.1866. The family included:

(1) Levi B. Zeigler, born c.1836. We found Levi listed as head of his own household in the 1870 census, as a saw-mill laborer. He had a wife, Julia, born c.1844, and three children:

(a) Lillian L. Zeigler, born c.1863

(b) Arthur E. Zeigler, born c.1867

(c) Herbert E. Zeigler, born c.1869

(2) Asa H. Zeigler, born c.1838. He is living in his parents' household in 1870, listed as a physician.

(3) Francis T. Zeigler, born c.1840; not found in the 1870 census, either at home or in his own name.

(4) John Wilson Zeigler, born c.1842. Listed only as Wilson in the earlier census reports, this is apparently John W. Zeigler as found at home in the 1870 census, listed as an engineer. Based solely on the arrangement of family members in the taking of the census of 1870, we believe that his wife was named Mary F., born c.1847 and that they had

three children at the time of the census; all living in the home of his parents:

- (a) Alva W. Zeigler, a daughter, born c.1866
- (b) Laura E. Zeigler, born c.1869
- (c) David F. Zeigler, born c.1870

(5) Mary E. Zeigler, born c.1844; perhaps the same who was married in Montgomery County November 7, 1867 to E. G. Harris

(6) David T. Zeigler, born c.1847; apparently the same as Davis S. at home in the 1870 census. (The initials are always difficult to read in census records).

(7) Jesse L. Zeigler, born c.1851. This child appears only in the 1870 census with the family, but is assumed to be a son, based on age ranges.

(8) Ida J. Zeigler, born c.1856; perhaps the same Ida J. Zeigler who was married January 23, 1877 to Ephraim G. Harris in Montgomery County.

(9) Alice B. Zeigler, born c.1862.

c. Isabella Hyatt, born January 17, 1818, died January 3, 1819

d. Theophilus Hyatt, born June 20, 1820, died February 3, 1821

e. Sary Ann S. Hyatt, born June 11, 1823, died July 4, 1823

f. Mary Ann Hyatt, born December 3, 1824

g. Leah Ann Willson Hyatt, born December 17, 1826, died July 19, 1827

h. Sarah Elizabeth Hyatt, born June 2, 1828

i. Lucinda Mariah Hyatt, born October 22, 1830

j. Willson Lee Hyatt, born April 5, 1833, died August 29, 1833

5. Susannah Hyatt, born February 15, 1790
6. Samuel Hyatt, born April 28, 1792
7. Polly Hyatt, born April 8, 1794
8. Charlotte Hyatt, born March 29, 1796
9. Eli Hyatt, Jr., born March 28, 1798
10. Mary Ann Hyatt, born June 26, 1800
11. Lloyd Hyatt, born January 11, 1803

Seth Warfield
1723-

This son of Richard Warfield and Marian Caldwell, was born c.1723 in Anne Arundel County, Maryland and married to Mary Gaither, daughter of John Gaither (1713) and Agnes Rogers. He settled on the tract called *Venison Park,* west of South River. In 1750, he acquired about fifteen hundred acres in Howard County, near Lisbon, and divided it between his five eldest sons. The youngest, Amos, inherited the homestead property. Typical of Colonial planters, Seth held indentured servants. The *Maryland Gazette* announced on September 8, 1757 that Seth Warfield, living in the fork of the Patuxent, near Snowden's Iron Works, in Anne Arundel County, reported a runaway convict servant, Thomas Rowling, about 25. Seth and his wife had several sons, each of whose given names contained but four letters, and who are the progenitors of the Warfield families now found in Howard County, Maryland:

1. Seth Warfield, Jr., married Ruth Welsh, born about 1754, daughter of Captain John Welsh, and had children:
    a. Seth Warfield, III, married Elizabeth Shipley, and had eight children.
        (1) Benjamin Warfield; married Eliza or Lethia Shipley and had two children:
            (a) John Warfield.
            (b) Samuel Warfield.
        (2) Charles Warfield, married Ann Regina Yost and had children:
            (a) Charles A. Warfield of Philadelphia.
        (3) Elizabeth Ann Warfield married Lorenzo Warfield.
        (4) Seth Warfield, IV, married Emeline Shipley.
        (5) Gustavus Warfield, married to his cousin, Lydia Welsh, daughter of Charles Welsh and Lydia Hammond Warfield (who were married February 1, 1821 in Frederick County).
        (6) Amelia Warfield, married Reuben Manaca.
        (7) Caroline Warfield, married Ephraim Buckingham.
        (8) Thomas Warfield, married Mary Blakely.
    b. John Warfield.

c.   Ann Warfield, married William Lansdale.
d.   Mary Warfield, married R. Dorsey.
e.   Ruth Warfield.
f.   Harriet Warfield.
g.   Amelia Warfield.
h.   Lydia Hammond Warfield, married to Charles Welsh, son of Reverend Henry Welsh. Children:
  (1)   Charles Stanhope Welsh.
  (2)   Ruth Welsh, married Hanson Franklin of Woodbine, Carroll County, Maryland.
  (3)   Mary Ann Welsh, died single.
  (4)   Columbus O'Donnell Welsh, born February 24, 1827. Married first Emily Harden and second Mrs. Ellen Webb, daughter of Ephraim Zepp, by whom he had ten children.
  (5)   Rezin Hammond Welsh, died young.
  (6)   Amelia Welsh, died young.
  (7)   Lydia Welsh, married to her cousin, Gustavus Warfield.

2.   Beni Warfield, married Ariana Dorsey, born February 24, 1755, daughter of Henry Dorsey (1712) and Elizabeth Worthington (1717), and had children:
a.   Charles Dorsey Warfield, owned *Bushy Park.* Married Mrs. Ruth Griffith Dorsey. She is probably the same who was born c.1794, died August 31, 1854, and is buried at New Market Methodist Church, in Frederick County.
b.   Daniel Warfield, married first Sarah Meriweather. and second Nancy Mactier, daughter of Alexander Mactier and Frances Crain of Scotland. Daniel is the direct ancestor of Elizabeth Wallace Warfield, the Duchess of Windsor. Through Ariana Dorsey, the ancestry has been traced back to William the Conqueror, with six Kings of England in line.
c.   Nicholas Dorsey Warfield, who married Rebecca Burgess daughter of Captain Vachel Burgess of Triadelphia, and had children:
  (1)   Alfred Warfield, born c.1825, and died January 13, 1896 at the home of sister Hettie, near Lisbon,

Maryland. He was single, and had lived most of his life in Missouri.

    (2)   Vachel Warfield.
    (3)   Beni Warfield.
    (4)   Louis Warfield.
    (5)   Hettie Warfield, married Henderson.
    (6)   Lucretia Warfield, married Warren Dorsey.

d. Sarah Warfield.
e. Margaret Warfield.
f. Maria Warfield.
g. Alfred Warfield, a judge, single, lived at Lisbon.
h. Elizabeth Warfield.

3. Bela Warfield, married July 25, 1785 to Achsah Dorsey, the daughter of Colonel Nicholas Dorsey (1712) and Sarah Griffith (1718) Children:

a. Nicholas Dorsey Warfield. Married to Deborah Gaither, who is referred to as a niece in the will of Beal Gaither, dated April 13, 1835, probated March 26, 1839, and filed in liber W at folio 154, will records of Montgomery County. The will of Deborah (Gaither) Ray (probated June 10, 1828) names Deborah Warfield, daughter of sister Mary Dorsey. From those wills, it would appear that the mother of Deborah was Mary Gaither, sister of Beal Gaither, and that her father was named Dorsey. There was apparently at least one daughter:

    (1)   Deborah Jane Warfield, named in the will of Samuel R. Gaither (liber JWS-1, folio 61, August 14, 1860, Montgomery County) as a niece and daughter of Nicholas Warfield.

b. Bela Warfield.
c. Joshua Warfield.
d. Mary Ann Warfield, born February 22, 1788, died February 26, 1856. Married September 19, 1807 to Rezin Welsh, born November 18, 1774 Anne Arundel County, Maryland, and died July 5, 1864 in Cromwell, Indiana. He was the son of Charles Welsh and a grandson of Captain John Welsh. Rezin and Mary Ann moved to Ohio in 1832 and to Indiana in 1849, and had children:

- (1) Greenberry Welsh, born 1809, died 1833, single.
- (2) Middleton Welsh, born 1810, died 1833, single
- (3) Rezin Welsh, Jr., born 1816, died 1896, single
- (4) Mary Ann Welsh, born 1820, died 1880. Married John Larimore and had children:
  - (a) Aldine Larimore, married Godfrey and had at least three children.
  - (b) Caroline Larimore, married Gericking and had at least three children.
  - (c) Rosine Larimore, married Perry and had at least one son born at Ft. Wayne, Indiana.
  - (d) Woodville Larimore, born Oakland, California. Married and had at least four children.
- (5) Cornelia Welsh, born 1822, married Ammon and had children, two of whom were:
  - (a) Rezin Ammon.
  - (b) Mary Ann Ammon.
- (6) Jeanette Welsh, born 1826, married Peter Draggo and had children:
  - (a) Ann Draggo.
  - (b) Jeannette Draggo.
  - (c) William Draggo.
  - (d) Jacob Draggo.
- (7) Caroline Welsh, born 1832, died 1900. Married to William Fenton and had children:
  - (a) Ann Fenton.
  - (b) Sufrona Fenton.
  - (c) Emmaette Fenton, married Carothers.
- e. Lucretia Warfield.
- f. Mary G. Warfield.
- g. Juliet Warfield.
- h. Rachel Warfield, married her cousin, Reuben Warfield.
- i. Achsah Warfield, also married Reuben Warfield, the Surveyor of Howard County.
4. Elie Warfield, married February 17, 1792 to Frances Dorsey (Chapman), daughter of Colonel Nicholas Dorsey (1712) and Sarah Griffith (1718), and had children:
- a. George Warfield.

b. Rezin Warfield.
c. Eli Gaither Warfield, married June 16, 1831 at St. Bartholomews Episcopal Church in Montgomery County to Ellen Bowie Magruder, born c.1800, daughter of Dr. Jeffrey Magruder. She was found in the 1850 census of Cracklin District of Montgomery County, with the Warfield surname, living in a household headed by Jeffery P. T. Magruder, born c.1805, with two children, apparently belonging to Ellen, who was perhaps a widow. Jeffery had no other family, and was perhaps her brother, considering the given name of one of the children. Also in the household was one James Gray, born c.1825, and a laborer. Two children in that census, and one other, were:
    (1) Fannie Warfield, married Engle.
    (2) Susan Warfield, born c.1833
    (3) Magruder Warfield, born c.1834
d. Seth Warfield.
e. Reuben Warfield, the surveyor, poet and genealogist.
f. Rufus Warfield.
g. Louisa Warfield, married James Henderson.
h. Eleanor Warfield, married Nicholas R. Warfield, son of Joshua Warfield.
5. Azel Warfield, married Elizabeth Welling and had children:
a. Richard Warfield.
b. Azel Warfield, Jr.
c. Henry Warfield.
d. William Warfield.
e. Charles A. Warfield.
f. Edmund Warfield.
g. George W. Warfield.
h. Elizabeth Warfield.
i. Mary Warfield, born 1797, died 1843. Married March 27, 1823 to John Fisher, born 1797, died 1883. They had at least seven children, one of whom was:
    (1) Lemuel Fisher, who married Eliza Hopkins and had children, one of whom was:
        (a) Mary Catherine Fisher, born c.1855, died October 27, 1916, buried Monocacy ceme-

tery, Montgomery County, Maryland. Married Hanson Thomas Miles, born March 25, 1850, and died June 18, 1926; buried Monocacy Cemetery, and of whom more following.
- j.   Eliza Warfield.
- k.   Matilda Warfield.
- l.   Sarah Warfield.
- m.   Nancy Warfield.

6.   Amos Warfield, inherited the home place near Laurel, Prince George's County. Married Sarah Warfield, daughter of Richard Warfield, Jr. and Nancy Gassaway. Children:

- a.   Seth Washington Warfield, born c.1805, formerly Sheriff of Howard County, Maryland. Married May 22, 1827 to Lydia A. Meredith, born c.1810, died March 20, 1896, the daughter of Thomas and Ruth Meredith, and had children:
  - (1)   Amos Wiley Warfield, born June 10, 1829, died March 27, 1866 in Tennessee. Married April 11, 1854 in Columbia, Tennessee to Cornelia A. Francis, and had children there:
    - (a)   John Francis Warfield, born December 3, 1854. Married February 16, 1880 to Mary D. McLemore and had four children.
    - (b)   Seth Washington Warfield, born December 19, 1856. Married June 8, 1887 to Chloe E. Boddie, and had three children.
    - (c)   Amos Wiley Warfield, Jr.; December 1, 1860
    - (d)   Mary Meredith Warfield; January 26, 1862
    - (e)   Amy Cornelia Warfield, born May 11, 1866. Married 1893 to W. J.Alexander, and had two children.
  - (2)   Ruth S. Warfield, married January 26, 1858 to Lebbeus Griffith, Sr., born February 11, 1804 in Montgomery County, Maryland, died 1888, the son of Howard Griffith (1757) and Jemima Jacobs of Prince George's County. Lebbeus moved to Frederick County about 1827, and Ruth S. Warfield was his third wife. By his first wife, Lebbeus had

three children, by his second six, and reportedly eight from his marriage to Ruth S. Warfield. For those interested in the earlier family of Lebbeus Griffith, prior to his marriage to Ruth Warfield, he appears as head of household in the 1850 census for New Market District of Frederick County, apparently with six of his children born by that date. He was a slave holder, and an extensive farmer. Six of the eight children born to Ruth were:

(a) Ida May Griffith, born November 22, 1858, died May 9, 1883

(b) Seth Warfield Griffith, born January 9, 1860, died November 4, 1935. Married to Eliza (Hopkins) Miller.

(c) Florence Griffith, born May 8, 1861. Married to F. Etchison and had three children.

(d) Robert Lee Griffith, born July 15, 1862. Married to Eliza Warfield, daughter of Garrison Warfield (1822) and Caroline Lewis (1835). There were reportedly three children, including:

    1. Forest India Griffith.

(e) Clarence Griffith, born November 17, 1863, died April 8, 1924.

(f) Varena Griffith, an infant death.

(3) John Thomas Warfield, born August 13, 1835, of whom more following.

(4) James Henry Harrison Warfield, a doctor, born 1841, served in the Confederate Army, and died March 6, 1883 near Laurel, at the home of his father, single.

(5) Isabella D. Warfield, born 1843, died December 5, 1919. Married December 12, 1873 to Zachariah L. Magruder of Montgomery County. No children.

(6) Randolph Ridgely Warfield, an attorney Baltimore.

b. Mary Warfield.

c. Lydia Warfield, born March 15, 1799. Married February 14, 1816 to Warren Welsh, born July 9, 1793, died February 25, 1867, son of Charles Welsh (1746). They lived and died in Maryland, and had six children:

(1) Amos W. Welsh, born September 16, 1818. Married to Julia Coale and had four children.

(2) Lycurgus Gassaway Welsh, born August 26, 1820 and died May 17, 1870. Married Elizabeth Ann Spear, born April 10, 1825, died November 11, 1908, and had twelve children.

(3) Washington Warfield Welsh, born September 2, 1823, died April 26, 1905 in Los Angeles, California. He was a minister for fifty-eight years. Late in life he married Mrs. Elizabeth Baker, a widow.

(4) Elizabeth Ann Welsh, born November 30, 1826, died December 31, 1882. Married James D. Lambden and had children. Married second Zack Lilley; no children.

(5) Brunette Welsh, born December 12, 1829, died April 3, 1872. Married to Reuben Warfield and had children.

(6) Mary Elizabeth Welsh, born June 3, 1837, married to Smith and had children. Married second John Henry Atchison and had two children.

   d. Catherine Warfield.

7. Daughter Warfield, married Edward Warfield of Philip.
8. Daughter Warfield, married Joshua Owings.
9. Daughter Warfield, died single.
10. Daughter Warfield, died single.

Hanson Thomas Miles
1850-1926

This son of James Hanson Miles (1810) and Elvira M. Beall (1811) was born March 25, 1850, and died June 18, 1926; buried Monocacy Cemetery. The 1860 census appears to read Henson T., born c.1852, which is obviously not correct, since he appeared in the 1850 census. He is listed with his parents in the 1870 census as Hanson T. Miles, born c.1850. This is probably the same Henson Miles appearing in the 1880 census for Montgomery County, born c.1850. His wife Mary Catherine Fisher was born c.1855, died October 27, 1916, buried at Monocacy, daughter of Lemuel Fisher and Eliza Hopkins. They have living with them in 1880 Henry Miles, born c.1848, listed as his brother (that would be Richard Henry). There is also a sister, Anna M. Miles, born c.1853. One child is there. In the 1900 census, the couple appears again, where she is listed as Kate, with the one son, and the statement that they have been married for twenty-two years, and are parents of four children, only one living, who was:

1. Howard Montgomery Miles, born September 12, 1879; died December 17, 1952. Married December 31, 1908 at Damascus to Ardella Mae King, born April 29, 1882, died November 10, 1959, daughter of Rufus Kent King (1850) and Emma F. Burdette (1862). The will of Howard Montgomery Miles, dated May 2, 1942, probated January 14, 1953, is found in liber WCC34, folio 11, in the records of Montgomery County, Maryland. He leaves his estate to his wife, with the suggestion that at her death, she divide it among their five children, without naming them. Her will, indexed under Della M. Miles, is filed in liber VMB 118, folio 418. Settlement of her accounts in Case #11,823 in the county reveals that she held real estate at or in the village of Clarksburg: 47 acres of *Warfield's Vineyard;* 65.22 acres of *Garnkirk;* and 16 acres, being part of *Richland* and *Woodport.* They had children:

   a. Howard Montgomery Miles, Jr., who was married to Eleanor Diamond, born January 24, 1915, died April 13, 1969, the daughter of Herbert Laurence Diamond and Marie Lyddane Jones. Eleanor is buried at the St. Rose Cemetery, Cloppers, Md., leaving a daughter:

      (1) Sandra Diamond Miles, married to Francis Easby Welter of Gaithersburg, and second Robert Eugene Campbell. Children:

          (a) Kelly Maureen Welter, married to Philip Arthur Passarelli.
          (b) Kate Frances Welter.
          (c) Julie Ann Welter, married to Gregory Thomas Smith.
          (d) Tricia Ann Welter.

b. Thomas Hanson Miles, born September 25, 1911, died on or about March 20, 1998 at Gaithersburg. Married Janet Etchison, and had children:
  (1) Janet Marian Miles, born October 25, 1943 in Frederick, died March 26, 1982 at La Plata, Maryland. Buried at Forest Oak Cemetery, Gaithersburg.
  (2) Thomas Etchison Miles, born March 2, 1947, and lived at Port Tobacco, Md.
c. Laura Virginia Miles, married Thomas Ashton Garrett and had children:
  (1) Sharon Ann Garrett, married George Debnam and had children:
      (a) Raney Debnam, who had two sons:
          1. Drew Debnam.
          2. Mark Debnam.
      (b) Audra Debnam.
  (2) Ashton Montgomery Garrett, married Sharon and had three children:
      (a) Ashley Garrett.
      (b) Laura Elizabeth Garrett.
      (c) Paige Garrett.
  (3) Jeffrey Moore Garrett, married Carolyn and had children:
      (a) Miles Garrett.
      (b) Molly Garrett.
  (4) Laurie Garrett, married to John Hall and had children:
      (a) Tagart Hall.
      (b) Kada Hall.
d. Mary Catherine Miles, born May 23, 1919. Married to December 31, 1941 to Ernest Jennet Whitaker, born September 30, 1916, and had children:
  (1) James Miles Whitaker, born November 15, 1942; married and divorced. One child:
      (a) Jamie Michele Whitaker, born 1972

(2) William Ernest Whitaker, born October 1, 1946. Married Sandra Dee Boules, born January 5, 1947 and had two daughters:
    (a) Corrine Dee Whitaker.
    (b) Stacey Kathryn Whitaker.
(3) Stephen Jennet Whitaker, born September 17, 1948. Married and divorced; one daughter:
    (a) Marie Katherine Jennet Worlow Whitaker.
(4) Thomas Michael Whitaker, born September 4, 1951. Married to Candace Beck and had children:
    (a) Stephanie Catherine Whitaker.
    (b) Nicholas Miles Whitaker.
    (c) Christopher Thomas Whitaker.
(5) David Miles Whitaker, born August 24, 1953. Married to Kerie Sheeran and had two sons:
    (a) Miles Sheeran Whitaker.
    (b) Jordan Cahill Whitaker.
(6) Patrick Joseph Whitaker, born March 15, 1954. Divorced; one son:
    (a) Ryland Grant Whitaker.

e. Henry Kent Miles, married July 5, 1953 in Washington, D. C., to Patricia Carol Duvall, born January 13, 1931, daughter of Alfred Ward Duvall (1906) and his first wife, Margaret Cecelia Beckwith. Children:
(1) Karen Anne Miles, born January 3, 1956. Married Dan English, born February 25, 1952; children:
    (a) Mathew Charles English: March 6, 1982
    (b) Katie Ann English: May 16, 1983
    (c) Sara Kendall English: December 5, 1984
(2) Kim Ardell Miles, born April 19, 1958. Married to Steve McLaughlin, and had children:
    (a) Brian Patrick McLaughlin, a twin, born November 6, 1983
    (b) Kevin Michael McLaughlin, a twin, born November 6, 1983
    (c) Brendan Kent McLaughlin: August 4, 1987
    (d) Kara Megan McLaughlin: June 27, 1990

(3)   Kendall Mae Miles, born June 30, 1960. Married to John Lupari and had children:
- (a)   Brooklyn Leigh Lupari: March 3, 1986
- (b)   Henry Lupari, twin: November 25, 1992
- (c)   Kierianne Lupari, twin: November 25, 1992
- (d)   Emerald Lupari: April 14, 1994
- (e)   Miles Lupari: October 19, 1995

(4)   Kathryn Patricia Miles, born June 25, 1963. Married to Mathew Starrett and divorced. Children:
- (a)   Breelyn Nicole Starrett: July 4, 1992
- (b)   Brandon Starrett: July 23, 1994

(5)   Kent Montgomery Miles, born August 27, 1965. Married to Teri Jensen; one child:
- (a)   Alexandra Miles, born June 4, 1991

John Thomas Warfield
1835-1921

    This son of Seth Washington Warfield (1805) and Lydia A. Meredith (1810) was born August 13, 1835 in that part of Anne Arundel County which is now Howard, and died November 29, 1921 at the home of his son-in-law, Greenbury G. Griffith. Buried with his wife at Goshen Methodist Church near Laytonsville, where they had lived. In the 1870 census for Brighton, in Montgomery County, Maryland, he was found in the household headed by Joshua W. Dorsey, born c.1783, his father-in-law. Living there also is Mary A. E. Dorsey, born c.1815, his mother-in-law. With John is his wife, there listed as Ginnie, and their four children at that time. John Thomas was married November 19, 1862 to Rachel Virginia Dorsey, born August 13, 1845, and died December 2, 1930, daughter of Joshua Warfield Dorsey (1783) and Mary A. E. Childs (1814). Services and burial were at the Goshen Methodist Church, near Laytonsville. Rachel Virginia left a will in Montgomery County, dated November 8, 1927, probated January 6, 1931 and filed in liber PEW 20 at folio 33, will records, in which she names her children. Information found in the family file of the Montgomery County Historical Society library in Rockville, taken from the Bible of Joshua W. Dorsey provides additional data. Cemetery records also list the burial of an infant child with the initials J. M. at twenty-eight days, as well as a second infant, who died at seven months. The book *Welsh-Hyatt and Kindred,* by Luther W. Welsh, 1928, reports only eight children in this family, but other sources mentioned here provide a total of twelve, including:

1.   Mary Washington Warfield, born August 26, 1863. Married January 25, 1888 Charles Prather Higgins of Brookeville, Maryland. Lived at Rockville, and had seven children:

    a.   Charles Edwin Higgins, born August 9, 1892. Married December 26, 1917 to Mary Emma Powell of Tennessee. They had children:

        (1)   Charles Austin Higgins; November 20, 1918

        (2)   Emma Catherine Higgins; December 12, 1921.

    b.   Annie Lucille Higgins, born August 20, 1894. Married December 28, 1916 to Wallace Jones Clark. Children:

        (1)   James Thomas Clark; December 28, 1917

        (2)   Wallace Jones Clark, Jr.; February 28, 1919

        (3)   Dorothy Garland Clark; September 17, 1923

        (4)   Beverly Eugene Clark; February 13, 1927

    c.   Thomas Warfield Higgins, married Ruth Davis England.

    d.   Daisy Cornelia Higgins, born August 19, 1898

    e.   Eugene Staley Higgins, born September 7, 1900. Married June 22, 1925 to Loretta Kathryn Schwartz. Children:

        (1)   Jeanne Dorsey Higgins, born July 4, 1926 at Washington, D. C.

    f.   Kenneth Crawford Higgins, born February 8, 1902.

    g.   Jesse Thomas Higgins, born December 12, 1903. Married June 26, 1927 to Evalyn Marie Thompson.

2.   Noel N. P. Warfield, born December 16, 1864, died January 25, 1874. On pages from an old ledger of the family, and in cemetery records, this child is listed clearly as Noel N. P. Warfield; another source listed Noah, incorrectly.

3.   William Thompson Warfield, born December 26, 1866, died December 20, 1945 at Woodfield, Maryland. Married February 10, 1904 to Lillian C. Griffith, born July 2, 1871, died May 1, 1956, daughter of Judge Charles Harrison Griffith (1840)) and Hester Dorsey (1834) of Laytonsville. Buried Goshen Cemetery. Lillian was a grand daughter of Elisha

Riggs Griffith (1805) and Elizabeth Gaither (the daughter of Frederick Gaither and Jane Gartrell). William Thompson Warfield left a will dated February 6, 1942, probated January 15, 1946 and filed in liber OWR 14 at folio 223, will records of Montgomery County, Maryland, naming his wife and daughter:

    a.   Mary Cornelia Warfield, born October 27, 1905, died October 20, 1972, single. Buried Goshen Cemetery, in Montgomery County.

4.   Seth Washington Warfield, born February 1, 1870, died December 23, 1951; buried at Mt. Olivet, Frederick. Married October 30, 1901 to Eugenia Waite Hanshaw, born October 17, 1873, died July 13, 1963; buried with her husband. His will, dated November 30, 1948, was probated January 15, 1952 and filed in liber WCC 31 at folio 5, will records of Montgomery County. He names his wife, two sons and two daughters. They lived on Warfield Road near Laytonsville, and had children:

    a.   Seth Henry Warfield, born May 16, 1903, died February 12, 1994 at a hospital near his home in Bridgman, Michigan. He was a consulting engineer, and formerly from Laytonsville, in Montgomery County, Maryland. He was married to Mabel L., who predeceased him. Two sons survived him, as well as a sister. A brother and a sister predeceased him. His two sons were:

        (1)   George Warfield, of California.

        (2)   Seth H. Warfield, Jr., of Bridgman, Michigan.

    b.   John Thomas Warfield, known as Jack, born November 13, 1904, died November 14, 1986 at Washington Adventist Hospital in Takoma Park. Raised on the family farm, he founded Jack's Roofing Co., a slate roofing business as a young man, in which he was active until his death. He also owned and operated a chain of roofing supply stores, known as Roof Centers. He had worked on the White House, Blair House and other major landmarks in the Washington area. Married 1937 to Anna Grace Beasley, born in Burke, Virginia, died July 12, 1975. Children:

      (1)   John T. Warfield, Jr. of Laytonsville.

      (2)   Seth Leonard Warfield, of Rockville.

      (3)   Eletheer Warfield, married Keith Decker of Silver Spring.

  c.   Eugenia Elizabeth Warfield, born December 17, 1907; married Harold Hargett.

  d.   Rachel Virginia Warfield, born July 27, 1912; married Claibourne Ferguson of Gaithersburg.

5.   Reuben Dorsey Warfield, born October 28, 1871, died October 19, 1959; buried at Goshen Cemetery near Laytonsville. Married November 25, 1915 to Mary Anna Rhodes of Lexington, Virginia,, born c.1886, died September 3, 1970; buried with her husband and other family members. One of their daughters married W. J. Neese and one married Leonard Miederlehner. Children:

  a.   John Rhodes Warfield, born October 19, 1916. Possibly the same individual who married Mildred Cooper, daughter of J. Edgar Cooper of Gaithersburg. She died October 23, 1977, leaving children:

      (1)   Phyllis Warfield, married Watkins.

      (2)   John R. Warfield, Jr.

  b.   Anna Belle Warfield, born July 9, 1917

  c.   Charles Preston Warfield, born June 23, 1920, died January 7, 1925. Buried with his parents.

  d.   Helen Virginia Warfield, born April 26, 1922

6.   Chloe Anne Warfield, born September 15, 1873. Married April 8, 1897 to Nathan Elwood Gott, who died October 11, 1917. Two children:

  a.   Muriel Virginia Gott, born February 15, 1898. Married January 31, 1920 to Dowell Jennings Howard, the son of Henry Howard and Florence Jones. Children:

      (1)   Dowell Jennings Howard, Jr.; April 2, 1924

      (2)   Marianna Virginia Howard, born Winchester, Va.

  b.   Louise Warfield Gott, born March 10, 1903. Married November 20, 1924 to William Asbury Bowman.

7.   John Thomas Warfield, Jr., born August 30, 1875, died May 5, 1877.

8. Cornelia Isabella Warfield, born September 7, 1877. Married in Montgomery County, November 5, 1908 to Greenbury Gaither Griffith, born April 10, 1874, son of Charles Griffith and Hester Dorsey. He had been first married to Elizabeth Tschiffely, by whom he had one son. They had a son:
   a. Wiley Gaither Griffith, born June 11, 1914.
9. Hannah Holland Virginia Warfield, born January 31, 1879. Married September 16, 1912 Staunton Pilcher of Petersburg, Virginia; moved to Jackson, Michigan; and had a child:
   a. Mary Virginia Pilcher, born January 19, 1916
10. James Meredith Warfield, born June 11, 1880, died July 7, 1880
11. Amos Wiley Warfield, born April 23, 1883, apparently died before his mother made her will.
12. Lee Clagett Warfield, born July 1, 1886, died April 4, 1973 at Montgomery General Hospital, Olney. Buried at Goshen cemetery. Buried with his wife at Goshen Methodist. Married April 1, 1915 to Isabell J. Parsley, born November 2, 1891, died November 4, 1981, daughter of John H. Parsley and his wife Cornelia. Three children, two of whom were:
   a. Lee Clagett Warfield, Jr., born May 19, 1916
   b. John Gordon Warfield, born March 30, 1920 in Gaithersburg. Married March 31, 1943 at St. Peter's Church in Poolesville to Mary Maxine White, born June 17, 1918 at Frederick, daughter of Frank Malcolm White (1890) and Ellen Percy Blake (1892). They had children:
      (1) Mary Lee Warfield, born July 2, 1947 at Frederick and married January 10, 1966 Raymond J. Dillon. They had a daughter:
         (a) Tracey Leigh Dillon, born November 16, 1967 at Frederick
      (2) John Gordon Warfield, Jr., born February 11, 1950 at Frederick. Married July 31, 1976 Laura J. Weismantel, and had children:
         (a) Andrea Warfield.
         (b) Benjamin Warfield.

(3)   Malcolm White Warfield, born December 2, 1954 at Frederick. He was married December 1, 1979 to Maryanne Ellinghaus and had a son:

        (a)   Joshua Warfield.

Hyattstown Christian Church
Hyattstown, Maryland

CHAPTER 4

Benjamin Warfield
1702-1753

This son of John Warfield (1673) and Ruth Gaither (1679), whose family and descendants were discussed in Chapter 2, was born c.1702 in Anne Arundel County and died c.1753. Married first October, 1731 to Rebecca Ridgely, daughter of Judge Nicholas Ridgely (1694) and Sarah Worthington (1696), and had five children. Married second Anne White, and had three children, all listed following. The *Maryland Gazette* of February 22, 1753 ran an announcement by Anne Warfield, executrix of the estate of Banjamin Warfield, late of near Elk Ridge, deceased, regarding the estate sale to he held at his late plantation. It appears also that after his death, Anne was married secondly to Acrid, in that on August 11, 1757, the paper announced that "Anne Acrid, administratrix of the estate of Benjamin Warfield, will sell much of the estate at his late plantation at Elk Ridge." The children of Benjamin were:

1. Nicholas Ridgley Warfield, captain. Inherited *Warfield's Range* and *Worthington Range*. He also obtained by warrant two hundred, twenty-eight and three quarters acres of the tract called *Errors Corrected* in Montgomery County, May 23, 1792. Little Seneca Creek passed through the property, as did the old Baltimore Road from Barnesville to Neelesville, and it was the home farm of Gassaway W. Linthicum. The will of Nicholas in 1814 left all of his lands in Montgomey County to Lloyd Warfield, son of his brother Vachel Warfield. In the event that Lloyd had no children, then to Philemon Dorsey Warfield, son of Vachel. Other bequests went to nieces and nephews. It appears that Nicholas Ridgely Warfield was not married.

2. Benjamin Worthington Warfield, born 1734, died 1778, a captain of the Revolution, Elkridge Battalion of Militia. Married Catherine Dorsey, born November 30, 1745, died 1769, daughter of Colonel Philemon Dorsey (1714) and Catherine Ridgely (1723). In 1758, Captain Benjamin built his home

called *Cherry Grove.* He also bought and extended *Fredericksburg.* His will was made July 8, 1806 and probated September 19, 1806. He names his three sons, and a granddaughter Kitty Warfield. Children:

a. Benjamin Warfield, who died young.

b. Beale Warfield, died 1815, who inherited all his father's land that lay on the south side of the main road, and all the personal estate in his possession at the time of his father's death, and of whom more following.

c. Philemon Dorsey Warfield, born 1776, died April 30, 1851, who inherited from his father the plantation called *Bite the Skinner.* He located at *Locust Grove* and bought part of the tract called *Ridgely's Great Range,* increasing his estate to more than fifteen hundred acres. Married January 2, 1816 to Lucretia Griffith Welsh, born September 7, 1799, died August 9, 1859, the daughter of Philip Welsh (1765) and Elizabeth Davis (1768). Children of Philemon and Lucretia were:

   (1)   Elizabeth Ann Warfield, born 1816. Married 1847 to John G. Crapster. Two children, infant deaths.

   (2)   Lemuel Warfield, born 1819; married 1846 Elizabeth Hood Owings, daughter of Dr. John Hood Owings. Thirteen children, three of whom were:

      (a)   Philemon Dorsey Warfield, married Carrie Dorsey, daughter of Basil Dorsey.

      (b)   John Hood Owings Warfield, married Annie Reed and had children.

      (c)   Lemuel Warfield, Jr., married Vallie Burgess, the daughter of Dr. Carter Burgess, and had children.

   (3)   Guy Trevelyn Warfield, single.

   (4)   Amanda Warfield, born August 12, 1821. Married April 12, 1843 Dr. Artemus Riggs of Brookeville, born c.1814, son of Colonel John Hammond Riggs (1771) and his second wife, Rebecca Howard. Dr. Riggs moved to Ohio, but returned to Brookeville, Maryland, where he had been born. They appeared in the 1870 census for the First District of Mont-

gomery County, with only a black domestic servant living in the household. Artemus was listed as a physician, with $7,000 in real estate and $6,000 in personal property. They had one daughter:

(a) Kate Riggs, born c.1844, according to the 1870 census of the First District of Montgomery County. She was married January 5, 1869 to Franklin Griffith, Lieutenant, 1st Maryland Cavalry, Co. A., CSA, born 1840, died 1892 and had two children. In the 1870 census, he is listed as a farmer, with his real estate valued at $10,000 and $2,600 in personal property. At the time, they have living with them Georgina White, born c.1848, as a domestic servant, and Mary Griffith, born c.1837, perhaps a sister of Artemus. There are also four black servants and farm laborers living in the household.

(5) Philemon D. Warfield, died young.

(6) Catherine Dorsey Warfield, born 1825. Married October 24, 1846 in Frederick County to Samuel Greenberry Davis of Carroll County, and had one daughter.

(7) Milton Welsh Warfield, a doctor, born July 20, 1827 at Lisbon, Maryland, died November 26, 1905. Married July 29, 1861 to Mary Elizabeth Dawley, daughter of John Dawley of Yorkshire, England, and his wife Adaline Cummings. They had children:

(a) Benjamin Dorsey Warfield, an attorney.

(b) Ridgely Brown Warfield.

(c) Anna Elizabeth Warfield, married June 15, 1892 to Dr. Archibald Carlyle Harrison, of Baltimore and had children.

(8) Augustus Warfield, born 1830. Married 1859 Kate A. Gaither, the daughter of Perry Gaither and Henrietta Poole. No children.

(9)   Lucretia Griffith Warfield, born 1832. Married 1847 Dr. James S. Martin, and had children.

(10)   Avolina Warfield, born 1833. Married 1857 Major Charles Wayman Hood of Carroll County. No children.

(11)   Joshua Dorsey Warfield, born July 1, 1838. Professor of English Literature, genealogist, author of the Warfield family history of 1898. Married first April 15, 1868 to Tonny Dawley and had children. Married second January 18, 1883 to Margaret E. Cooke, daughter of Dr. Septimus J. Cooke and Mary Dalrymple. Both were said to be of Prince George's County. His children were:

    (a)   Eldred Dudley Warfield, Captain, Co. D, 5th Md Volunteers, Spanish-American War.

    (b)   Marian Serenah Warfield.

    (c)   Mary Octavia Warfield.

    (d)   John Breckinridge Warfield.

    (e)   Bernard Dalrymple Warfield.

    (f)   Margaret Clare Warfield.

d.   Joshua Warfield, born September 11, 1781, died March 19, 1846, their youngest son, inherited the *Cherry Grove* property. Married first January 29, 1807 to Rachel Griffith Welsh, born 1790, died 1815, daughter of Samuel Welsh and Rachel Griffith. Two sons and a daughter were born. Married second March 12, 1816 to Lydia Dorsey Welsh, born October 23, 1790 in Anne Arundel County, Maryland (in an area that later became Howard County), daughter of John Welsh and Lucretia Dorsey. They had two children. The children of Joshua from his two marriages included:

(1)   Benjamin Warfield, died young.

(2)   Nicholas Ridgely Warfield, died 1860; married Eleanor Warfield, the daughter of Elie and Frances Warfield. No children.

(3)   Avolina Warfield, born May 8, 1813, died February 23, 1883. Married September 26, 1833 Elisha Riggs, born July 6, 1810 on *Bordley's Choice* in

Montgomery County, died July 16, 1883 at *Annandale*, near Florence, Howard County, son of Thomas Riggs (1772), and Mary Riggs (1776) of Elisha. Elisha lived at *Rockland* on the Patuxent River in Montgomery County, formerly owned by his father. Elisha and his wife appear in the 1850 census for the First District of Montgomery County with the first four of their children. They are also in the 1860 census for the same District, although the entry could be overlooked. Only the name of Elisha is correct; the enumerator has listed his wife as Eveline; a daughter Eve; a son Joshua; and a daughter Kate; all of whom can be identified if one knows the names. The couple appears next in the 1870 census of the First District, where he is said to be a retired farmer, with $6,000 in real estate and $500 in personal property. Only the daughter called Eva is at home, who appears to be Avolina, according to the age stated. Elisha and Avolina are buried in the Warfield cemetery at *Cherry Grove* in Howard County. Seven children:

(a) Mary Olivia Riggs, born August 7, 1834, died September 9, 1863. Married November 12, 1856 Dr. Lloyd Thomas McGill of city of Frederick.

(b) Rachel Griffith Riggs, born July 9, 1836. Married January 8, 1856 Evan Aquila Jones and had four children.

(c) Avolina Riggs, born July 7, 1838, died January 25, 1892 in Howard County. Married June 28, 1871 to Captain Festus Farmer Griffith, 8th Virginia Infantry, Co. H., CSA, born July 12, 1838 at *Edgehill* near Unity, Montgomery County, the son of Thomas Griffith and Elizabeth (Griffith) Griffith.

(d) Joshua Warfield Riggs, born March 4, 1844, private, 43rd Virginia Cavalry, (Mosby's Rangers), CSA. Married October 2, 1867 to

Matilda S. Dorsey, born Feburary 9, 1849, daughter of John A. Dorsey and Margaret Banks. Two children.

(e) George Thomas Riggs, born November 1, 1847, lived twenty-nine days.

(f) Nicholas Ridgely Warfield Riggs, born March 4, 1849, died April 22, 1849.

(g) Catherine Augusta Riggs, born June 8, 1850. Married June 8, 1870 to Humphrey Dorsey of Montgomery County.

(4) Albert Gallatin Warfield, born February 26, 1817 of whom more following.

(5) Catherine Dorsey Warfield, inherited *Cherry Grove.* Married James Baxley and had a son.

3. Vachel Warfield, married to Sarah Dorsey, born September 9, 1747, daughter of Colonel Philamon Dorsey (1714) and Catherine Ridgely (1723). Lived on *Partnership* and *Good Range.* Children:

a. Lloyd Warfield, a bachelor, who in 1814 inherited lands in Montgomery County under the will of his uncle, Captain Nicholas Ridgely Warfield.

b. Philemon Dorsey Warfield, named in that will. In his own will, he left various bequests to family members.

c. Joshua Warfield, also named in his uncle's will. Received the tract of *Good Range* under the will of his brother, Philemon Dorsey Warfield, on which the brother lived.

d. Greenberry Warfield, who received from his brother's will the tracts of *Exchange* and *Partnership.*

e. Allen Warfield, who received two hundred dollars under the will of his brother Philemon Dorsey Warfield. He was married and left two children. This may be the same Allen who was married in Montgomery County July 26, 1808 to Mary Dugan. The children were:

(1) Greenberry Warfield.

(1) Allen Warfield, Jr.

f. Catherine Warfield, married Lancelot Linthicum and had children, named in the will of Philemon Dorsey Warfield:

(1) Vachel W. Linthicum.

      (2)   Lloyd W. Linthicum.

      (3)   Sarah Linthicum.

      (4)   Mary Linthicum.

4. Elisha Warfield, a member of the Committee for Observation for Anne Arundel County in 1775. He was first married to Elizabeth Dorsey, born February 15, 1743, daughter of Henry Dorsey (1712) and Elizabeth Worthington (1717), and had three children. Married second Ruth Burgess, daughter of Captain Joseph Burgess of the Elkridge Militia of 1776. Her mother was Elizabeth Dorsey, the daughter of Michael Dorsey and Ruth Todd. In 1790, Elisha and Ruth moved to Kentucky, and had children, the last twelve listed following:

  a. Polly Warfield, born December 18, 1772. Married July 31, 1795 to William Ford of Fayette County, Kentucky. They had three children, apparently born there:

      (1)   Charles Ford.

      (2)   James C. Ford, a prominent business man in the city of Louisville. Married Mary J. Trimble.

      (3)   Eliza P. Ford.

  b. Sally Warfield, an infant death.

  c. Nicholas Warfield, an infant death.

  d. Elisha Warfield, Jr., married in 1800 to Mary Barr, the daughter of Robert Barr and Rebecca Tilton. Children:

      (1)   Rebecca Tilton Warfield.

      (2)   Thomas Barr Warfield.

      (3)   William Pollock Warfield.

      (4)   Elisha Warfield.

      (5)   Anne Eliza Warfield.

      (6)   Mary Jane Warfield.

      (7)   Caroline Barr Warfield.

      (8)   Julia Genevive Warfield.

      (9)   Laura Ruth Warfield.

  e. Nicholas Warfield, a doctor, married Susan Orr of Bourbon County,Kentucky. Children:

      (1)   Mary Ellen Warfield.

      (2)   Rebecca Warfield.

      (3)   RuthWarfield.

      (4)   Caroline Warfield.

f. Benjamin Warfield, married first Sallie Caldwell of Paris, Kentucky and had five children. Married second Nancy Barr, no children. His children were:
   (1) Elisha Nicholas Warfield, married Elizabeth Brand of Lexington, Kentucky.
   (2) William Warfield, married Mary Breckinridge.
   (3) Ruth Warfield.
   (4) Sarah Warfield.
   (5) Benjamin Warfield, Jr.
g. Lloyd Warfield, a doctor of Lexington, married first to Mary Barr and had children, only five of whom reached maturity; the first five listed following. The three surviving sons served in Confederate forces, and died single. He married second Elmira Burbank and had children:
   (1) Rebecca Pollock Warfield.
   (2) Mary Jane Warfield.
   (3) Lloyd Warfield, Jr.
   (4) Edward R. Warfield.
   (5) Henry N. Warfield.
   (6) Robert Warfield.
   (7) Elisha Warfield.
   (8) Charles Chase Warfield.
   (9) Elizabeth Church Warfield.
   (10) Burgess Barr Warfield.
h. Henry Warfield was an attorney and died young. Married Eliza Millar of Cynthiana, Kentucky. Two children:
   (1) Henry Warfield, Jr.
   (2) Eliza Warfield, married to Magee.
i. Eliza Warfield, married General James Coleman.
j. Sarah Warfield.
k. Rebecca Ridgely Warfield, married William Pollock.
l. Harriet Burgess Warfield, married to Colonel William Brown of Cynthiana, Kentucky. They had children born in Kentucky, and moved the family to Illinois.
m. Ann Warfield.
n. Ruth Warfield.
o. Nancy Dorsey Warfield.

5. Mary R. Warfield, married Thomas Dorsey, born March 15, 1737, son of Henry Dorsey (1712) and Elizabeth Worthington (1717). They had at least these children:
  a. Benedict Dorsey, born c.1768 and married to Margaret Watkins, daughter of Jeremiah Watkins (1739). Children:
    (1) Thomas Dorsey.
    (2) Washington Dorsey, married Hannah Chapman and settled in Wilmington, Delaware.
    (3) Elizabeth Ann Dorsey, born October 20, 1795, married November 22, 1814 in Baltimore to George Wilmer Ford, son of John Ford and Millicent Hyland. Lived in Cecil County.
  b. Elizabeth Dorsey, married October 6, 1781 to Joshua Warfield, born April 27, 1761 in Queen Caroline Parish, Anne Arundel County, son of John Warfield and Rachel Dorsey. They had a child, following. Joshua married second January 13, 1783 Mary Ann Jones, daughter of Captain Isaac Jones of South River, and had ten more children. The one son of Elizabeth and Joshua was:
    (1) Thomas John Warfield, married Sarah Sellman.
6. Caleb Warfield.
7. Daughter Warfield, married Charles Banks.
8. Daughter Warfield, married John Lansdale.

Beale Warfield
died 1815

This son of Benjamin Warfield and Catherine Dorsey was born in Anne Arundel County and died 1815, intestate. Married to his cousin, Amelia Ridgely, daughter of William Ridgely of Elk Ridge, and Elizabeth Dorsey. They had three children:
1. Catherine Dorsey Warfield. Married to her cousin, Warner Washington Warfield, born c.1787, died 1867. He bought the tract called *Bagdad* near Sykesville. Served in the War of 1812. He was the son of Joshua Warfield (1761) and his second wife, Mary Ann Jones. Children:

a. Marcellus Warfield, married Josephine E. Lawrence, daughter of Colonel John Lawrence, Jr. of Linganore, and Martha West of *The Woodyard*. Two daughters.

b. William Henry Warfield, a merchant in Laurel, married Charlotte Duvall, born 1835, the daughter of Dr. Mareen Merriken Duvall (1807) and Harriet Evans. No children.

c. Manelia E. S. Warfield, married October 27, 1869 to Henry Jenkins. No children.

2. George W. Dorsey Warfield, single.

3. William Ridgely Warfield, born c.1807 in Anne Arundel County. Married after December 18, 1830 to Eleanor C. Watkins, daughter of Colonel Gassaway Watkins (1752) and his third wife, Eleanor Bowie Clagett (1782). Children:

a. Rosalba Warfield, married Reverend Mosely Beale of Mississippi, and had a daughter:
   (1) Bertha Mosely.

b. Beale A. Warfield, born March 21, 1834, died October 19, 1910, buried at Poplar Springs cemetery. A surveyor, he was married to Cordelia R. England, born May 10, 1839, died January 5, 1920, buried with her husband; daughter of Abram England. No children.

c. Bowie Clagett Warfield, married to Julia Gregory and lived at Sandoval, Illinois. He was a horticulturist and the originator of the "Warfield Strawberry". Children:
   (1) Alverta Warfield, married Rhodolphus Crapster.
   (2) Alice Warfield.

d. Eleanor Amelia Warfield, married the Reverend William Crapster, and had children. Married second to Captain Richard Watkins of California. Her children were:
   (1) William Channing Crapster.
   (2) Emma Crapster, married Taylor.
   (3) Florence Crapster, married Shields.

e. Gassaway Watkins Warfield, died single.

f. Emma Warfield, married John R. Kenley. Children:
   (1) Edna Kenley.
   (2) Nelly Kenley.

g. Camsadel Warfield, married George England, son of Abram England. Children:

(1)   Elizabeth England, married Sollers

(2)   Cordelia England.

h.   Alberta Clay Warfield, married Samuel Sharretts, and died as a bride.

i.   William Ridgely Warfield, Jr., a hydraulic engineer who was in charge of the Harlem River Tunnel; single.

j.   Georgietta Warfield, married Mortimer Dorsey Crapster, the only son of Rhodolphus Crapster and Elizabeth Dorsey. Children:

(1)   Rhodolphus Crapster.

(2)   Ernest Crapster.

(3)   Eleanor Crapster.

(4)   Mary Blanche Crapster.

(5)   Thaddeus Crapster.

(6)   Mortimer Dorsey Crapster, Jr.

(7)   Alice Crapster.

(8)   Emma Crapster.

(9)   Bowie Crapster.

(10)   Robert Gordon Crapster.

Albert Gallatin Warfield
1817-1891

This son of Joshua Warfield (1781) and Lydia Dorsey Welsh (1790) was born February 26, 1817, died November 6, 1891. Just two months before his death, there was a newspaper announcement that he was 74 years old, and lived at Florence, Howard County. Married August 25, 1842 to Margaret Gassaway Watkins, died August, 1897, daughter of Colonel Gassaway Watkins (1752) and his third wife, Eleanor Bowie Clagett (1782). Colonel Watkins served seven years in the Revolutionary War and was in command of forces at Annapolis during the War of 1812. In 1838, Albert Gallatin Warfield built his home called *Oakdale* in Howard County, Maryland, and served as School Commissioner of the county for several years. He owned a number of slaves, but freed each of them when they reached the age of forty. Ten children:

1.   Albert Gallatin Warfield, Jr., born 1843, died 1883, who also served in the Confederate Army as a Major, according to some

reports. However, in *Marylanders in the Confederacy,* by Daniel D. Hartzler, Albert was reported as a private in the 1st Maryland Cavalry, Co. A, CSA. After the war, he became a well-known civil engineer; went to Japan in 1873 as a member of the American Scientific Commission, and died in 1883, as a result of exposure in the mountains of West Virginia while building the West Virginia Central Railroad. Married Celina Duperu of California, and had children:

a. Albert Gallatin Warfield, III.

b. Catherine Warfield.

c. Frances Warfield.

2. Joshua Nicholas Warfield of Howard County, born September 3, 1845. Married December 8, 1881 at St. John's in Mechanicsville, to Lucy W. Hutton, daughter of Enoch B. Hutton. Children:

a. Margaret Warfield.

b. Joshua Nicholas Warfield, Jr., born February 28, 1885 in Howard County, Maryland. He was secretary/treasurer of the Eureka Life Insurance Co. of Baltimore until April of 1923, and later held those offices with the Woodbine Canning Company; and was involved in numerous other business enterprises. In addition, he farmed more than six hundred acres in Howard County. Graduated from the University of Maryland in the class of 1902. Married in Baltimore on March 6, 1908 to Mary Nicodemus, daughter of Frank Nicodemus and Mary Weeks.

c. Norman Warfield.

3. Gassaway Watkins Warfield, born 1846, CSA army; died in the Union prison in 1864 at Camp Chase.

4. Edwin Warfield, born May 7, 1848 in Howard County, died March 31, 1920. President of the Maryland Senate in 1886 and Surveyor of the Port of Baltimore. He owned the family homestead of *Oakdale.* Governor of Maryland from 1904 to 1908, president of the Fidelity and Deposit Company. Married November 24, 1886 to Emma Nicodemus, daughter of J. Courtney Nicodemus of Baltimore, and his wife, Mary J. Montandon. Children:

a. Carrie Warfield, born January 12, 1888. Married William Hugh Harris and had children:
   (1) Rosalind Harris.
   (2) Louise Harris.
   (3) Barbara Harris.
   (4) Virginia Harris.
   (5) William Hugh Harris, Jr.
b. Louise Warfield, born February 27, 1889. Married Count Vladimir Ledochowski, and had three children. She married second Charles D. Morgan. Her children were:
   (1) Therese Ledochowski.
   (2) Yadwiga Ledochowski.
   (3) Stanislaus Ledochowski.
c. Edwin Warfield, Jr., born June 28, 1891; president of the Daily Record Publishing Co. of Baltimore. Married to Katherine Lawrence Lee and had children:
   (1) Katherine Warfield.
   (2) Edwin Warfield, III
   (3) Francis Warfield.
d. Emma Warfield, born March 27, 1899. Married to Frank Gramkow and had children:
   (1) David Gramkow.
   (2) Edwin Gramkow.
5. Alice Warfield, born May 28, 1849 the oldest daughter. Married M. Gillet Gill of the firm of Martin, Gillett & Co., tea importers. On their wedding trip, she visited Japan, being the first American lady on the island. Children:
   a. M. Gillett Gill, Jr., served in the Spanish-American War.
   b. Howard Gill.
   c. Royal Gill.
   d. Mildred Gill.
6. John Warfield, born 1850, died single, an attorney, and editor of the *Daily Law Record* of Baltimore.
7. Frank Warfield, born March 5, 1854
8. Clarence Warfield, born December 8, 1855
9. Margaret Gassaway Warfield, born April 28, 1858, married Herman Hoopes of West Chester, Pennsylvania. Children:
   a. Marian Hoopes.

    b.   Edward Hoopes.

    c.   Albert W. Hoopes.

10. Marshall T. Warfield of Howard County, born August 20, 1861. Inherited part of the original tract of *Fredericksburg,* and in 1898 was single.

CHAPTER 5

Edward Warfield
1710-

This son of John Warfield (1673) and Ruth Gaither (1679) was born August 11, 1710 in Anne Arundel County, Maryland; died December 31, 1786. His will was dated April 20, 1782 and probated in Anne Arundel February 13, 1787. He there named his wife, leaving her the home plantation of *Venison Park,* containing 200 acres which he had inherited from his father. He left to three of his sons; Robert, Levin and Edward; the tract called *Additional Chance Increased,* to be equally divided. He left some of his negroes to various of his children. He was married October 6, 1741 in Anne Arundel County to Rachel Riggs, born June 11, 1724 in Anne Arundel County, died April 16, 1794 daughter of John Riggs and Mary Davis. Many of the later generations of this family, including those who moved to Tennessee, are discussed in *The Riggs Family of Maryland,* by John Beverly Riggs, published in Baltimore 1989, to which the reader is referred. We include here only the first few generations. Children of Edward Warfield (1710) were:

1. Ephraim Warfield, born August 23, 1742, served in the Revolution and died October 22, 1832, single.
2. Edward Warfield, Jr., born January 8, 1745, died December 19, 1768, single.
3. Achsah Warfield, born June 4, 1747; married Joseph Hall.
4. Robert Warfield, born May 1, 1749, died in 1818 without children.
5. James Warfield, born September 21, 1751, inherited the home property of *Venison Park.* Married Ann Gassaway, daughter of Brice John Gassaway and Dinah Warfield and had children. Ann was married secondly after August 1, 1814 in Anne Arundel County to Nicholas Worthington, and moved to Tennessee, apparently with her children. The children of James Warfield were:

a.   Laban Warfield, moved to Tennessee. Married Huldah Metcalf and second Ann Alensworth. One son born to his first marriage, none to the second:
   (1)   William Wallace Warfield, married to Adelia Boyseau and had three children.
b.   James Harvey Warfield, a major in the Mexican War, he received large tracts of land in Texas; died there, single.
c.   Henry Warfield.
d.   George Hanson Warfield, married after May 7, 1827 to Susan Waters, daughter of Colonel Jacob Waters of Annapolis, and his wife Elizabeth Wells. Married second to Elizabeth J. Johnson. Moved to Tennessee in 1825 and had four children from his first marriage and nine from the second:
   (1)   James Harvey Warfield, married Sarah E. Reid and had six children.
   (2)   Anne Elizabeth Warfield; married to George R. Browder and had five children.
   (3)   Susan Virginia Warfield, married to Thomas E. Browder and had five children.
   (4)   George Waters Warfield, married Dora Pollard and had seven children.
   (5)   Amanda Warfield, married D. P. Sypert and had one child.
   (6)   Charles P. Warfield, married Mary Rice and had three children.
   (7)   Joseph Gassaway Warfield, married Eddie Northington and had two children.
   (8)   Nannie M. Warfield, married Mack Meriweather and had a son.
   (9)   Martha H. Warfield, married David Hendrick and had five children.
   (10) Samuel J. Warfield, died single.
   (11) Luther Laban Warfield, a doctor, died single. He lived at Clarksville, Tennessee.
   (12) Alexander Guen Warfield, married Sarah Wood and had three children.
   (13) Unknown child.

e. Luther Warfield.
f. Charles Milton Warfield, moved to Tennessee as a youth. Married first Jane Trigg and second Mary C. Hutchings. He had three childlren from his second marriage:
   (1) Henry Clay Warfield, married Barbara Gun.
   (2) William C. Warfield, married Ann Sadler.
   (3) Elizabeth Walter Warfield, married J. R. Young and had a daughter.
g. Elizabeth Ann Warfield, married January 2, 1826 to Walter Warfield Waters of Maryland, son of Ignatius Waters and Nancy Warfield. Moved to Tennessee; no children.
6. Levin Warfield, born December 11, 1753, and of whom more following.
7. Ruth Warfield, born February 6, 1756, died single.
8. Catherine Warfield, born July 22, 1758, died single.
9. Rachel Warfield, born July 23, 1760 at *Venison Park*, the family plantation in Anne Arundel County, Maryland, and married Noah Hobbs, son of Joseph Hobbs and Elizabeth Higgins. At least nine children:
a. Ephraim Hobbs.
b. Amos Hobbs.
c. Dennis Hobbs.
d. Warfield Hobbs, born c.1794.
e. Rachel Hobbs, married Leach.
f. Elizabeth Hobbs.
g. Ruth Hobbs, married to Caleb Hobbs, who died 1837, the son of Thomas Hobbs, and had children:
   (1) Gustavus Warfield Hobbs, a minister.
   (2) Rezin Thomas Hobbs.
   (3) Henry Macken Hobbs.
   (4) Remus Riggs Hobbs.
   (5) Samuel Adams Hobbs.
   (6) Sarah Jane Hobbs.
h. Anna Hobbs.
i. Hannah Hobbs.
10. Sarah Warfield, born May 15, 1762 at *Venison Park*, married August 29, 1781 to Zachariah Gaither, the son of John Gaither

and Agnes Rogers. Zachariah served as an Ensign in the company of Captain Basil Burgess, Elk Ridge Battalion, during the Revolutionary War, under a commission issued March 30, 1779. He and Sarah had children:

a. Rachel Gaither.

b. Zachariah Gaither, Jr., died December 28, 1834 in Wharton Township, Fayette County, Pennsylvania, where he is buried. Married January 11, 1805 in Washington County, Maryland, to Elizabeth Garver, born 1786 at Hagerstown, buried February 12, 1827 at Clear Springs, Maryland, daughter of Samuel Garver. About 1824, they moved to Fayette County, Pennsylvania. They had children, probably born in Washington County:

    (1) Samuel Gaither, born October 27, 1806 in Washington County, Maryland, died November 5, 1890 in Somerset County, Pennsylvania. Married there April 1, 1832 to Lydia Hugus, daughter of Michael Hugus and Elizabeth Ankeny. They had seven children, probably all born in Somerset County, where Samuel was an attorney at law.

    (2) William Gaither, married Garret.

    (3) Hezekiah Gaither.

    (4) Millicent Gaither, married Brown.

    (5) Sarah Gaither.

    (6) Elizabeth Gaither, single.

c. Greenberry Gaither, born December 3, 1792. Married and had at least six children, one of whom was:

    (1) Matilda Riggs Gaither, who was married to James Holliday Rawlings and had at least one son.

d. James Gaither, married, lived in Cincinnati, Ohio and had at least three children, one son being:

    (1) Thomas B. Gaither, a major, born c.1827, died November 3, 1902 in Baltimore. He was Clerk of the Superior Court of Baltimore for forty years. Married first Mary Olivia Zachary, who died October 17, 1864, the daughter of Captain William Zachary of Baltimore; and second to Lucretia D.

Thomas had four children from his first marriage and two from the second.

e. Lucy Gaither, died young.

f. Edward Gaither.

g. Evan Gaither, married to Mary Ann (Hinkle) Gibson, a widow of Philadelphia. They had a large family, including these two daughters:

   (1) Caroline Riggs Gaither, born 1848

   (2) Sarah Warfield Gaither, died single.

h. John Gaither.

11. Elizabeth Warfield, born August 23, 1764; married to James Ray. No children.

12. Edward Warfield, the Younger, born June 5, 1769 on the home plantation of *Venison Park* in Anne Arundel County, Maryland; died in March, 1853. He is noted in the family as the first genealogist, recording much of the family history up to that date in an 1828 record. He took up the tract called *Additional Chance Increased.* Married to Mary Ann Warfield, daughter of Davidge Warfield (1729) and Anne Dorsey; (of Alexander Warfield and Dinah Davidge); and had children:

a. Anna Warfield, born September 8, 1795, died July 18, 1852, single.

b. Ephraim Warfield, born February 15, 1797, a Methodist minister, died May 7, 1860. Married Catherine Browne, born February 17, 1807, died April 16, 1853 (or 1859). They are buried at Howard Chapel cemetery near Lisbon, Howard County, Maryland. They had children, all of whom died without issue:

   (1) Margaret Ann Warfield, born March 5, 1837 and died December 21, 1888, according to her tombstone at Howard Chapel cemetery. She appears to have first been married to a Browning, and secondly married by license dated June 24, 1869 at Ellicott City to Nathan J. Burdette, born May 9, 1827 and died April 4, 1904. He was a son of Benjamin Burdette (died 1833) and Elizabeth Brown (1792). The couple appear in the 1880 census of Howard County, with one child. The 1900

census for Hyattstown, in Montgomery County, carries a couple who may be these two; Nathan at age 74, and Mary J. at age 63. While the name of Nathan's wife is not correct in the census, the ages correlate with known facts. Their daughter was:

(a) Ida E. Burdette, born c.1872

(2) Mary Warfield, born October 6, 1841, died January 20, 1891, single.

(3) Martha Warfield, born July 18, 1845, died February 16, 1867, single.

c. John Davidge Warfield, born March 4, 1799, died July 31, 1865 near Poplar Springs, Howard County, Maryland. Married Corilla Elizabeth Hobbs, born March 3, 1806, died July 23, 1880 at or near Lisbon. Both are buried in the Oak Grove Cemetery, at Glenwood, Howard County. She was a daughter of Gerard (or Jared) Hobbs and Ellen Shipley. Children:

(1) Mary Ellen Warfield, born November 25, 1827, died December 8, 1893, single. Buried Oak Grove.

(2) Thomas Wallace Warfield, born August 24, 1833, died April 9, 1898 at Easton, Maryland. Buried with his wife at Mt. Olivet cemetery, Frederick, Maryland. Reportedly, he had inherited the seal ring of Richard, the Immigrant, which showed a warrior on horseback; although we have found no evidence that the Warfield family was entitled to bear Arms. Married to Rebecca A. Trail, born November 24, 1840, and died November 20, 1909, daughter of Oscar Trail and Sarah Kemp. They had children:

(a) Louis Edwin Warfield, born July 2, 1864, died February 28, 1936; buried at Mt. Olivet in Frederick. The records there spell his name as Lewis, rather than Louis. Married May 2, 1892 to Alice McMillan, daughter of Hugh McMillan of Detroit, and had two children.

(b) Nina Harding Warfield, born April 24, 1866, died June 6, 1922, single.

(c) Rebecca Elizabeth Warfield, born February 19, 1868. Married Charles Campbell Patterson of England. Two children.

(d) Thomas Wallace Warfield, Jr. born May 27, 1875. Married first Julia (Watson) Hoone of Pittsburg, and secondly in May, 1934 to Elizabeth (Colston) Randall.

(e) Mary Josephine Warfield, born August 10, 1877. Married first Hugh McMillan, son of James McMillan of Ontario, Canada. Two children were born of that marriage. Married second Dr. Walter Dent Wise of Baltimore.

(f) John Davidge Warfield, born November 14, 1880, died May 21, 1934.

(3) Ruth Elizabeth Gaither Warfield, born December 3, 1836 in Anne Arundel County, died April 24, 1910. Married to Leonidas Magruder Griffith, born May 8, 1835, died April 14, 1906, son of Jefferson Griffith, and Cordelia Magruder. Children:

(a) Mary Warfield Griffith, born January 16, 1861, died July 23, 1861.

(b) Florence May Griffith, born May 31, 1862. Married November 20, 1888 to Ephraim Butzer, of Tuscarora, New York.

(c) John Jefferson Griffith, born May 21, 1865, died July 25, 1903. Married December 29, 1897 to Mildred Messenger; no children.

(d) Cordelia Elizabeth Griffith, born January 4, 1867. Married June 25, 1891 to George Ellsworth Miller of Amos, West Virginia. Two children.

(e) Rosalie Griffith, born May 11, 1869, died April 20, 1902. Married June 24, 1895 to Dr. Charles Thatcher Waggoner and had two children.

(f) Columbia Magruder Griffith, born August 24, 1870, died June 16, 1931. Married January 24, 1893 to William T. Knickerbocker and second November 3, 1898 Rolland McCaslin. Apparently there were no children.

(g) Leonidas Magruder Griffith, Jr., born August 6, 1876. Married first Flora Golden and second March 10, 1926 to Amelia Lee Johnson.

(4) Cecilius Edwin Warfield, born August 15, 1841, died September 8, 1915, buried with is wife at Mt. Olivet cemetery in Frederick. A merchant of Baltimore, he married Janury 18, 1870 in Frederick to Laura Winters Thomas, born December 1, 1844, died January 19, 1912, daughter of David Ogle Thomas and Elizabeth Stauffer of *Rose Hill* at Frederick, Maryland. After the marriage, Cecilius Edwin and his wife lived there. They had children:

(a) John Ogle Warfield, born May 12, 1871 at *Rose Hill* near Frederick. An Episcopal minister, holding an Honorary Doctor of Divinity degree from St. John's College in Annapolis, he was married October 26, 1898 to Louyse Duvall Spragins, born November 19, 1869 in Baltimore, daughter of Stith Bolling Spragins and Elizabeth Ann Hamilton. Six children.

(b) Frederick Howard Warfield, born August 28, 1874 in Baltimore, died April 5, 1928 at Bala-cynwdy, Pennsylvania. Married at Baltimore, November 28, 1903 to Julia Rogers Warner, born there January 7, 1876, daughter of Henry Warner and Mary Godey. Frederick was a graduate of Johns Hopkins (as was his brother John Ogle) and was a prominent attorney in Baltimore. Two children.

(c) Cecilius Edwin Warfield, Jr., born October 17, 1880, died September 15, 1897; buried with his parents.

Levin Warfield
1753-1812

This son of Edward Warfield and Rachel Riggs was born December 11, 1753 and died about 1812. He held the tract called *Additional Chance Increased* in Howard County. Levin wrote a will dated April 21, 1812, and perhaps died not too long thereafter. He stated that he was then of Anne Arundel County, and was sick of body. Apparently his wife had predeceased him, not being mentioned. He was married under license dated October 6, 1779 in Anne Arundel County, Maryland, to Anna Hobbs, the daughter of William Hobbs. However, he does mention his brothers, Robert Warfield and Edward Warfield, and named several children with bequests to each of them. Each of the three daughters received one feather bed and furniture, one cow and calf, one sow and pigs, one chest, and one Linen wheel. He also provides for the ultimate freedom of his slaves: Sam, Becky, Frank, Tuase, Harry and Hen. Children were:

1. Edward Warfield, died c.1836, the eldest son, received all of the lands in Montgomery County, and of whom more in Chapter 6.
2. Greenbury Warfield. He and Robert received the dwelling plantation whereon Levin then lived. Greenbury also received a horse and second choice as to a clock standing in the house. Married October 8, 1824 in Frederick County Sarah Adams.
3. Levin Warfield.
4. William Warfield.
5. Robert Warfield, born March 4, 1790 in Anne Arundel County, died May 23, 1842. He received the dwelling plantation with his brother Greenbury, a horse and first choice as to the black walnut cupboard in the house. He was married after February 1, 1831 to Sarah Griffith, born April 27, 1792 in Montgomery County, and died there October 1, 1857, daughter of Captain Samuel Griffith (1752) and Ruth Berry (1762). In the 1850 census for Montgomery County, there is a household headed by Sarah Lyon, with Israel Griffith Warfield living with her. Her age matches reasonably close to that of his mother, who was married January 13, 1845 to Benjamin Lyon,

a second marriage for Sarah Griffith Warfield. Robert and Sarah had two sons:

    a.   Israel Griffith Warfield, born February 17, 1832 and of whom more following.

    b.   Robert H. Warfield, born in July, 1835, died in February, 1846

6. Rispah Warfield.

7. Rachael Warfield, married April 16, 1812 William Etchison, and was to receive the sum of fifteen pounds as soon as convenient.

8. Anna Warfield, married December 13, 1804 to John Etchison.

9. Mary Warfield, who received in addition to the items mentioned above, the sum of thirty pounds to be paid at arriving to the age of twenty-one, or at marriage, whichever was first.

10. Sarah Warfield, who also received the sum of fifty pounds at the age of twenty-one or marriage. Married to Duvall.

11. Achsah Warfield, born c.1781 in Anne Arundel County; received a negro girl named Dinah under her father's will. She was married February 7, 1801 in Montgomery County to Daniel Browning, born January 31, 1779 in Anne Arundel County, Maryland and died January 31, 1839 in Ross County, Ohio; the son of Archibald Browning (1753) and his first wife, Sarah Johnson. Daniel served as private under Captain Nicholas Hall, 2nd Reg., 1st Cavalry Div., War of 1812. Daniel died January 31, 1839 in Ross County, Ohio, the father of at least two children:

    a.   Greenberry Browning, born c.1814 in Montgomery County, Maryland, died September 28, 1850 in Ross County, Ohio. Married there January 17, 1838 to Eleanor Bourne.

    b.   Wesley Browning, born c.1820 in Ross County and married there June 10, 1841 Julia Ann Hines, born c.1820 in Ohio.

Israel Griffith Warfield
1832-1907

This son of Robert Warfield (1790) and Sarah Griffith (1792) was born February 17, 1832, perhaps in Howard County, and died February 27, 1907 at Laytonsville in Montgomery County, having moved there at about the age of six with his parents; buried with his wife at the Laytonsville Cemetery. In the 1850 census of the Cracklin District of Montgomery County, Israel was found living with Sarah Lyon, born c.1794, and she was listed as head of household. In the 1860 census for Laytonsville District, Israel is listed as head of household, by his initials only, born c.1833, which appears to be the same individual. He there had a wife, Maria G., born c.1838. He was listed then as owning real estate valued at $2,500 and personal property valued at $2,000; not too bad for a young man, just twenty-seven years old, and recently married. Married at St. Bartholomew's Episcopal Church June 7, 1860 to Maria Gaither Griffith, born May 28, 1838 and died October 30, 1903, daughter of Elisha Riggs Griffith (1805) and his wife Elizabeth Gaither (1805). By the census of 1870, Israel was found living in the Brighton area of Montgomery County, with his wife, and five children. They had others, born after the taking of the census:

1. Robert Clarence Warfield, born June 15, 1861 at Laytonsville, died April 6, 1943 at Rockville. A dentist in Rockville, he was first married February 15, 1888 to Margaret Webb, born November 9, 1861, died May 12, 1913 at Rockville, daughter of Francis Ignatius Devereaux Webb (1833) and Mary T. Postley (1838) by whom he had five children before her death. Dr. Robert and Margaret are buried at Rockville. He was married second in Philadelphia August 30, 1916 to Susan Natalie Dutrow, born August 14, 1872 in Ohio, died August 25, 1963 at Potomac, Maryland, daughter of Amos W. Dutrow and Sarah Howell. Robert Clarence left a will dated March 8, 1943, probated April 20, 1943 and filed in liber JWN 2 at folio 113, will records of Montgomery County. He names his wife Susan, and his three surviving sons. Children were born to his first marriage only:

a. Robert Leroy Warfield, of Frederick, who founded a Ford auto dealership there in 1916. Born c.1889, died October 5, 1970 in a Palm Beach, Florida hospital. Before entering the auto business, he was an attorney in Rockville. Married Mabel Poole, and had two sons:
   (1) John Clark Warfield, of Frederick.
   (2) Robert Warfield.
b. Helen Elizabeth Warfield, born December 18, 1889, died February 11, 1894.
c. Clarence Griffith Warfield, an Admiral in the US Navy, Died June 28, 1982; married to Kathryn Knight and had a daughter:
   (1) Kathryn D. Warfield, married O'Neill.
d. Webb Warfield, died as an infant October 11, 1891; buried with parents.
e. Gaither Postley Warfield, a minister, born February 13, 1896, died August 16, 1986 at his home in Rockville. He had been a Methodist Missionary in Poland, where he met and married his wife in 1928. She was Hania M. Drodiowski, born January 18, 1906 in Lvov, died March 16, 1995 in Rockville. In September, 1939, he was interned by the Russians and exchanged to the Germans; finally in 1942, being exchanged to American forces. He and his wife were co-authors of *Call Us to Witness*, an account of their experiences. One daughter:
   (1) Monica Warfield, born c.1937, probably in Poland, married to Kulp of Vermont.

2. Elisha Griffith Warfield, born May 15, 1863 at Laytonsville, died March 19, 1953; buried at Laytonsville. Baptized at Rockville Methodist Church September 4, 1864. In 1884, he made his way to Boston, and in 1891 moved to New York City, where he managed the Mallory Steamship Line with noted success. In 1910, with others, he organized the Seaboard and Gulf Steamship Company, of which he was the vice-president and general manager. Married May 14, 1890 to Harriet Sophia Sargent of Boston, Massachusetts, and had at least two daughters:

a. Helen Elizabeth Warfield, married to Allen O. Mogensen and had two children:
   (1) James Mogensen.
   (2) Jean Mogensen.
b. Mary Adams Warfield, married to Mac Baker. Children:
   (1) Lee Baker.
   (2) Robert Baker.
   (3) Patricia Baker.
   (4) William Baker, a twin.
   (5) Paul Baker, a twin.
3. Elizabeth Worthington Warfield, born February 8, 1865 at *The Cedars,* Laytonsville, Montgomery County, Maryland; died September 4, 1972. Her name is shown in some records as Elizabeth Washington Warfield, but we believe that to be incorrect. Married July 15, 1890 Francis Clarence Webb, born September 27, 1866, died March 11, 1957, son of Francis Ignatius Devereaux Webb (1833) and Mary T. Postley (1838). Two children:
   a. Gladys Elizabeth Webb, born May 24, 1891, died July 31, 1954. Married September 10, 1917 to Thomas H. Patterson. One child:
      (1) Harriet Elizabeth Patterson born October 29, 1922 and married May 12, 1944 to Pierce S. Ellis, Jr. Three children:
         (a) Robert P. Ellis, born April 13, 1948. Married January 23, 1971 at Succasunna, New Jersey to Joan Marie Kirchgessner.
         (b) Catherine Elizabeth Ellis, born September 17, 1951. Married July 25, 1970 in Ottawa, Canada to Mark Kenneth Lloyd.
   b. Francis Warfield Webb, born October 15, 1893, and died 1974. Married November 16, 1925 to Adelaide Horine and had two daughters:
      (1) Constance Ann Webb, born November 9, 1926. Married May 2, 1953 to Jack Visscher St. John and had three children:
         (a) Robert Warfield St. John: February 15, 1954
         (b) Susan Elizabeth St. John: Apri 19, 1956

(c)   Richard William St. John: August 12, 1961
    (2)   Miriam Horine Webb, born November 19, 1930. Married November 15, 1952 to James Noble Kilb and had two children:
       (1)   Deborah Sue Kilb, born June 13, 1958
       (2)   Clifford Francis Kilb, born March 30, 1960

4. Alfred Griffith Warfield, born November 4, 1867, died September 2, 1877. Buried Methodist cemetery, Laytonsville.

5. Israel Griffith Warfield, Jr., a doctor, born November 18, 1869, died August 11, 1918. Buried at Laytonsville. Married November 3, 1897 at Ascension Chapel, Gaithersburg, to Mrs. Kate L. Shaw Church, born c.1870, died February 14, 1936. Two children:
   a.   Charles Warfield.
   b.   Courtney Warfield.

6. Lena Matthews Warfield, born May 15, 1872, died August 14, 1940; buried Monocacy Cemetery at Beallsville. Married October 25, 1898 to Dr. Vernon Hilleary Dyson and lived in Laytonsville. No children.

7. Martha Jane Warfield, born July 25, 1874, died December 17, 1879. Buried at Laytonsville.

8. Bertha Warfield, born March 21, 1876, died December 11, 1876. Buried at Laytonsville.

9. Frederick Gaither Warfield, born June 15, 1879, died July 30, 1881

CHAPTER 6

Edward Warfield
died 1836

This son of Levin Warfield (1753) and Anna Hobbs, was married in Montgomery County, Maryland, December 4, 1805 to Eunice Etchison, according to *James Day of Browningsville and his descendants, A Maryland Family,* by Jackson Harvey Day; and according to *The Warfields of Maryland,* by Professor Joshua Dorsey Warfield, 1898. Edward may have been married twice, however, in that his wife is named Elizabeth in his will, dated June 9, 1836, probated October 18, 1836 and filed in liber U at folio 399 in Montgomery County. It was later transcribed into liber VMB 4 at folio 56 in the office of the Register of Wills. In the will, it is first provided that the one third of his wife Elizabeth be first taken out, followed by various bequests. He gives to his wife the negro girl named Kitty for her personal use. We will first list the children of the family, followed by detailed discussions of each of them having descendants. The children were:

1. Caleb Warfield, born c.1806, of whom more as Child 1.
2. Elizabeth Warfield, born c.1810, died single. This is perhaps the same Elizabeth buried at Kemptown Methodist Church. Her stone records her birth as August 28, 1812, and she died March 15, 1878.
3. Horace Warfield, born April 7, 1814, of whom more as Child 3, following.
4. John M. Warfield, born July 17, 1816, of whom more as Child 4, following.
5. Hamilton G. Warfield, born December 17, 1817, of whom more as Child 5, following.
6. Mahlon H. Warfield, born July 11, 1819, of whom more as Child 6, following.
7. Garrison Warfield, born c.1822, of whom more as Child 7.
8. Mary Ann Warfield, born April 15, 1809, of whom more following as Child 8.

9. Asbury Warfield, under 21 in 1836. Asbury was born c.1827, according to the 1850 census for the Clarksburg District of Montgomery County, Maryland. He is listed there with his wife, Angeline. Asbury Warfield and Angeline appear next in the 1860 census, with Elizabeth Lewis (born c.1840) living in the household with them. No record of children. Married in Frederick County November 11, 1848 to Angeline Lewis, born September 11, 1828, died March 14, 1898, daughter of Jeremiah Lewis (1781) and Mary Windsor (1787). After the death of Asbury, she was married October 6, 1870 to Edmund L. Windsor, born September 14, 1810, died November 6, 1872, son of Zadock Windsor (1781) and Jane Lewis (1776).
10. Edward Stansbury Warfield.
11. Edna James Warfield.

CHILD 1

Caleb Warfield
1806-1863

This son of Edward Warfield (died 1836) was born c.1806 and died February, 1863, and was said to have lived on the home plantation. His father's will provided that Caleb could remain on "my plantation where he presently lives." . He appears as head of household in the 1850 census for the Eighth Election district of Frederick County, with his wife and three children. According to the census, Caleb owned 70 acres of improved land and 10 acres of unimproved land, valued at one thousand, eight hundred dollars. He had 3 horses, 2 milch cows, 1 other cow and 8 swine, not very much in the way of animals. His largest crop appears to have been tobacco, poducing 800 pounds of that during the previous year. He produced 200 pounds of butter, probably for his own use. Married November 1, 1834 to Harriett A. Purdy, born c.1815. This family must have suffered a severe illness, in that Caleb and his first two daughters died within a matter of one or two months; the two girls only ten days apart. His children were:
1. Frances Ann Warfield, born 1836, died January 13, 1863, single.

2. Lydia Augusta Warfield, born 1839, died January 23, 1863, single.
3. William R. Warfield, born 1844

CHILD 3

Horace Warfield
1814-1873

This son of Edward Warfield (died 1836) was born April 7, 1814, died April 11, 1873, buried at Kemptown Methodist Church. Under his father's will, Horace received a bay stud horse, a cow and furniture. He is listed as head of household in the 1850 census for the Clarksburg District of Montgomery County, born c.1812, and a farmer, with real estate valued at $1,800. His wife, Sarah R, was born c.1817, and they then had four children living at home, assumed to be theirs. Also living with them were Hamilton G. Warfield, born c.1820 (actually 1817), and Elizabeth Warfield, born c.1810, a brother and sister. Horace was married December 1, 1843 at Rockville to Sarah Rebecca King, born March 6, 1818, died July 10, 1902 at Kemptown, daughter of John Duckett King (1778) and Jemima Miles (1782). The descendants of John Duckett King are the principal subjects of *Our Maryland Heritage, Book Five, The King Families,* one of the earlier books in this series. Horace is found again in the 1860 census for Damascus with his wife and six children. Also in the household is Elizabeth Warfield, apparently the same from the 1850 census, although there she is reported as born c.1813, not too bad for census reports. The family appears next in the 1870 census for Damascus, with both parents, and now reporting seven children at home, and again, Elizabeth. At that time, he was said to be a farmer, with real estate valued at $2,500 and $2,031 in personal property. Horace left a will dated February 10, 1873, probated April 29, 1873 and filed in liber RWC-6 at folio 23, Montgomery County will records. He mentioned his wife, and several children:
1. Martha Warfield, born February 22, 1845, died April 15, 1906, buried Damascus cemetery. Married after December 7, 1875 to Franklin B. Day, born November 10, 1836, the

youngest child of James Day (1762) and his third wife, Sarah Mark (1799). Franklin B. Day was apparently first married to Ellen Monroe about March 26, 1861 while living in Washington County, Maryland. No children.

2. John E. Warfield, born c.1846, died about July 10, 1925, according to his obituary in the *Frederick Post*. He was buried at Providence Methodist Episcopal Church in Kemptown, Maryland. He was married at City Hotel in Frederick County, April 28, 1887 to Mary E. Molesworth, born 1847, died 1921, buried with her husband, and had no children. She was apparently the daughter of Josiah (1819) and Elizabeth A. Molesworth (1823), who are found with their family in the 1860 census for Clarksburg District of Montgomery County. John E. Warfield was found in the 1900 census for Damascus, living with his mother. The census reports that he had been married for seventeen years. His mother is listed as Mary E., born 1818, which does not fit with any other information available, as to the name.

3. Amanda Warfield, born c.1849, not in the 1870 census. In her father's will, she is listed as Amanda Purdum and of whom more following.

4. William Warfield, born c.1851

5. Bradley Warfield, born c.1854. Spelled Pradby in 1870 and in cemetery records. In the obituary of his mother, he is listed as Bradley Warfield. Died April 24, 1915; buried at Kemptown Methodist Church, with his wife, Mary E, with no dates on her stone. With them is one daughter. Bradley's wife was Mary E. Browning, born 1858, the daughter of John William Browning (1832) and Lucinda Brandenburg (1832). Bradley and Mary appear in the 1900 census for Damascus, with her mother living in their household, and the one living daughter:

    a. Bessie Warfield, born 1885, died July 30, 1885.

    b. Mamie E. Warfield, born 1888

6. Eveline Warfield, born c.1859. Spelled Exeline in 1870. married February 22, 1881 in Montgomery County, Maryland, to Jacob M. Allnutt.

7. Mary E. Warfield, born c.1856. Not shown in any census but the 1870, when she should have been in 1860.

8.   Edward D. Warfield, born c.1853. Not shown in any census but the 1870, when he should have been found also in 1860.

Amanda Warfield
1849-1941

This daughter of Horace Warfield (1812) and Sarah Rebecca King (1818) was born c.1849 and married to Columbus A. Purdum, born c.1838 and died May 31, 1917, son of Joshua Purdum (1801); buried at Kemptown. Columbus Purdum was assigned the post office position under Grover Cleveland, which was held in Al Smith's store and called Purdum Post Office, from which the name of the village derived. They were first found in the 1870 census for the Second District of Montgomery County, with their first child. Living with them was George W. Hobbs, born c.1856, listed as a farm laborer. They appeared next in the 1880 census for Montgomery County, with two children. In his household at the time is Joshua Purdum, born c.1801, listed as his father. They appear again in the 1900 census for Damascus, Montgomery County, with four of their children. From the census and other sources, we list following two daughters; Lynee and Sallie L., who may in fact be a single individual. Only Sallie L. appears in a census record, and we suspect that Lynee may be her middle name; it is possible that she was married twice, to the two husbands and with the descendants attributed to the two daughters listed. Further research is warranted. Columbus and Amanda had children:

1.   Eunice Elizabeth Purdum, born September 18, 1869, died June 25, 1870; buried at Kemptown.
2.   Leah W. Purdum, born c.1870, died May 19, 1877 at the age of 7 years, 9 months, 11 days. Buried at Kemptown.
3.   Hepsi Gertrude Purdum, born June 2, 1875, died May 15, 1951; buried at Kemptown. Married February 22, 1894 to Reuben Newton "Knute" Poole at Mountain View Church in Montgomery County, and had children:
      a.   Gertrude Poole, married William Johnson. Children:
            (1)   Guy Johnson.
            (2)   James V. Johnson, married Mary Stanley, and had children:

(a) Larry E. Johnson.

(b) Vernon "Pete" Johnson. Married to Melody Brown.

(3) Ruth Johnson, married to Lindy N. Beall, son of Barry Beall.

(4) Dorothy Lillian Johnson, born June 3, 1928. Married June 29, 1946 at Mountain View Church to Franklin Webster King, born March 31, 1927, the son of Harvey Webster King (1890) and Martha Pauline Burdette (1893). They had children:

(a) Dorothy Ann King, born May 20, 1949, and married November 29, 1968 to Robert Lee Anderson, born December 8, 1948, the son of James William Anderson and Elizabeth E. Fox (1920); and had a daughter:

1. Heide Lynn Anderson: October 5, 1969

(b) Frank Robert King, born January 28, 1951; married twice, and had children.

(5) Walter Johnson.

b. Lucy Poole, married to William Haller King, born May 18, 1893, died November 11, 1972; buried at Mountain View Cemetery in Montgomery County, his first wife. He was a son of Holady Hix King (1857) and Amy Jane Musgrove (1860). We have not identified whether or not Lucy was the mother of any of his children. He was married second to Daisy I. Price, born c.1891 and died February 8, 1974. She had first been married to Wesley R. Smith, by whom she had a daughter and a son. William Haller's will was dated April 5, 1972 and probated in Montgomery County, in which he names his wife, and both of her children from her first marriage. Only one daughter is named in the will, Lucille M., and a daughter-in-law, Eileen M. King. He also names a grandson, Robert M. King, and two granddaughters: Catherine Jones and Patricia Lucille King. His stepchildren and children appear to have included:

(1)   Haller Howard King, born December 9, 1912; married to Eileen M., and father of the grandson and granddaughter bearing the King name:
(a) Robert M. King.
(b) Patricia Lucille King.
(2)   Lucille M. King, married to Junkin.
(3)   Frances Lucille King, born May 29, 1914, perhaps married to Jones, and mother of the granddaughter bearing that name mentioned in the will.
c.   Purdum Poole, married Ethel Mullinix.
d.   Roger Poole, born May 14, 1905. Married Susie Gue.
e.   Robert Poole, married Pearl Gartrall.
f.   Wallace Poole.

4.   Urner S. Purdum, born 1878, died 1963. Married December 25, 1902 to Olea Burdette, born 1882, died 1956, daughter of Franklin Burdette (1854) and Columbia (Burdette) Burdette (1862) of Bartholow, in Frederick County. Buried at Kemptown. They were found in the 1920 census for Frederick County, where he was listed only by his initials, with his wife and two sons. They had two children:

a.   Roscoe Franklin Purdum, born September 3, 1904 on the Johnson farm, died July 19, 1991 in Woodbine. He was a police office in Montgomery County and owned and operated a Firestone store in Damascus for many years. He was one of the organizers of the Damascus Volunteer Fire Department in 1944, and served as its first Chief. He was also a charter member of the Damascus Lions Club. Married in Frederick County, Maryland on September 20, 1924 to Mary Adaline Mullinix, born February 12, 1907 on Mullinix Mill Road in Montgomery County, died November 15, 1975, daughter of Joseph H. and Molly Evea Mullinix. Three children:

(1)   Allan R. Purdum, born October 12, 1934 in Gaithersburg, Maryland. Married August 20, 1966 to Linda Monee. Lived in Dania, Florida.
(2)   David Burk Purdum, an infant death July 31, 1936 buried with his parents at Damascus Methodist
(3)   Urner F. Purdum, born February 15, 1951.

b. Claude Rufus Purdum, born April 17, 1913, died October 28, 1987 and lived at Clarksburg, where he is buried at the Methodist Church with his wife. Married August 30, 1934 to Mary Evelyn Purdum, born May 3, 1912, died March 19, 1988, daughter of James F. Purdum (1876) and Nettie Estelle Burdette (1882). Children:
   (1) Catherine Purdum, born 1936; married to Darryl Armstrong and had a son.
   (2) Jefferson L. Purdum, born 1940 and had children.

5. Alma C. Purdum, born 1881, died 1928. Married Robert L. Stanley, born 1874, died 1925. Children:
a. Mary Lee Stanley, married August 30, 1927 John Lewis King, born March 7, 1905 at Woodfield, Maryland, son of James Rufus King (1871) and Della Waters Woodfield (1879). John Lewis and Mary Lee had children:
   (1) Sandra Lee King, born September 18, 1940, and married Willard Coulson Speace, born 1937, and had children:
      (a) Stanley Coulson Speace, born July 1, 1968
      (b) Brandon King Speace, born 1972
   (2) John Lewis King, Jr., born March 23, 1942. Married Roberta Ann Messer, born 1941; children:
      (a) Kimberly Ann King, born June 1, 1963 and married Matthew James Kempel. Children:
         1. Megan Ann Kempel, born 1987
         2. Matthew James Kempel, Jr., born 1989
      (b) Kenneth Stanley King, born March 4, 1965, and married Jill Marie Kempel. Children:
         1. Pamela Beth King, born 1988
         2. Donald John King, born 1989
      (c) Karl Lewis King, born March 19, 1969
b. Esther Stanley, married Edwin Warfield.
c. Louise Stanley.
d. Roland Stanley, never married.
e. Estelle Stanley, married Steve Thomson.
f. Jeanne Stanley, married Bryan Falcone.

6. Martha A. Purdum, born c.1883

7. Lynee Purdum, born c.1886. Married Reverend Noah C. Clough. See discussion above relative to possibility that this child may in fact be the same as the one following. In the 1920 census for Carroll County, his mother-in-law is living in the household. They later lived in Washington County, Maryland, and had children:
    a. Elizabeth Clough.
    b. Hobart Clough.
    c. Eunice Clough.
8. Sallie L. Purdum, born April 29, 1886, died March 13, 1966. As mentioned just above, further review is called for relative to this child and child 7. Married to Archie W. Souder, born January 15, 1884, died July 1, 1933 at Damascus. They had children:
    a. Ruth Souder; married Irving Gue, a prominent builder and businessman, and had a son:
        (1) John Gue, married Nancy Davay.
    b. Jane Souder; married Hubert Snapp, who was also a lo-cally well-known builder of quality homes and small communities. They had children:
        (1) Carol Snapp.
        (2) James Snapp.
        (3) John Snapp.
    c. Helen Warfield Souder. In 1989, she was invited to be-come the first woman member of the Damascus Lions Club. Married March 20, 1954 to Doctor Milton McKendree Boyer, born March 25, 1907, son of George Milton Boyer (1872). Children:
        (1) Sally Ann Boyer.
        (2) George Milton Boyer, II.
        (3) McKendree Warfield Boyer.
    d. Dorothy Laurene Souder, born 1912. Married Roger William Burdette, born 1909, son of William Hubert Burdette (1872) and Beda Cassandra King (1873). They had children:
        (1) Roger William Burdette, Jr.
        (2) Richard Souder Burdette.

e. Grace Wilson Souder, born July 23, 1913; married Clark Fout King, born August 16, 1910, son of Filmore Clark King (1890) and Emma Jane Lydard (1890). He is a retired Corporate Counsel, living in Damascus, and had children, born in the city of Washington, D. C.:

(1) Daniel Clark King, born August 30, 1939; married to Daria Nadja Hentish, born in the Ukraine, and had children, born in Washington, D. C.:
(a) Michael Andrew King: July 4, 1966
(b) Christine Anne King: January 19, 1968

(2) John MacDonald King, born June 2, 1942. Married February 18, 1962 in Reingold, Georgia, to Alice Keith Myers, born June 2, 1942 at Knoxville, Tennessee, daughter of Richard Myers and Sara Nell Hasson. Children, born in Washington, D. C.:
(a) Mark Sheridan King: October 19, 1962
(b) Bryan MacDonald King: October 19, 1965

CHILD 4

John M. Warfield
1816-1886

This son of Edward Warfield (died 1836) was born July 17, 1816, died November 13, 1886; buried with his wife at Damascus Methodist cemetery. Married October 31, 1848 in Frederick County, to Lucetta Burdette, born August 5, 1829, and died October 28, 1907, according to cemetery records; daughter of Hazel Burdette and Elizabeth Miles (1795). John was found as head of household in the 1850 census for Clarksburg District of Montgomery County, Maryland. With him was his wife Lusetta, born c.1829. They are found next in the 1860 census for Clarksburg, but then with three children. The transcription of that census found in the library of the Montgomery County Historical Society spells her name Luzzetta, which is apparently incorrect. They are next found in the 1870 census for Damascus, with her name spelled as in 1850, and five children at home. The family included:

1. Ida V. Warfield, born c.1853
2. Titus W. Warfield, born c.1856 in Montgomery County, according to census records. He is probably the same who is buried at the Montgomery Chapel cemetery, Clagettsville, where he was reported as born c.1849, died 1936 (which fits the probabe date of his will). Married November 26, 1885 to Annie C. Molesworth, born c.1857. Records of Montgomery Chapel cemetery at Claggettsville report the burial of Sarah C. Watkins Warfield, wife of Titus W. Warfield. She was born October 10, 1861, died January 23, 1942, and is buried with her first husband, John W. C. Watkins (1859). It appears that Titus W. Warfield married her as his second wife. Titus and Anna appear in the 1900 census for Damascus, with their daughter. In that census, Anna C. is listed as born c.1850 and the mother of only one child, then living. Titus and Annie are living in the 1920 census for Damascus, with one Ella V. Pearre, born c.1858, living with them, listed as a sister-in-law. The will of Titus W. Warfield was dated November 15, 1933, probated August 25, 1936 and filed in liber HGC 11 at folio 485, will records of Montgomery County, Maryland. He names his wife, and his daughter. One child, born to the first marriage:
   a. Della Elizabeth Warfield, born December 20, 1887; perhaps the same who was married July 11, 1909 to Edgar B. Gue at Kemptown. They are buried at Claggettsville Methodist Church, where stones indicate he was born 1879 and died August 19, 1941. They appear in the 1920 census for Damascus with one daughter. His will, dated July 14, 1939 was probated September 3, 1941 and recorded in liber HGC 40 at folio 89 in Montgomery County will records. It names only his wife, and the one daughter listed following. They had children, born near Kemptown, including:
      (1) Mabel Elizabeth Gue, born July 13, 1915. Married October 15, 1935 at Woodlawn Methodist parsonage to Paul Wesley Brown of Ridgeville.
3. Laura E. Warfield, born c.1858

4. Elizabeth J. Warfield, born c.1862, died 1939. Married December 30, 1882 to Basil Edward Boyer, who died 1920 at Newport, Maine. They lived at Kemptown, and he moved alone to Massachusetts. They appear in the 1900 census of Montgomery County, with five children. Also living with them was his mother, Elizabeth A. Boyer, born c.1827, a widow who had four children, all of them living at the time of the census. There were apparently a total of six children:

a. Raymond Boyer, born March 21, 1884, died June 2, 1884. (Deceased prior to the 1900 census.)

b. Norman Day Boyer, born December 2, 1885, died November 3, 1948, and buried at Browningsville. Married December 25, 1906 to Mamie Cleveland Watkins, born July 7, 1884, daughter of Tobias C. Watkins (1859) and Catherine C. Swartz. They had children:

    (1) Catherine Elizabeth Boyer, born September 23, 1909. Married June 12, 1933 to Charles Sigsbee, born August 31, 1908. A son:

        (a) Charles Norman Sigsbee: December 31, 1940

    (2) Nellie Day Boyer, born August 8, 1914. Married October 21, 1934 to William Willard Easterday, born September 2, 1912, died October 2, 1938 and buried at Sharpsburg, Maryland. A son:

        (a) William W. Easterday: September 2, 1935

c. Muller W. Boyer, born c.1888

d. Elsie Boyer, born October 16, 1890, died December 8, 1890. (Deceased prior to 1900 census.)

e. Rudy Wendell Boyer, born 1895 at Kemptown, and died December 4, 1956. Married Minnie Currier, born 1896 at Benton Harbor, Michigan. Buried Providence Churh, at Kemptown. Children:

    (1) James William Boyer, born January 4, 1921. Married January 1, 1943 to Nannie Louise Sharp, born June 6, 1919 at Waverly, West Virginia, and had children:

        (a) James Lee Boyer: September 22, 1944

        (b) Carolyn Sue Boyer: September 11, 1946

    (2) Muller W. Boyer, born December 18, 1921

(3)   Harold R. Boyer, born February 8, 1923

(4)   Rudy W. Boyer, born January 14, 1931

f.   William C. Boyer, born June 1, 1897, died November 11, 1961. Married June 2, 1921 to Edna Sophia Jaeger, born January 16, 1903. A daughter:

    (1)   Helen Elizabeth Boyer, born October 26, 1923. Married August 30, 1952 to Russell Lee Craig, Jr., born January 15, 1920. One child:

        (a)   Terry Lee Craig, born October 1, 1953

5.   Edna G. Warfield, born April 15, 1868 and died March 14, 1931. Married July 27, 1892 to Charles Lewis, born c.1860. This is perhaps Charles H. Lewis born August 3, 1860, died September 14, 1906, son of Caleb Lewis (1817) and Ascenah S. King (1825). Charles and Edna are buried at Damascus Methodist Church. In the 1900 census for Damascus, they are living alone, and it reports that they have been married eight years, own their farm free and clear, and had one child, who died before 1900.

CHILD 5

Hamilton G. Warfield
1817-1882

This son of Edward Warfield (died 1836) was born December 17, 1817, died September 8, 1882; buried at Bethesda Methodist Church at Browningsville. As mentioned above, Hamilton was found living in the household of Horace Warfield (1812) during the 1850 census for the Clarksburg District of Montgomery County, Maryland. In the 1860 census, Hamilton is living in his own household, next door to Horace, and presumed to be his brother. According to the two reports, he was born about 1818 to 1820. His wife is Harriet C. Williams, to whom he was married November 9, 1858 in Frederick County, and they had one son. She was born January 29, 1839, died February 27, 1897; buried at Browningsville Methodist Church. After the death of Hamilton, Harriet was married secondly August 20, 1889 to Joshua Molesworth, born October 18, 1818. In the 1870 census for Damascus, Hamilton had three children. Also living in the household was Mary A. Miller, born c.1803. Cemetery records indicate that he was born December 17, 1817, died September 8, 1882, and bured at Browningsville Methodist Church. Children:

1.   Basil T. Warfield, born August 24, 1859, of whom more.
2.   Lydia E. Warfield, born c.1861; probably the same who was married December 21, 1880 to Luther James Moore.
3.   William H. Warfield, born c.1868, died 1939. Buried at Damascus Methodist cemetery. Married December 22, 1890 to Emma C. Burdette, born 1870, died February 10, 1955, daughter of Nathan James Burdette (1842) and Rispah Ann Lewis (1844). They are shown in the 1900 census, with one child, and again in the 1920 census with a son. The will of Emma C. Warfield was dated September 27, 1940, and filed in liber WCC 49 at folio 454, will records of Montgomery County. She names her son and his wife; and her daughter and her husband. They had a son and a daughter:

a.   Ethel P. V. Warfield, born August 20, 1894, died August 3, 1978 at Westminster Nursing Home. Married to Elisha S. Warfield, born November 6, 1893, died January 1, 1965 at his home in Damascus, Montgomery County, Maryland; buried in the Damascus Cemetery. He is found as head of household in the 1920 census for Damascus, there listed as Elisha G. with his wife and one son. Also in the household was his father, George W. Warfield (1864). The son was:

(1)   Donald Elisha Warfield, born August 19, 1918 at Damascus, died September 3, 1985 while on vacation in Nova Scotia. Married October 10, 1946 to Julia Louise Kemp, born July 18, 1920 at Woodfield, Maryland, and died October 18, 1990, daughter of James Raymond Kemp (1898) and Mary Frances King (1900). Children:

(a)   James Harvey Warfield, born August 25, 1947 at Frederick. Married November 29, 1974 Jennifer Lynn Hamm, born May 13, 1954 at Fairfield, Alabama, daughter of

James Hamm and Florence Y. Anthony.
There were children:
1. Sarah Elizabeth Warfield, born November 5, 1981.
2. Jennifer Lynn Warfield, born November 11, 1987.
   (b) Diane Louise Warfield, born October 2, 1948 at Frederick.
b. William Edwin Warfield, born c.1909 at Damascus and taught school for a number of years before being called into service during the second world war. Served as Lieutenant Colonel, Twenty-ninth Division, and killed in action June 10, 1944 in France. Awarded the Silver Star, posthumously. He left a will dated February 9, 1938, probated September 6, 1944 and filed in liber OWR 6 at folio 134, will records of Montgomery County, Maryland. He named only his wife, Esther Gertrude, in his will. He had two children:
(1) Natalie Jo Warfield, born c.1937
(2) Robert E. Warfield, born c.1940

Basil T. Warfield
1859-1931

This son of Hamilton G. Warfield (1817) was born August 24, 1859, died May 19, 1931; buried at Mt. Lebanon with his wife. Married December 24, 1886 to Alice Flavilla Mullinix, born February 28, 1867, died March 22, 1955, daughter of John Joseph Mullinix (1839) and Emily Jones Purdum (1843). Note that Mullinix is sometimes found as Mullineaux in this family. His will was dated January 2, 1926, probated June 2, 1931 and filed in liber PEW 20 at folio 143, will records of Montgomery County, Maryland. He left the home farm to his wife for her lifetime, and the use of a tenant house and farm property to his son Raymond at the same rent he was then paying for as long as he chose to remain. His four children were all named in the will:
1. Raymond Lafayette Warfield, born 1890, married first to Bessie M. Allnutt, born 1886, died 1931, and had two chil-

dren. Both buried at Mt. Lebanon, Methodist. Married second July 14, 1932 to Dorothy Elizabeth Watkins, born April 28, 1900 and died September 28, 1970, daughter of Alonzo Claggett Watkins (1867) and Mary Luana Boyer (1870). Buried in the Damascus Methodist Church cemetery. Three children were born to the second marriage, the last three listed here. The five were:

a. Basil Thomas Warfield, born December 30, 1917, died April 20, 1938. Buried with his parents.
b. Clyde Gardiner Warfield: March 26, 1925
c. Dorothy Elizabeth Warfield, born August 9, 1934.
d. Raymond Lafayette Warfield, Jr., Born April 23, 1937. Married October 3, 1971 Carolyn Jane Ray, born Arpil 19, 1945 at Olney.
e. Ellis King Warfield, born January 19, 1942, died June 5, 1942. Buried with his mother.

2. Mamie E. Warfield, married Charles Murphy of Ijamsville and had children:
a. Cortney Murphy.
b. Mary Alice Murphy.
c. Merhle Murphy.
d. Casper C. Murphy.
e. Rockney E. Murphy, married Arnold.
f. Harry A. Murphy.
g. Wilford Murphy.

3. Bessie C. Warfield, married April 5, 1919 at Kemptown to Raymond L. Murray, who died January 1, 1946. One son:
a. Calvin M. Murray.

4. Merhle Basil Warfield, born June 11, 1898 in Damascus and died there January 25, 1977. Married January 29, 1920 to Mary Elizabeth Leishear, born August 14, 1895 at Brighton, died February 4, 1975 at Damascus. Buried at the Mt. Lebanon Cemetery. She was the daughter of Thomas Leishear and Mary F. Molesworth. Records of St. John's Episcopal Church at Olney report their marriage. The witnesses to the wedding were Miller Leishear and Lucretia Leishear. Children:
a. Merhle Basil Warfield, Jr., born February 26, 1927 at home near Etchison, Maryland. Married September 2,

1948 to Gloria Alvin Moxley, born December 20, 1930 near Kemptown the daughter of Raymond Merson Moxley (1909) and Effie Madeline Day (1912). Children:

(1)   Merhle Wayne Warfield, born December 15, 1950. Married June 19, 1971 to Sharon Lee Smith, born May 8, 1951 at Damascus, daughter of Clayton Otis Smith (1913) and Betty Lee Watkins (1924). Two children:

(a)   Jason Edward Warfield: April 8, 1979
(b)   Kristin Leanne Warfield: July 26, 1984

(2)   Raymond Curtis Warfield, born January 20, 1952. Lived at Gaithersburg.

b.   Lavinia Leishear Warfield, born c.1926. Married Truman Leo Kelley, born March 18, 1927, son of Leslie Norris Kelley (1895) and Marguerite Elizabeth Penn (1898).

c.   Ruth Warfield, married Davis.

CHILD 6

Mahlon H. Warfield
1819-

This son of Edward Warfield (died 1836) was born July 11, 1819. Head of household in the 1850 census for Clarksburg District of Montgomery County, Mahlon was born c.1818. He was a farmer, and his wife was Sarah A, born c.1824. She was Sarah Ann Beall, died April 30, 1862, daughter of Elisha Beall (1800) and Aleathea Ann Lewis (1806); and they were married November 27, 1849. According to the census they had been married within the year. Also living with them was one Horace Beall, born c.1825, who may prove to be a brother of Sarah. In the 1860 census for Clarksburg, the couple now appear with four children. Sarah is listed at thirty years old, thus born between 1824 and 1830 according to the two census reports. They had children:

1.   Lucretia Warfield, born May 9, 1851; died April 5, 1929. Married October 17, 1875 to Josiah Wolf Lawson, born April 9, 1849 and died September 10, 1928. They appear in the 1900 census of Damascus District, Montgomery County, with

two daughters. In the 1920 census for the same area, daughter Claudia is still living in the household. The two daughters were:

a. Claudia Olivia Lawson, born April 20, 1883, died June 9, 1973. Married October 14, 1920 to Silas Young Browning, born May 12, 1870. and died January 18, 1941; lived at Poolesville, and is buried at Damascus United Methodist cemetery with his wife. He was a son of Mahlon Browning (1821) and Sarah F. Smith (1826). The 1900 Soundex of the census for Montgomery County includes a household headed by Silas Y. Browning, said to have been born May, 1867, which is reasonably close to the date of birth of Silas Young Browning, listed here. In the household at the time are three females: Sarah F. Browning, born April, 1837, his mother (although her date of birth has apparently been erroneously recorded); Sarah J. Browning, born March, 1875, his sister; and Frances G. Browning, born January, 1880, also a sister. The will of Silas, dated July 2, 1930, was probated February 4, 1941, filed in liber HGC 33 at folio 361, Montgomery County. It is very simple, leaving his entire estate to his wife, said to be of Damascus as of the date of making the will. Her will, dated November 17, 1961, was filed in liber WES 7403 at folio 872 in the will records of Montgomery County. She names as her heirs her daughter, listed following, and a sister, Ola Blanche Smith. One daughter:

(1) Frances Lucretia Browning, born June 26, 1923 in Washington, D. C.; married April 6, 1942 to Alfred Davis Broadhurst, born February 21, 1921, from Bethesda. They had children:

(a) Alfred Wayne Broadhurst, born April 27, 1943. Married December 10, 1963 to Judith Diane Walker, born July 12, 1944, of Garrett Park. Three children:

1. Matthew Dwane Broadhurst, born November 14, 1970

2. Justin Marshall Broadhurst, born April 2, 1973

3. Preston Wade Broadhurst, born August 24, 1977

(2) Claudia Marlene Broadhurst, born June 20, 1948. Married July 21, 1968 to James Irvin McCauley, Jr., born October 1, 1947, from Pennsylvania. Two children:

    (a) Christine Margaret McCauley: May 22, 1973

    (b) Erica Marlene McCauley: October 22, 1975

(3) Brian Eugene Broadhurst, born October 30, 1955, died the same day.

(4) Joyce Ann Broadhurst, born February 3, 1958

(5) Jeffrey Scott Broadhurst, born June 30, 1961; married to Gail Sanders of Hyattsville, Prince George's County.

(6) Lisa Christine Broadhurst: October 12, 1963

b. Ola Blanche Lawson, born February, 1887 according to the 1900 census, and married September 4, 1912 to Murray Baker Smith. In at least one other report we have seen, this daughter was assigned the same birth date as her sister, suggesting twins, which does not appear to be the case.

2. Mary E. Warfield, a twin, born August 15, 1855; died October 27, 1929. She was married September 12, 1896 as the second wife of John Wesley Boyer, born December 21, 1854 at Kemptown, Maryland, who was first married to Zeru Clarke Day (1855), by whom he had five children. Mary E. had no children.

3. Martha A. Warfield, a twin, born August 15, 1855; died June 25, 1874; buried at Kemptown Methodist Church. Perhaps the same who was living in the household of Jackson Day (1831) in 1870 census for Damascus.

4. Edward Dorsey Warfield, born c.1858, died 1925. Married January 11, 1894 to Verta K. Mullinix, born 1872, died 1919, daughter of James Luther Mullinix (1843) and Mary Evelyn Young (1842). He is listed as head of household in the 1900 census for the Hyattstown area, with his names reversed; listed

as Dorsey E., with the correct birth year. His wife, however, is there listed as Gertrude K., born c.1873, which is perhaps an error in the transcription. In any case, he appears to have been married only once. The census states that they have been married six years, own their farm free and clear, and have had three children, all then living at home. Living with them was Bradley W. Warfield, born c.1879, listed as a cousin. He was perhaps Bradley Winfield Warfield. At least these children:

a. Edward Ray Warfield, born December 31, 1894, and christened March 14, 1899 at Clarksburg.

b. Jesse Winstead Warfield, born February 3, 1900, died July 7, 1900, a twin.

c. James Paul Warfield, a twin, born February 3, 1900 at Boyds, died September 16, 1991 at Shady Grove Hospital, in Montgomery County. Married to Avie C. Watkins, born c.1903 at Cedar Grove, died March 15, 1989 at Shady Grove, daughter of John Oliver Thomas Watkins (1860) and Eva Lee King (1864). Buried at the Clarksburg Methodist Cemetery. Children:

   (1) Jane Warfield, married to Wiener.

   (2) John P. Warfield, of Clarksburg.

   (3) Joseph Watkins Warfield, born March 29, 1941, and died May 7, 1968 at New Market, Maryland in an automobile accident. Married Connie L. and had children:

      (a) Terri Warfield.

      (b) Jodi Warfield.

   (4) James Earl Warfield, born September 8, 1923 at Boyds, Maryland, died May 3, 1979 at Suburban Hospital from injuries received in an auto accident. Buried Clarksburg Methodist Church cemetery. He had two daughters:

      (a) Cheryl Ann Warfield, who was married to McDonough and had a son: Wesley Joseph McDonough.

      (b) Joy Marie Warfield.

d. Linda Virginia Warfield, born October 3, 1908; married Gordon of Frederick.

CHILD 7

Garrison Warfield
1822-1895

This son of Edward Warfield (died 1836) was born c.1822, died May 19, 1895, buried at Hyattstown Methodist cemetery. He was a farmer of Frederick County, and was married February 2, 1848 to Caroline Lewis, born c.1835, died November 20, 1902, daughter of Jeremiah Lewis (1781) and Mary Windsor (1787); buried with her husband. Caroline was reportedly also married May 14, 1885 in Frederick County to Singleton Lewis King (1843), his third wife, which does not seem likely. Garrison appears in the 1850 census for the New Market District of Frederick County, with his wife Caroline and their first child. He is there listed as Garrettson Warfield, which could be the correct spelling, or a mistake on the part of the census enumerator. Garrison was father of, at least:

1. Frances L. Warfield, born 1849, married John T. Dixon, the son of Thomas Dixon (1818) and Lucy A. Rine of Frederick County. At least two children:
   a. Florence Dixon.
   b. Lillian Dixon.
2. James Latimer Warfield, born September 25, 1850, died October 20, 1899; buried at Hyattstown. Married March 27, 1884 to Annie Elizabeth Lewis, born September 8, 1857, died March 6, 1944; buried at Hyattstown Methodist Church; daughter of John A. Lewis (1832) and Julia Ann Shaw (1832). In the 1900 census, she is listed as a widow, owning her farm free of mortgage. She was the mother of two children, both living at home. Also in the household was her mother, Julia A., also a widow. Two children:
   a. Charles Edwin Warfield, born December 14, 1884, died April 18, 1958, single. Buried at Hyattstown Methodist.
   b. Edith L. Warfield, born August 14, 1889; listed as Edith S. Lewis in the 1900 census; married Oscar Tabler and had children:
      (1) Bernice Tabler, married Bernard Hillard.

(2) Harold Tabler, born at Waldorf, Maryland. He was married and had two sons.

3. Luther Day Warfield, born July 30, 1853, died June 24, 1906 and buried at Hyattstown Methodist Church. Luther was survived by a wife and a daughter. He was married March 3, 1887 at the Lutheran Parsonage in Frederick, to Ella B. Tabler, born December 12, 1860, died January 17, 1919. Both were said to be from Montgomery County and both are buried at Hyattstown Methodist cemetery. Luther left a will, dated May 31, 1906, stating he was then of Frederick County, probated July 10, 1906 and filed in liber PEW 14 at folio 318, will records of Montgomery County, Maryland. Their only child, a daughter, was buried with them:
   a. Carrie Olivia Warfield, married to Ira Lynnwood Davis.

4. Mary Eunice Warfield, married Dr. J. D. Norris, Major and Surgeon, Fourth Regiment of Militia, Baltimore. Children:
   a. Chester Norris.
   b. Lester Norris.
   c. Hazel Norris.
   d. Eunice Norris (or Eloise Norris).

5. William Warfield, married Nannie Simmons. Children:
   a. Lucille Warfield.
   b. Eloise Warfield.

6. Edwin Alonzo Warfield, born August 30, 1859, minister, married Mary E. Button of Lynchburg, Virginia, daughter of Charles W. Button and Mary E. Zollikoffer.

7. Ida Fidelia Warfield, born May 28, 1861. Married November 8, 1887 to William D. Bell, and had children:
   a. Ethel Bell.
   b. Mary Bell.
   c. Garrison Bell.
   d. Lewis Bell.
   e. Maud Bell.

8. Eliza Warfield, married to Robert Lee Griffith, born July 15, 1862, son of Lebbeus Griffith, Sr. (1804) and his third wife, Ruth S. Warfield (who were married January 26, 1858 in Frederick). There were reportedly three children, including:
   a. Forest India Griffith.

9. Caroline Warfield, married G. Wallace Davis, son of George W. Davis (1837) and Elizabeth Price. Children:
   a. Malcolm Davis.
   b. Kathleen Davis.
   c. Stanley Davis.

CHILD 8

Mary Ann Warfield
1809-1886

This daughter of Edward Warfield (died 1836) was born April 15, 1809, and died April 10, 1886. Married March 15, 1831 to Jefferson Day, born November 4, 1807 at Browningsville, Maryland, and died Januay 5, 1863. He was a son of James Day (1762) and his second wife, Sarah Warfield (died 1821). Their numerous descendants are treated in *James Day of Browningsville and his descendants, A Maryland Family,* by Jackson Harvey Day, 1976, Columbia, Maryland, to which the reader is referred for details. Suffice to say here that they had eight children:

1. Luther Day, born January 16, 1832, died February 16, 1897. Married after June 4, 1867 to Ann Eliza Lewis, born September 12, 1848, died March 21, 1918, daughter of Jeremiah Lewis of Levi and Sarah Jane Claggett. Ten children.
2. Wellington Day, born February 4, 1834, died February 18, 1860 of tuberculosis, single.
3. Hamilton Day, born November 30, 1836, died September 4, 1857 of appendicitis, single. He was reportedly the first person buried at Kemptown Cemetery.
4. James Edward Day, born c.1838, single.
5. Washington Lafayette Day, born September 8, 1840, died January 23, 1921. Married to Louana T. Boyer, born September 6, 1854, died March 9, 1917, the daughter of William Boyer (1821) and Jane E. Browning (1819). No children.
6. Survila Augusta Webster Day, born c.1842, died 1923, single.
7. Eunice Ann Day, born October 1, 1845, died June 12, 1927. Married George Wolfe Price, born September 15, 1840, died May 16, 1918. Four children.

8. Sarah Warfield Day, born c.1848, died 1927. Married to Charles Price, born February 20, 1838, died July 27, 1896. Two children.

CHAPTER 7

Richard Warfield, Jr.
1677-1755

This son of Richard Warfield (1646) and Elinor Brown was born in Anne Arundel County about 1677.

In the *Maryland Gazette* of February 27, 1755 it was announced that *"Richard Warfield, age 79, died last Sunday of the Pleurisy, at his plantation on the Patapsco Road about 9 miles from Annapolis. He served many years as magistrate and representative of the Assembly."*

Married 1698 to Ruth Crutchley, born 1683, died 1713, daughter of Thomas Crutchley and Margaret Baldwin. She inherited the estates of *Baldwin's Addition* and *Theodora's Chance,* and died in 1713. He served in the legislature and in other civic and religious capacities. He was one of the organizers of the first county public school system in 1732. They had children:

1. Alexander Warfield, married December 3, 1723 to Dinah Davidge and had children. He left a will in Anne Arundel County dated June 12, 1773 and probated November 28, 1773, naming his children. His property was known as the tracts named *Stringer's Chance* and *Wincopen Neck.* His estate was valued at over one thousand pounds, which included fifteen slaves and personal items such as his sword, pistol and books. *Anne Arundel Gentry,* Volume 1, by Harry Wright Newman, contains extensive information relative to the descendants of Alexander Warfield and Dinah Davidge. The reader is referred to that detailed work. Their children were:
    a. Joshua M. Warfield, eldest son, of whom more following.
    b. Azel Warfield, born June 24, 1728, of whom more.
    c. Davidge Warfield, born February 15, 1729, of whom more following.
    d. Rachel Warfield, born July 10, 1731, died 1745
    e. Absolom Warfield, born April 30, 1733. Married to Elizabeth Scrivener. He settled in what was then Frederick County, on the lands known as *Bear Garden* and

Spring Garden, and apparently had no children. After his death, Elizabeth married George Snell.

f.   Sarah Warfield, born November 28, 1734. Married to Thomas Price.

g.   Ann Warfield, born April 9, 1736, and married to John Marriott. She married second Richard Cole.

h.   Charles Warfield, born August 30, 1738, of whom more.

i.   Rezin Warfield, born May 16, 1740, died 1767. Married c.1762 to Honour Elder Howard, born March 27, 1740, daughter of Sir Henry Howard and Sarah Dorsey. They had children. After the death of Rezin, his widow married second to John Davidge, son of Robert Davidge and Rachel Warfield. The children of Rezin were:

(1)   Beale Warfield, single.

(2)   Anne Warfield, married March 22, 1780 to Richard Lawrence, born 1757 after the death of his father of *White Hall*, son of Levin Lawrence and Susannah Dorsey (1717).

(3)   Sarah Warfield, married after July 10, 1790 to Charles Warfield of Linganore.

j.   Dinah Warfield, born March 28, 1742. Married to William Woodward. At least two daughters:

(1)   Maria Woodward.

(2)   Elizabeth Woodward.

k.   Philemon Warfield, born April 15, 1744. Married Asenah Waters, daughter of Joseph Waters of *Snowden's Manor*. Philemon served as Quartermaster of the militia during the Revolutionary War, commissioned Lieutenant. He died without a will, and had two daughters:

(1)   Mary Warfield, inherited the home property, and married Lancelot Warfield, Jr.

(2)   Ann Warfield, married Richard Dorsey.

l.   Basil Warfield, married to Mary Hanson. He went to the Eastern Shore of Maryland as a surveyor. Children:

(1)   John Warfield.

(2)   Joshua Warfield.

(3)   Basil Hanson Warfield.

m. Sophia Warfield, married to Richard Simpson. At least one daughter:

    (1)   Anne Simpson.

2. Ruth Warfield, married Joseph Hall. Under her father's will, she inherited two hundred acres of *Warfield's Contrivance*.
3. Rachel Warfield, married Robert Davidge.
4. Lydia Warfield, married first Samuel Stringer, and second Colonel Charles Ridgely (1702), his second wife. Children:
    a.   Samuel Stringer, born 1734, died July 11, 1817, a doctor of Albany, New York. Married Rachel Van Der Heyden.
    b.   Rachel Stringer, married Major Stephen Lush.

Joshua M. Warfield

This son of Alexander Warfield and Dinah Davidge was a doctor, and was married August 6, 1751 to Rachel Howard, born April 2, 1732, died 1792, daughter of Sir Henry Howard (1710), British Consul at Elk Ridge Landing, and his wife, Sarah Dorsey (1715) and had children:

1. Dinah Warfield, married to Caleb Dorsey, who died before 1789, son of Ely Dorsey and Deborah (Dorsey) Dorsey (1722)
2. Joseph Warfield, born February 19, 1758, of whom more in Chapter 8.
3. Sarah Warfield.
4. Ruth Warfield.
5. Rachel Warfield. Married Lieutenant Nicholas W. Dorsey, and had at least one son:
    a.   Joshua Warfield Dorsey, born c.1783. Married to Mary A. E. Childs, born c.1814, and had at least one daughter:
        (1)   Rachel Virginia Dorsey, born 1845. Married November 13, 1862 to John Thomas Warfield, born 1835, son of Seth Washington Warfield (1805) and Lydia A. Meredith (1810). They had numerous descendants, who were treated under their father's name in Chapter 3, which see.

Azel Warfield
1728-

This son of Alexander Warfield and Dinah Davidge was born June 24, 1728. Married February 26, 1751 to Sarah Griffith, who died December 24, 1765, daughter of Charles Griffith and Catherine Baldwin, by whom he had six children. He was married second May 19, 1768 to Susanna Magruder, by whom he had two more children, for a total of eight. He owned the plantation containing part of *Yate's Contrivance* and part of *Second Addition to Snowden's Manor*. Azel also held indentured servants on his plantations, as did many prosperous Colonial planters. The *Maryland Gazette* of December 24, 1760 reported that "Daniel Stephenson, in Bladensburg, Prince George's County, reports a runaway convict servant named James Fairbanks who formerly lived with Mr. Azel Warfield on Elk Ridge." Azel and his wife had children:

1. Charles Alexander Warfield, born December 3, 1751, died March 29, 1813 at his home. A doctor, he was married November 21, 1771 to Elizabeth Ridgely, born September 25, 1752, died September 8, 1808, daughter of Major Henry Ridgely (1728) and Ann Dorsey (1730). He was the builder in 1753 of *Glenwood*, which many years later was destroyed by fire. On March 27, 1813 in the *Fredericktown Herald*, his sons Gustavus and Charles Alexander advertised the sale of negroes at the home of their late father. Children, including:

   a. Elizabeth R. Warfield, married December 26, 1834 to Major Richard N. Snowden, son of Washington's friend, Colonel Edward Snowden of Prince George's County. Eliza won title to *Glenwood* by casting lots with her brother, Gustavus.

   b. Henry Ridgely Warfield; admitted to the Bar 1797 in Montgomery County; represented Frederick County in the House of Delegates 1797 and 1798; served in Congress during 1820. Perhaps the same Henry R. who died March 18, 1839 in Frederick County.

   c. Walter Warfield, a doctor, served in the Revolution, and settled in Virginia.

d.   Charles Alexander Warfield, established mills at Sykes-ville, and then moved south.
e.   Gustavus Warfield, a doctor. He was the builder of *Longwood*, within sight of *Bushy Park.* Married Mary Thomas of Philadelphia and had nine children.
f.   Ann Warfield, married Samuel Thomas. They made their home at *Roxbury Hall.*
g.   Peregrine Warfield, a doctor, and Justice of the Peace, married May 7, 1806 in Frederick County to Harriet Lucy Sappington. He lived in Georgetown.
h.   Charles Alexander Warfield, Jr., a merchant in Sykes-ville, married Eliza Harris and had children. They moved to New Orleans.

2.   Dinah Warfield, born April 4, 1753. Married to Brice John Gassaway.

3.   Catherine Warfield, born April 7, 1757, died April 14, 1796. Married November 14, 1775 to Hezekiah Griffith, born November 25, 1752, died July 28, 1825, son of Greenbury Griffith (1727) and Ruth Riggs (1730). In 1777, Hezekiah was commissioned a first Lieutenant in the Montgomery County Militia. They had children:

a.   Ann Griffith, born September 27, 1776. Married to Jonas Clark and had children:

(1)   Katherine Clark, born December 27, 1798
(2)   Hezekiah Clark, born August 29, 1802. This is perhaps the same individual who was found at the age of 48, in the 1850 census of Berry District, Montgomery County, living in the household of James Smith (1822) and his wife Mary Ann (1823) with five Smith children. Could Mary Ann have been a daughter of Hezekiah?
(3)   Sarah Clark, born July 25, 1804
(4)   John Clark, born April 14, 1807
(5)   Robert Clark, born November 24, 1809
(6)   Mary Clark, born April 14, 1812
(7)   Lydia Clark, born October 7, 1814
(8)   Bazaleel Clark, born September 7, 1816

b. Sarah Griffith, born May 17, 1778, died July 10, 1839.
Married in 1797 to Bazaleel Wells, and had children:
   (1) Catherine Wells, born April 17, 1798, died September, 1843. Married October 8, 1818 to John W. McDowell.
   (2) Rebecca Wells, born October 11, 1799. Married November 10, 1822 to Philander Chase.
   (3) James Ross Wells, born October 8, 1801, died October 23, 1846. Married April 17, 1834 to Ann Eliza Wilson, who died in 1868.
   (4) Samuel D. Wells, born October 8, 1803, died December 13, 1849, single.
   (5) Alexander Wells, born September 16, 1805, died January 6, 1839, single.
   (6) Bazaleel Wells, Jr., born August 6, 1808.
   (7) Hezekiah Griffith Wells, born January 16, 1811. Married to Achsah Strong.
   (8) Frank A. Wells, born September 4, 1813. Married to Jane Boggs.
   (9) Ann C. Wells, born August 28, 1813, died 1885. Married the Reverend Ezra Kellogg.
   (10) Sarah Griffith Wells, born January 11, 1818, died August 24, 1866. Married the Reverend Dudley Chase.
   (11) Mary Wells, born February 12, 1822, died March 3, 1822.
c. John Belford Griffith, born December 28, 1780
d. Walter Griffith, born February 3, 1783
e. Lydia Griffith, born December 10, 1785, died April, 1815. Married George Fetter who died in September, 1817, and had children:
   (1) Daniel Fetter, born May 31, 1807
   (2) George Fetter, Jr., born October 6, 1809
   (3) Hezekiah Fetter, born November 1, 1811
   (4) Roderick Fetter, born February 16, 1814
f. Roderick Griffith, born December 8, 1787, died May 26, 1817.

g. Hezekiah Griffith, Jr., born November 1, 1790, died August 13, 1840. Married to Lydia Mobley, who died April 16, 1874. Children:
    (1) John Griffith, born November 8, 1814.
    (2) Roderick R. Griffith, born July 21, 1816, died August 6, 1889. Married first Isabel Clark, and had three childlren. Married second Mary Tillman and had six children.
    (3) Anne E. Griffith, born June 15, 1815. Married to Jesse V. Bramwell.
    (4) Randolph Griffith, married Eliza J. Barfield.
    (5) Rebecca Griffith, born February 4, 1824. Married Ezra Bramwell.
    (6) Rachel Griffith, born June 13, 1827. Married to Samuel Hovens.
    (7) Catherine Griffith, born July 30, 1829, died July 24, 1851, single.
    (8) Hezekiah Griffith, 3rd, born May 2, 1832. Married to Mary Ann Stevens.
    (9) Alexander W. Griffith, born July 7, 1835
    (10) Lydia Griffith, born December 11, 1837. Married Joseph Renier.
h. Charles Greenberry Griffith, born July 3, 1792, died May 24, 1864. Married Jane Johnson and had children:
    (1) Sarah Griffith, born December 29, 1817. Married three times: A. Arnick; M. C. Maynard; and Smith Vowler.
    (2) James J. Griffith, born November 13, 1819, died November 7, 1855.
    (3) Margaret Griffith, born November 20, 1820. Married to McKeehan.
    (4) Samuel Griffith, born November 26, 1822. Married to Elizabeth Goltha.
    (5) Hezekiah Griffith, born August 19, 1824
    (6) Mary Griffith, born August 31, 1826. Married to Johnson.
    (7) Anna Griffith, born November 31, 1828, died November, 1860. Married to J. Chase.

103

(8)   Charles Greenberry Griffith, Jr., born August 19, 1830. Married to McKeehan.

(9)   Rachel Griffith, born August 10, 1832. Married to W. C. Soper.

(10)   Jennie Griffith, born March 31, 1833.

i.   Jane Griffith, born November 3, 1794.

4.   Walter Warfield, born June 17, 1760. He was a surgeon in the Revolutionary War. Moved to Virginia and was married to Sarah Winston Christian, niece of Patrick Henry. They moved on to Kentucky. Children:

a.   Anne Henry Warfield.

b.   Charles Alexander Warfield, a doctor.

c.   William Christian Warfield, Baptist Minister. Married Rachel Edwards, daughter of Benjamin Edwards of Montgomery County, and had children.

5.   Ann Warfield, born June 28, 1762. Married Ignatius Waters.

6.   Zachariah Warfield, born January 6, 1765, died c.1832 in Montgomery County, single, with a will, dated March 8, 1832, probated April 3, 1832 and filed in liber S at folio 205; refiled in liber VMB 3 at folio 479. He named his sister Sarah and his brother George Fraser Warfield as his heirs. He also provided that his negro woman Bett and her son George were to be set free, provided George agreed to care for his mother.

7.   George Fraser Warfield, born March 13, 1769, died December 11, 1849. Buried at Eldersburg Wesley Chapel Methodist Church, with his wife. He is perhaps the same George F. Warfield who, on October 12, 1811, advertised the sale of 20 negroes at his dwelling plantation, living on Elk Ridge, between Snell's Bridge and Richard Owing's mills. Married to Rebecca Brown, born October 24, 1774, died March 4, 1852, the daughter of Abel Brown of Carroll County, Maryland. He built *Groveland* near Sykesville, Carroll County, and they had children:

a.   George W. Warfield, a doctor, married October 21, 1835 to Sarah Brooke Bentley, daughter of Caleb Bentley.

b.   William Henry Warfield, lieutenant. This is probably the same William Henry who was born August 3, 1807, died March 25, 1857, and is also buried at Eldersburg.

c. Rebecca Warfield.
d. Susannah Warfield, born c.1796, died at *Groveland,* February 14, 1890, single. Buried at Eldersburg with her parents. According to her obituary, one of her sisters was married to Richard Holmes.
e. Ann E. Warfield.
8. Sarah Warfield, married to John Waters of Tennessee and had children.

Davidge Warfield
1729-

This son of Alexander Warfield and Dinah Davidge was born February 15, 1729. Settled on *Snowden's Manor,* and married Ann Dorsey, born February 7, 1741, daughter of Judge Henry Dorsey (1712) and Elizabeth Worthington (1717). In 1778, Davidge Warfield had surveyed in his name, four hundred and eighty-five acres of *Warfield's Good Luck.* They had children:

1. Henry Warfield, married June 21, 1790 to Anne Hammond, the daughter of Vachel Hammond, and settled in Frederick County. Children.
2. Sarah Warfield, married October 22, 1783 Michael Burgess, son of Captain Joseph Burgess and Elizabeth Dorsey (1735).
3. Mary Warfield, married Edward Warfield, the younger, born June 5, 1769, son of Edward Warfield (1710) and Rachel Riggs (1724). Their children are treated under the name of their father in Chapter 5, which see.
4. Thomas Warfield, born c.1770, died October 17, 1855; buried in the Simpson family cemetery with his wife. Married March 20, 1802 to Delilah Simpson, born c.1759, died November 16, 1841; buried in the Simpson family cemetery at Libertytown. No surviving children.
5. Ann Warfield, or perhaps Nancy Ann Warfield, married Obed Leeke.
6. Rebecca Warfield, married after January 13, 1801 to Joshua Simpson.
7. Basil Warfield, married after February 16, 1803 in Montgomery County to Nancy Cecil, daughter of Philip Cecil. Basil and

his wife lived in Baltimore at the time of the 1850 census, both said to be 70 years of age (born c.1780).

8. Dinah Warfield, married William James after March 10, 1807.
9. Absolom Warfield, died 1806 in Frederick County, single, with a will.

Charles Warfield
1738-1790

This son of Alexander Warfield and Dinah Davidge was born August 30, 1738, died 1790, and is buried at Sams Creek cemetery, located near the boundary line between Frederick and Carroll Counties, east of Libertyville. Married Elizabeth Warfield, daughter of Richard Warfield of *Brandy*, and Sarah Gaither. They settled in Frederick County and he was one of its leading citizens, serving as Quartermaster in General Johnson's Brigade, and in 1777 as First Lieutenant in the Linganore Battalion of Militia. His home plantation was part of *Warfield's Vineyard* and part of *Stringer's Chance*. They had ten children. On April 12, 1792, Elizabeth married second to Joshua Howard. The children were:

1. Alexander Warfield, born c.1764, probably in Frederick County, died January 6, 1835 at the age of 70 years, 9 months and 6 days. Buried at Sams Creek cemetery, located on the boundary line between Frederick and Carroll Counties, east of Libertytown. Represented Frederick County in the State Legislature during 1818 and 1819. Married after December 5, 1788 to his cousin, Elizabeth Woodward, daughter of William Woodward and Dinah Warfield; and second after March 14, 1797 to Jemima Dorsey, born c.1775, died November 26, 1847 at *Pilgrim's Retreat* in Frederick County, daughter of Michael Dorsey and Honour Howard. Jemima is buried with her husband at Sams Creek. Two children from the first marriage and eleven from the second, not necessarily in this order:

   a. Charles Alexander Warfield, married Ann Hollingsworth of Baltimore, and had children. He died in Butte County, California. The children were:
      (1) Mary Hollingsworth Warfield.
      (2) Margaret Warfield, married Hammond; St Louis.

(3)   Martha Warfield, married Hamilton of Texas.

(4)   John A. Warfield.

(5)   Charles A. Hamilton Warfield.

b.   Joshua Warfield, married Evelina Johnson; six children.

c.   Jesse Lee Warfield, born November 27, 1801, died February 9, 1887 in Baltimore County. A doctor, married first to Hannah Yellott and had one child. Married second Anne Marie Bond and third Olivia Baker. His child was:

(1)   Francina H. Warfield, married Gorsuch.

d.   Honor Warfield, married first March 7, 1825 to Richard Green Dorsey, born April 18, 1799, died December 12, 1832 in Frederick County, son of Lloyd Dorsey (1772) and Anna Green (1770). Honor married second to Andrew Nicodemus. She and Richard Dorsey had one son, and one daughter was born to her second marriage:

(1)   Alexander Warfield Dorsey, born December 27, 1828, and died January 2, 1868 at Westminster, Maryland. A doctor, he was married to Mary R. Webster, born 1830, died 1892. Two children:

(a)   Richard Green Dorsey, Jr.

(b)   Lloyd Dorsey, born March 10, 1856 at St. Louis, Missouri, died August 29, 1942 at Baltimore, Maryland. Married February 6, 1884 to Mary Augusta Canter, born February 22, 1859, died May 12, 1942. Children, born in Baltimore.

(2)   Cecelia Nicodemus, married Reverend J. P. Hentz.

e.   Asbury O. Warfield.

f.   Cecilia Warfield, married August 4, 1834 to Frederick A. Davis.

g.   Sarah Warfield, married Thomas H. W. Moore.

h.   Mary Catherine Warfield.

i.   Henrietta Warfield, married February 1, 1819 to Thomas I. Worthington, and had children, including:

(1)   Charles Alexander Worthington.

j.   Elizabeth Warfield, married April 25, 1827 to Upton Higgins.

k.   Dennis Warfield.

1. Juliet Warfield, married John Howard, son of Joshua Howard, of Baltimore. At least one daughter:
     (1) Jemima Howard, married Archibald Lamar of Martinsburg, West Virginia.
   m. William Woodward Warfield, died young.
2. Mary Warfield, married after January 13, 1791 to Elisha Bennett in Baltimore County.
3. Sarah Warfield, married May 10, 1792 to James Pearre, born March 10, 1761, the owner of *Pearre's Retreat* in Frederick County, and had children.
4. Elizabeth Warfield, married Samuel Johnson.
5. Anne Warfield, married December 7, 1796 Joshua Jones of Sam's Creek, Frederick County.
6. Elijah Warfield, died c.1814. He was a captain during the War of 1812; later removed to Kentucky and died there.
7. Lancelot Warfield, known as Lott, born in that part of Frederick County which became Carroll. A minister, he located in Easton, Maryland and died 1834. He married June, 1807 to Elizabeth White and had at least one daughter. Apparently married second in 1817 to Mrs. Anna Needles Harris and had children.
8. David Warfield, died September 4, 1821, single, in Baltimore. He was also a captain during the War of 1812. He had become quite wealthy operating a merchandising house in the city, and for the period, his will left rather large legacies to various members of his family, totalling well over one hundred thousand dollars, in addition to substantial properties.
9. Charles Warfield, died c.1848, a minister in Baltimore.
10. Dennis Warfield, born c.1784, died c.1806, single, in Havana, Cuba.
11. Rezin Warfield.

CHAPTER 8

Joseph Warfield
1758-1837

This son of Joshua M. Warfield and Rachel Howard was born February 19, 1758 near Elk Ridge, Anne Arundel County and died October 19, 1837. Pages 440 and 441 of *Anne Arundel Gentry,* Volume 1, by Harry Wright Newman, contains a listing of the seven children, and thirty-eight grandchildren, with dates of birth and marriage, taken from the records submitted by the widow Elizabeth in 1839 in her application for pension. It appears that Joseph was granted pension for Revolutionary service about 1832, soon after the Act for payment of such pensions. The records indicate that he served as a Lieutenant in the Maryland line, and was to receive $85.97 per year pension payment.

Additional information relative to this family was found in the family file at the library of the Montgomery County Historical Society. He enlisted September 25, 1776 as a Cadet in Captain James Disney's Company, Colonel Josia C. Hall's Maryland Regiment, and was discharged November 30, 1776. Married August 6, 1778 to Elizabeth Dorsey, born December 8, 1761, the daughter of Nicholas and Elizabeth Dorsey, and moved to Montgomery County about 1801, where he taught school. His wife left a will, dated December 8, 1843 and probated January 21, 1851 in Montgomery County. She there named a son and two daughters, as well as several grandchildren. Among those listed were: Mary Elizabeth Beall, a great grand-daughter; and Evelina Beall, a grand-daughter; indicating that one of her daughters married a Beall. Children, born in Anne Arundel County:

1. Elizabeth Warfield, born June 4, 1782, married April 20, 1802 to Andrew Offutt, and had children:
   a. Evelina Offutt, born August 19, 1803
   b. Edwin Offutt, born October 4, 1805
   c. Harriet Offutt, born July 24, 1807
   d. Joseph Wesley Offutt, born June 3, 1809
   e. Elizabeth E. Offutt, born May 27, 1811

f.   Charlotte Ann Offutt, born September 1, 1813
g.   Juliet William Offutt, born November 20, 1815
h.   Joshua Warfield Offutt, born October 10, 1817
i.   Zachariah Offutt, born July 12, 1826
2. Juliet Warfield, born May 18, 1785, married September 10, 1805 to Alpheus Williams, and had children. This daughter was referred to as Juliet Davis in the will of her mother dated 1843, and was perhaps married twice:
a.   Achsah Elizabeth Williams, born September 27, 1809. Married February 14, 1827 to Charles McCubbin, born January 18, 1807, died June 25, 1891 at Mexico, Missouri. At least one son and a daughter:
   (1)   Joseph Nicholas McCubbin, born May 28, 1839 at Redlands, California.
   (2)   Elizabeth Achsah McCubbin.
b.   Eswell Williams (questionable spelling).
c.   Benjamin Joseph Williams, born April 29, 1813
d.   Nicholas Williams, born August 26, 1815
e.   Alpheus B. Williams, born March 19, 1818
3. Harriet Warfield, born July 2, 1787
4. Nicholas Dorsey Warfield, born May 25, 1789, of whom more
5. Elizabeth Dorsey Warfield, born September 10, 1791
6. Charlotte Warfield, born October 25, 1793, died August 8, 1831. Married September 7, 1824 to Richard Lawrence and had children:
a.   Nicholas Otho Lawrence, born June 27, 1825
b.   Richard Joseph Lawrence, born October 1, 1827
c.   Warfield Lawrence, born April 9, 1831
7. Sarah Warfield, born September 25, 1798.

Nicholas Dorsey Warfield
1789-

This son of Joseph Warfield (1758) and Elizabeth Dorsey (1761) was found as head of household in the 1850 census for the Rockville District of Montgomery County, Maryland. He was born May 25, 1789, and his wife Mary was born c.1786; they were married March 12, 1816. Also in the household was one Elizabeth

Warfield, born c.1761, his mother, apparently widowed. Nicholas is also listed in the census as the owner of three slaves. Living with them were two daughters. In the 1860 census for Darnestown, Nicholas D. is apparently a widower, owning real estate valued at $2,300 and personal property at $4,700. His will was dated February 4, 1860, probated October 15, 1861 and filed in liber JWS-1 at folio 88, Montgomery County. He mentions his wife Mary; who did not appear in the 1860 census and must have predeceased him by a matter of months; both daughters and his son Edwin. Joshua is not named in the will, nor are either of the twin sons, who must have predeceased their father. The children were:

1. Elizabeth Anne Warfield, born April 6, 1817. Living in the household of her father in the 1860 census, with the surname Hawkins, and personal property valued at $1,000. She inherited part two of the farm, containing 117 acres of *The Resurvey on William and John,* and *Susannah.* This is perhaps the same Elizabeth A. who was married February 12, 1851 to James Hawkins, Jr., who is listed in the 1850 census for the Rockville District of Montgomery County at the age of 52, and thus born c.1798, who perhaps was deceased by 1860.

2. Edwin Warfield, born November 8, 1818, died May 7, 1891. He was married January 5, 1847 to Sarah Ann Darby at St. Peters Church in Poolesville, born c.1826, died February 6, 1885. His wife and children inherited from his father a lot in Dawsonville; part of *Small Purchase* and part of *The Resurvey on William's Range;* and all remaining real estate. Found in the 1850 census for Cracklin District (Laytonsville), born c.1820. He was a farmer, with property valued at $1,000, and they then had two children. In the census, Edwin is listed as owning 90 acres of cleared land, and 117 acres of unimproved land. He had 2 horses, 1 milch cow, and 10 hogs, his livestock being valued at $100. He raised 40 bushels of wheat, 650 bushels of Indian corn, 150 bushels of oats, 400 pounds of tobacco, 5 bushels of peas and beans, 30 bushels of Irish potatoes, 40 bushels of buckwheat, and 80 pounds of butter. The value of animals slaughtered for the year was listed at $100. He appears also in the 1860 census for the Goshen Post Office area, with his wife, and five children. The family next appears

in the 1870 census for the Third District near Poolesville Post Office. He then owned real estate valued at $2,925 and $1,140 in personal property. There were five children living at home, as well as Elizabeth Hawkins, born c.1816 (his sister Elizabeth Anne Warfield just above) and two black servants. Their children were:

a. Alice Virginia Warfield, born c.1848; listed as Alice V. in the 1850 census, and as Virginia in the 1860 census; born the same year in both cases. Married November 25, 1864 to James L. Lodge. Not at home in the 1870 census, and not found in her own household.

b. Mary E. Warfield, born c.1850

c. Sarah Lavinia Warfield, born October 3, 1852, died October 9, 1914. Buried Darnestown Presbyterian Church.

d. John Alexander Warfield, born August 29, 1855, died March 12, 1906. Baptized July 24, 1859 at Darnestown Presbyterian Church, where he is buried. He may be the same John A. who married January 18, 1893 to Jennie Rider of Baltimore County.

e. William Wright Warfield, born September 17, 1858, baptized July 24, 1859 at Darnestown Presbyterian Church, died at *Oak Grove* November 15, 1874. Buried Darnestown Presbyterian Church.

f. Gracie L. Warfield, born c.1864

3. Mary Eliza Warfield, born September 17, 1820, living at home in 1860, died December 27, 1880, apparently single. Buried at Darnestown Presbyterian Church. She inherited part one of the farm, containing 99 and 3/4 acres of *The Resurvey on William and John,* and *Susannah.*

4. Twin son Warfield, born November 23, 1822

5. Twin son Warfield, born November 23, 1822

6. Joshua D. Warfield, born November 29, 1823. Perhaps the son of Nicholas Dorsey Warfield (1789) discussed here, this individual is found listed as Joshua Warfield, head of household in the 1870 census for Brighton in Montgomery County, born c.1824. His wife Elizabeth was born c.1826, and they then had four children:

a. Edna Warfield, born c.1862

b.   George Warfield, born c.1864. Perhaps the same George W. Warfield found in cemetery records of Damascus Methodist Church. Born August 7, 1864, died April 23, 1954. Buried with him is his wife, Mary E., born March 29, 1869, died March 28, 1914. In the 1900 census for Damascus, George has been married seven years, and owns his farm free and clear. His wife Mary E. has been the mother of one child, then living at home. The mother of George is living with them, widowed. They are found again in the 1920 census of Damascus, with his mother still living with them, and one son:

(1)   Elisha S. Warfield, born August, 1893, and died January 1, 1965 at his home in Damascus, Montgomery County, Maryland; buried in Damascus Cemetery. He married Ethel P. V. Warfield, born August 20, 1894 and died August 3, 1978 at Westminster Nursing Home. She was a daughter of William H. Warfield (1868) and Emma C. Burdette (1870). They had children:

(a)   Donald Elisha Warfield, born August 19, 1918 at Damascus, died September 3, 1985 while on vacation in Nova Scotia. Married October 10, 1946 to Julia Louise Kemp, born July 18, 1920 at Woodfield, Maryland, and died October 18, 1990, daughter of James Raymond Kemp (1898) and Mary Frances King (1900). Children:

1.   James Harvey Warfield, born August 25, 1947 at Frederick. Married November 29, 1974 Jennifer Lynn Hamm, born May 13, 1954 at Fairfield, Alabama, daughter of James Hamm and Florence Y. Anthony. There were children:

a.   Sarah Elizabeth Warfield, born: November 5, 1981.

b.   Jennifer Lynn Warfield, born November 11, 1987.

2. Diane Louise Warfield, born October 2, 1948 at Frederick.
c. Walter Hamilton Warfield, born c.1865, of whom more
d. Charles Warfield, born c.1867

Walter Hamilton Warfield
1865-1937

This son of Joshua D. Warfield (1823) was born c.1865 at Damascus, Montgomery County, Maryland, and died January 10, 1937 at Ijamsville, Maryland. He was married April 17, 1890 to Frances Mary Day, born October 18, 1872 near Morgan, and died October 1, 1941, daughter of John Fletcher Day (1849) and Elizabeth Leatherwood (1851). Walter and his wife are buried at Mount Prospect Cemetery in Mt. Airy, and had several children:

1. Eunice Etchison Warfield, born April 15, 1891 at Mt. Airy, died April 7, 1969. Married December 21, 1913 to Nathan Monroe Clary, born September 1, 1888, died February 28, 1973. One son:
   a. Robert Clary, born August 14, 1925 at Frederick. Married December 10, 1944 to Lorraine Condon, born February 25, 1926 at Woodbine. Children:
      (1) Robert Wade Clary, born July 17, 1946, died July 20, 1969 responding to a fire call with the Lisbon Volunteer Fire Company.
      (2) Dennis Blaine Clary, born February 17, 1951. Married September 8, 1972 Kathleen A. Collins, born May 19, 1954 at Silver Spring, Maryland.
      (3) Bonnie Marlene Clary, born August 16, 1955
      (4) Kay Lorraine Clary, born January 21, 1963
2. Bessie Frances Warfield, born September 9, 1892. Married April 9, 1914 to Herbert Monroe Gosnell, born December 31, 1886 in Carroll County, died August 8, 1955. Children:
   a. Ethel Mary Gosnell, born September 2, 1916 on the farm near Taylorsville. Married March 31, 1938 to John Henry Holsten, born May 23, 1916 at Baltimore. They had children:

        (1)   Ethel Maree Holsten, born November 3, 1939. Married November 28, 1957 Leslie Edward Singleton, born Wilmington, Delaware. She married second September 20, 1974 Jorge Vazquez, born in Puerto Rico.

        (2)   John Henry Holsten, Jr., born January 6, 1943. Married December 21, 1962 to Doris Lee Tew, born in Wilmington. Married second June 30, 1972 to Clara Louise Jones, also born there.

        (3)   Leo Gosnell Holsten, born January 2, 1946 at Baltimore. Married June 3, 1966 to Annette Crites, born at Wilmington. Married second April 12, 1975 to Helga Leister Hall, born in Germany.

    b.   Leo Monroe Gosnell, born June 2, 1918. Married August 25, 1962 to Ruth Farver, born March 2, 1927 at Taylorsville.

    c.   Betty Gosnell, born June 26, 1923. Married August 5, 1955 to John Winn, born December 6, 1916 Baltimore.

    d.   Doris Marie Gosnell, born May 8, 1929. Married September 1, 1950 to Oliver E. Bullen, Jr., born December 30, 1919 at Baltimore. Children, born at Baltimore:

        (1)   Randy Oliver Bullen, born December 27, 1951

        (2)   Candace Marie Bullen, born January 28, 1956

        (3)   Nancy Lynn Bullen, born September 20, 1967

    e.   Peggy Webb Gosnell, born April 25, 1932. Married November 17, 1950 to Charles Ball, born June 2, 1928 in Ammons, Kntucky. Children:

        (1)   Vera Lynn Ball, born June 22, 1954

        (2)   Charles Earl Ball, born May 3, 1958

3.   Roy Day Warfield, born December 5, 1893. Married 1916 to Naomi Hood, born June 4, 1898 at Mt. Airy, died December 22, 1964. Buried at Bel Air, Maryland. Children:

    a.   Ernest Warfield, born March 13, 1917 at Mt. Airy and married to Jane Clark.

    b.   Carroll Warfield, born August 18, 1919 at Mt. Airy and married to Catherine Proctor.

    c.   Ada Belle Warfield, born April 13, 1921 at Mt. Airy and married to H. Webster Standiford.

d. Roy Day Warfield, Jr., born September 21, 1923 at Mt. Airy; married to Barbara Reaser.

4. Ruth Ethel Warfield, born March 15, 1895. Married October 11, 1916 to Roby Hurt Mullinix, born August 15, 1895 at Mt. Airy, died November 22, 1965. Buried at Howard Chapel. They had children:
   a. Frances Margaret Mullinix, born September 10, 1917. Married June 24, 1939 to John Sylvester Smith.
   b. Everett Warfield Mullinix, born December 11, 1921. Married Janice Watkins.

5. Raymond C. Warfield, born October 26, 1896, died July 7, 1972 at the Frederick Nursing Home. Married to Annie Marie Murray, born July 4, 1900 at Long Corner, Maryland, died December 29, 1974, daughter of Joseph and Hannah Murray. Buried at Prospect Cemetery. Children:
   a. Donald M. Warfield, married Mildred Pickett.
   b. Vera M. Warfield, married Bernard Dischinger.
   c. Dana Rudelle Warfield, married Patricia Dent.
   d. Margaret Ann Warfield, married Robert Ellis.
   e. Joseph E. Warfield, married Maggie Verdi.
   f. Douglas C. Warfield.

6. Charles Carroll Warfield, born July 5, 1898 at Mt. Airy, died February 12, 1976 at Avalon Convalescent Home in Hagerstown. Married Helen Martin. Children:
   a. Roland M. Warfield, married Dorothy Purdum.
   b. C. Holmes Warfield, married Cora Smith.
   c. Ballinger D. Warfield, married Dorothy Roe.
   d. Martin Warfield, married Audrey Sherman.
   e. Frances Mae Warfield, married Purnell Klapp.
   f. Paul M. Warfield.

7. Amy Louise Warfield, born March 5, 1900 near Mt. Airy, died there October 2, 1990. Married February 2, 1919 to Joseph Edwin Murray, born there November 25, 1897, died March 15, 1968. A daughter:
   a. Arlene Louise Murray, born January 5, 1924. Married five times: Curtis Zimmerman; C. C. Tyson; Samuel Henley; Thomas Owens; and David Helm.

8. Edgar Warfield, born June 1, 1901, died January 1, 1962 at Mt. Airy. He was a farmer and auctioneer. Married Lucy Virginia Mullinix; no children.

9. Byrtle Warfield, born September 24, 1903, died December 21, 1962. Married to William Tobias Martin. Children:
   a. William Warfield Martin, married Margaret Rout.
   b. Alton M. Martin, married Shirley King.

10. Elizabeth May Warfield, born May 1, 1905 at Mt. Airy. Married November 14, 1925 to Roger Holmes Martin, born near there September 29, 1903. He was a grocer, retired and moved to Clarksburg. They were divorced after five children. She married second Jesse M. Burrell, and moved to Pennsylvania. Her children were:
    a. Gloria Eileen Martin, born April 27, 1927. Married January 9, 1948 to Lawrence Buzi, born December 5, 1920 in Baltimore. Children:
       (1) Tanya Lee Buzi.
       (2) Lawrence Martin Buzi.
    b. Velma Mae Martin, born September 27, 1928. Married January 19, 1946 to John Burdette, born November 28, 1927.
    c. Joyce Denore Martin, born April 21, 1929. Married March 30, 1951 to Vernon Stup. Children:
       (1) Suzanne Joyce Stup.
       (2) Dwayne Vernone Stup.
    d. Phyllis Ann Martin, born December 31, 1933. Married March 21, 1952 to Glenn Moser, born August 22, 1933 in Baltimore. Children:
       (1) Judy Denise Moser.
       (2) Pamela Ann Moser.
       (3) Thomas Alan Moser.
    e. Shirley Marie Martin, born December 13, 1935. Married Clarence Whalen.

11. Hazel Eveline Warfield, born February 21, 1907 at Mt. Airy. Married November 14, 1925 to Milton Gosnell Penn, born June 17, 1903 at Winfield. Children:

a. Nancy Mae Penn, born April 30, 1930. Married June 10, 1950 to William Edward Moss, born July 14, 1920 at Leesburg, Virginia. Children:
   (1) Billie Rose Moss, born March 20, 1953. Married January 6, 1973 to Roger William Tabler and had a child:
      (a) Roger William Tabler, Jr., born September 27, 1975
   (2) Sallie Malvina Moss, born May 28, 1956
   (3) Clinton Oscar Moss, born May 3, 1958
   (4) William Peery Moss, born October 21, 1960
b. Thomas Milton Gosnell Penn, born May 25, 1936 at Mt. Airy. A pharmacist.
c. Monte Brooke Penn, born January 22, 1947 Frederick. Married May 27, 1971 to Maxine Alexis Cannoni, born June 5, 1947 at Charleroi, Pennsylvania.

12. Gladys Marie Warfield, born January 28, 1915 near Prospect, died January 3, 1988. Married October 9, 1937 to John Hardy Warfield, born July 29, 1915 near Shaffersville, Howard County, Maryland, died March 24, 1984 at Sinai Hospital, son of John Hebb Warfield and his wife Elizabeth H. Warfield. They had children:
a. Richard Hardy Warfield, born September 7, 1946. Married August 14, 1971 to Jane Marie Farrall, born April 10, 1946 in Washington, D. C. and had a child:
   (1) Adrian John Warfield, born August 3, 1974
b. James Stuart Warfield, born June 9, 1952, died October 30, 1987.

CHAPTER 9

Warfield Families of Frederick County

As has been the case with most of the families studied in our series under the general heading *Our Maryland Heritage,* of which this is Book Fifteen, many of them have lived back and forth across the boundary line between Montgomery and Frederick Counties. Prior to 1776, Montgomery was a part of Frederick, which was created from Prince George's County and a part of Baltimore in 1748. Early movement of colonists from the counties along the Chesapeake carried them into this area, and there they have remained through several generations.

For several years after its formation, Frederick was still wilderness country, unsettled, and unsafe. As late as August 4, 1757, the *Maryland Gazette* reported that: "Alexander M'Keasy was shot by an Indian on July 27th near his house, within 16 miles of Frederick Town, near Tom's Creek. He will probably not live. His son was carried away as a prisoner." The same issue reported: "Samuel Wilson, about age 17, was shot and scalped about 3 weeks ago near the house of George Pow, not far from Anti-Eatam (sic). Pow, his wife and eight children escaped, but his house and all possessions were burnt."

Despite these hardships, the Colonists continued to arrive in the western areas of Maryland. Among them were Warfields.

William F. Warfield
1856-1923

William F. was born July 28, 1856, died September 7, 1923, and is buried at Mt. Olivet cemetery in Frederick, with his wife. He was married December 1, 1895 to Nannie Simmons at Urbana, in Frederick County. She was born January 11, 1870, and died April 11, 1957. Birth records, Montgomery Circuit of the Methodist Church, identify three children:

1. Russell S. Warfield, born August 13, 1899

2. William F. Warfield, Jr., born February 1, 1902, died December 8, 1918. Buried with his parents.
3. Janet V. Warfield, born April 16, 1905

James R. Warfield

Identified only by cemetery records of their children, James R. was married to Mary C., and they had at least these children:
1. Scott Welty Warfield, born December 28, 1890, died February 29, 1892. Buried at Mt. Olivet cemetery in Frederick.
2. Robert Meredith Warfield, born March 19, 1898, died October 17, 1902; buried at Mt. Olivet cemetery.

Lavinia Warfield

Lavinia was the daughter of John and Elizabeth Warfield of Frederick County. Her father died intestate in Frederick County about 1763, and her widowed mother Elizabeth was married second to John Saffell. Lavinia was married October 8, 1780 to William Clarke, born at *Locust Thicket* on the Patuxent, son of Henry and Elizabeth Clarke. William died intestate in Prince George's County before July 17, 1783, when his personal estate was appraised. There is some reason to believe that she later married a kinsman of her deceased husband, and apparently had two more children. Lavinia and William had one child, and she had three more from her second marriage, also to a Clarke:
1. Elizabeth Clarke, married after May 23, 1798 in Anne Arundel County to William Clarke, son of Abraham Clarke. He obtained title to *Locust Thicket* through his wife, and by purchase from her mother. In 1835, he purchased parts of *Pleasant Grove* and *Locust Park,* adjoining his plantation. In 1807 he was named Constable for the district, and served in that capacity on other occasions. They had children:
   a. George Clarke.
   b. Abraham Clarke.
   c. Henry Clarke.
   d. William Clarke.
   e. Samuel Clarke.

120

f. Ann Clarke, married James H. Denson.
g. Elizabeth Clarke, married to E. Jacob.
h. Daughter Clarke, married Browning. At least one child:
    (1) Mary Ann Browning.
2. Tilghman Warfield Clarke, married Jane Lewis.
3. Ariana Clarke, born August 2, 1789, died December 22, 1858. Married James Atkinson, born August 1, 1769, died July 9, 1838. They had children:
    a. Samuel A. Atkinson, born August 27, 1816 at Ellicott Mills. Married Margaret Anna Webster, born September 24, 1821 at Baltimore, died April 20, 1897.
    b. James F. Atkinson, born February 25, 1819
    c. Elizabeth Ann Atkinson, born January 21, 1824
    d. Thomas Jefferson Atkinson, born June 27, 1827
4. Drady Clarke, probably married to Stinchcomb.

Alexander Warfield
1805-

Alexander was found as head of household in the 1850 census for the Woodsboro District of Frederick County. The district is located northeast of Frederick City. He was born c.1805 and had a wife Eliza, born c.1811, and eight children. Also living with them was Mary Dicus, born c.1790, not otherwise identified. She could have been the mother of the wife of Alexander, but that is simply a guess at this point. The children were:
1. Margaret A. Warfield, born 1832
2. Mary C. Warfield, born 1834
3. Learnard E. Warfield, born 1836 (which could be Leonard).
4. Owen B. Warfield, born August 10, 1838, died August 11, 1864; buried at Haughs Lutheran Church, Ladiesburg, in Frederick County. Probably the same who was married August 6, 1861 to Mary E. Fritz.
5. Jemima A. Warfield, born 1841, probably the same who was married December 30, 1861 in Frederick County to George V. Fitez.
6. Joanna R. Warfield, born 1843
7. Sarah Warfield, born 1845

8. Lloyd A. Warfield, born February 11, 1847, died June 8, 1904 and buried at Johnsville Beaver Dam Brethren Church in Frederick County. Married to Mary E., born 1852, died 1923 and buried at St. Peters Rocky Hill Lutheran Church, Woodsboro.

George W. Warfield
1817-

This George W. was listed as a merchant in the 1850 census of the New Market District of Frederick County. He was born January 17, 1817, died November 23, 1887, and is buried at Mt. Olivet in Frederick, with his wife. Hester Ann was born July 17, 1824 and died October 15, 1913. In 1850, they had two small children. Also listed with them was Elizabeth Moss, born 1836, designated mulatto. The children were:
1. Georgianna Warfield, born 1847
2. Earnest W. Warfield, born 1849

Mary Elizabeth Warfield
1808-

Her parents are yet to be located, but Mary Elizabeth was married in Frederick County, Maryland, August 29, 1832 to Ephraim Creager, born c.1808. They are found in the 1850 census for the Woodsboro District, with several children. He was a farmer with property valued at eight thousand dollars in 1850. Living with them was one Eliza Bussard, born 1822. In the next dwelling listed in the census was Daniel Creager, born c.1779, who could be the father of Ephraim. Children:
1. Daniel Alexander Creager, born c.1834, infant death.
2. Francis Asbury W. Creager, born 1835
3. Manelia S. Creager, born 1837; married April 17, 1861 to Frederick A. Markey, Sr.
4. George E. Creager, born 1839
5. Alcinda H. Creager, born 1841
6. Noble H. Creager, born 1843
7. Lancetta V. Creager, born 1845, died c.1918
8. Caroline E. Creager, born 1847

9. Mary Elizabeth Creager, born c.1851, died 1853
10. Octavia Creager, born 1853, died 1854

Ann Maria Warfield
1825-

Ann Maria was born c.1825 and married December 9, 1844 to Joshua Troxel in Frederick County. He appears as head of household in the 1850 census for Emmittsboro, born c.1815, listed as a butcher, with real property valued at three thousand, five hundred dollars. They then had three children:
1. Columbia Troxel, born 1845
2. Emma H. Troxel, born 1846
3. Thomas W. Troxel, born 1848

Caroline Warfield
1818-1852

Caroline was born c.1818, probably in Frederick County, and died there May 6, 1852. Married January 5, 1841 to William S. Bantz, born c.1818. He is head of household in the 1850 census for the city of Frederick, listed as a tanner, with real estate valued at four thousand, five hundred dollars. There were then four children:
1. William A. Bantz, born 1843
2. Henry H. Bantz, born 1844
3. Mary W. Bantz, born 1846
4. Clarence Bantz, born 1850

Catherine A. Warfield
1826-

Catherine was born c.1826, probably in Frederick County. Her mother was also Catherine A., born c.1783, died February 23, 1848, and buried at Jefferson Union cemetery. Her father has not yet been identified. Catherine of 1826 was married October 29, 1839 to Michael Keefer at Frederick. He is shown as head of household in the 1850 census for the city of Frederick, born c.1821. If the ages stated in the census are correct (and thus the years of birth), and if the marriage record date is also correct, then when they were married, Michael was but eighteen years of age, and Catherine was thirteen. Not impossible for the times, of course. In the census record, the oldest of the three children living at home was then seven, thus born when Catherine was seventeen. Michael was listed as an inn-keeper, operating a hotel, with real estate valued at fifteen thousand dollars. He then had three children, and a list of some thirty-three hotel occupants in the census. The three children were:

1. Albert W. Keefer, born 1843
2. Ellen C. V. Keefer, born 1846
3. Michael C. Keefer, born 1849

Elizabeth Ann Warfield
1817-1873

Elizabeth Ann was born c.1817 and died January 22, 1873. Married in Frederick County February 10, 1845 to Henry Culler, Jr., born c.1817. They appear in the 1850 census for the Jefferson District of the county, with their first child. Henry is listed as a farmer with real estate valued at four thousand dollars. Also in the household is David Culler, born c.1816, perhaps a brother of Henry. The child was:

1. William C. Culler, born 1846

Sarah Warfield
1797-

Sarah was born c.1797 and married September 24, 1833 to Jacob Young, born c.1796. They are found in the 1850 census for the Eighth Election District of Frederick County, with two children. They are found again in the 1870 census for Damascus, in Montgomery County, at which time Miranda Warfield, born 1835, and Wesley G. Warfield, born 1859, are living with them. There are three different children listed in the 1870 census, with ages that would indicate at least two of them should have been included in 1850. However, the age of their mother appears to be at least seven years lower than it should be, so we assume the children were incorrectly listed as well. Children, from the two census reports, appear to include:

1.   David W. Young, born 1836
2.   Emanuel J. Young, born 1844
3.   Mary E. Young, born 1844 (or somewhat later)
4.   Joseph D. Young, born 1845 (or somewhat later)
5.   Sarah A. Young, born 1850 (or somewhat later)

Salem United Methodist Church
Cedar Grove, Montgomery County, Maryland

126

CHAPTER 10

Miscellaneous Warfield Family Members

A number of family members have been found in various records, primarily of Maryland, in the counties with which we are concerned, but not yet fit into any family group. They are presented here for the record, and further research.

John F. Warfield
died 1957

John left a will dated January 6, 1955, probated and filed in liber EA 81 at folio 110, will records of Montgomery County, Maryland. According to the papers therein he died June 2, 1957. He names his wife, Isabella Josephine Warfield and two daughters:
1. Freda Warfield, married to Mullen.
2. Louise Warfield, married to Garrett.

James Albert Warfield
died 1943

The will of this individual was written October 28, 1937, probated September 21, 1943 and filed in liber JWN 2 at folio 299, will records of Montgomery County, Maryland. According to those papers, he died August 6, 1943. His wife was Virginia A., and they had several children. He left his estate jointly to his children, after the death of their mother, with the request that it remain in the family generation to generation; providing that should any child wish to dispose of their portion, they would do so only to siblings. Children:
1. Opray O. Warfield, married to White.
2. Algetha May Warfield, married to Quander.
3. James Albert Warfield, Jr.
4. Florence Evelyn Warfield.

Cost J. Warfield
1851-1933

This individual has not yet been placed in a family group, but he was born July 2, 1851, apparently in Montgomery County, and died there September 3, 1933. Buried at Mt. Lebanon cemetery with his wife, Georgetta, born 1854, died 1930. His will, dated May 30, 1931, was probated September 26, 1933 and filed in liber HGC 5 at folio 173 in will records of Montgomery County. It lists a number of small bequests to various individuals, but does not identify them as to their relationships. He names one sister, Fannie E. Day in a separate bequest. Later in his listings, there is a Bradley J. Day, who may have been her husband. At least some, if not all of those listed, were his children:

1. Effie A. Warfield, born 1887, died 1966. Buried Mt. Lebanon.
2. Mary Olive Warfield, born 1884, died July 7, 1963 at her home near Etchison. Mt. Lebanon cemetery.
3. Raymond C. Warfield, born 1892, died 1969. Mt. Lebanon.
4. Laura Warfield, married Molesworth.
5. Ella Warfield, married Hardy.
6. Rosalie Warfield.
7. Louise Warfield.
8. Thurman R. Warfield.
9. Louise Warfield, married Johnson and had four children.

Joshua D. Warfield
1822-1899

This Joshua was born June 21, 1822 and died September 3, 1899, and is buried at Damascus Methodist cemetery, Montgomery County, Maryland. He is probably the same Joshua D. who was married in the county January 17, 1849 to Delilah H. Duvall, daughter of Lewis W. Duvall (1775) and Sarah Wyville. Joshua and Delilah had at least one daughter:

1. Louisa A. Warfield, married to Hopwood, and had a son:
    a. William Mareen Hopwood. Note the use of the middle name, Mareen, suggesting descent from the almost legendary *Mareen Duvall of Middle Plantation.*

Alice Warfield
1841-1891

Alice was married to James Thomas Holland, born 1833 and died 1911. He was a son of Charles Holland and Nancy Griffith, and they are believed to have lived in Anne Arundel County, Maryland, although some of the Holland kin moved to Ohio. They had children:
1. Charles Griffith Holland, born September 16, 1867, married to Florence Clark. No children.
2. Lloyd Walter Holland, born November 17, 1869
3. Ann Holland, born December 12, 1871; married Sam Owings and had at least one daughter:
   a. Alice Dorsey Owings, married Guy Wood and had a son:
      (1) Guy Holland Wood.
4. James Philip Holland, born May 11, 1874; married Margaret Henderson and had children:
   a. Thomas Henderson Holland.
   b. Amos Holland.
   c. Hester L. Holland.

William E. Warfield
died 1966

William E. died April 26, 1966 at Laytonsville, and is buried at Parklawn Cemetery near Rockville, Maryland. His wife was Katherine M., who predeceased him, and they had children:
1. Elsie E. Warfield, married Thompson.
2. Wilson E. Warfield.
3. John W. Warfield.
4. G. Thomas Warfield.

Catharine Warfield
1816-

Catharine was born c.1816 and married January 26, 1843 in Montgomery County, Maryland, to Lewis H. Duvall, born there c.1814, son of Lewis W. Duvall (1775) and Sarah Wyville. Lewis

H. died before April 1, 1856, when his brother, Mareen Duvall, was named Guardian of the children. All four of them are found living with Mareen Duvall in the 1870 census of the Second District. Lewis and Catharine are listed in the 1850 census for Cracklin District of the county, with three children. Lewis was a farmer, owning 60 acres of improved land and 15 acres unimproved. He had 2 horses, 1 milch cow and 2 other cattle, and 12 swine. In the previous year he raised 20 bushels of wheat, 200 bushels of Indian corn, 40 bushels of oats, 5 bushels of buckwheat, 5 bushels of Irish potatoes, and 1,000 pounds of tobacco. His children were:

1. Catharine S. Duvall, born 1844, married Baker and second to Grimes.
2. Sally Elizabeth Duvall, born 1846, married Baker and second W. F. Glaze.
3. Mary F. Duvall, born 1849, married Easton.
4. Lewis Dorsey Duvall, born 1851 after the census; died single.

William Hinks Warfield
1815-1879

Head of household in the 1850 census for Clarksburg District of Montgomery County, William H. was born c.1815. His wife was Ann, born c.1824, and they then had three children. She was Ann Miller, born 1824, died November 28, 1910. According to records of Rockville cemetery, he died July 5, 1879, and the two of them, with at least two of their children, were buried there. He was listed as an overseer, and the owner of one slave. He also appears in the 1870 census for the Rockville District, with his wife and six children. Living with them at the time was Zachariah T. Clagett, born c.1839, a carpenter; his wife Sarah Ann, born c.1844; and one child, Mary E. Clagett, born c.1864. Marriage records of Montgomery County report the marriage of Zachariah T. Clagett on January 10, 1861 to Sarah A. Warfield, establishing a family relationship. The children of William Hinks Warfield were:

1. Sarah A. Warfield, born c.1843; probably Sarah Ann, married January 10, 1861 to Zachariah T. Clagett,, born c.1839 and living with her parents in 1870, with their first child:
   a. Mary E. Clagett, born c.1864

2. Josephine Warfield, born c.1846
3. Jane R. Warfield, born c.1848, died July 12, 1927
4. Mary E. Warfield, born c.1852
5. David H. Warfield, born c.1857. This is probably David Hanson Warfield, who was born 1857 and died October 5, 1924. Buried at St. Mary's Catholic cemetery in Rockville. He was first married October 7, 1886 to Nannie Lyddane, born August 23, 1858, died November 12, 1888, third daughter of Stephen M. Lyddane. Married second November 23, 1892 at St. Mary's to Katherine Rebecca Fields, born 1868, died December 16, 1945, youngest daughter of R. G. Fields; buried with her husband. He left a will dated July 12, 1921, probated October 21, 1924 and filed in liber PEW 2 at folio 253, will records of Montgomery County, Maryland. He names only his wife and two of his sisters as legatees, being: Ada Warfield and Emma Warthen. The will of his wife was filed under the name Kate R. Warfield, dated September 11, 1941, probated January 2, 1946 and filed in liber OWR 14 at folio 206. It names as sole legatee her niece, Rebecca Fields. Apparently, there were no children.
6. Ada Warfield, born 1861, died January 2, 1928
7. Emma Warfield, born c.1864

Lewis M. Warfield
1837-

In the 1850 census for Cracklin District of Montgomery County, Lewis is found listed as born c.1837, a student, living in the household headed by Elisha G. Hall, born c.1818, teacher, and his wife, Mary B. Hall, born c.1810, three children, and a number of other students.

Elizabeth Warfield
1798-

The 1850 census for the Clarksburg District of Montgomery County, Maryland, carries a household headed by Elizabeth, born c.1798. She is listed as owning real estate valued at $1,000. With her in the household is one Mary L. Norwood, born c.1806, also with real estate valued at $1,000, and several individuals all bearing the surname of Murphy: Priscilla Murphy, born c.1775; William W. Murphy, born c.1807; Sarah A. Murphy, born c.1834; John B. Murphy, born c.1836; and Thomas H. Murphy, born c.1846. There is also one Henrietta Davis, black, born c.1838. Family relationships are not stated.

Green Warfield

Found by reference in the obituary of his wife, Green was married to Drusilla, who was born c.1832 and died March 3, 1906 at the home of her son, Watkins Warfield, near Florence, Maryland. Buried at Poplar Springs Church. Eight surviving children:
1. Daughter Warfield, married Fuller Wright and lived near Cooksville, Maryland.
2. James Warfield, lived near Florence.
3. Robert Warfield, lived near Florence.
4. Daughter Warfield, married Gaither Lakins, and lived near Poplar Springs.
5. Daughter Warfield, married Arthur Davis, of Mt. Airy.
6. Daughter Warfield, married Eldridge Moxley, and lived near Long Corner, Howard County, Maryland.
7. Watkins Warfield, of near Florence.
8. Daughter Warfield, married Clifford Unglesbee, and lived near Long Corner.

Augustus L. Warfield
1862- 1929

Augustus was born April 10, 1862 in Howard County, died October 5, 1929, a son of Lemuel Warfield. He is buried at the Warfield Burying Ground at *Cherry Grove* in Howard County. Married to Sarah Elizabeth Dorsey, born November 30, 1873 in the county, daughter of Humphrey Dorsey and Catherine Augusta Riggs (1850). Children:
1. Bowie Warfield.
2. Joshua Dorsey Warfield.

3. Robert Warfield.
4. Mary Catherine Warfield.
5. Augustus Warfield.
6. Margaret Rachel Warfield, married Jeffrey Martin. A son:
   (a) Jeffrey Martin, Jr.

Warfield

The following brothers and sisters were found in the obituary of the first listed, with no reference to the parents. Places following each name are residence as of 1983:

1. Virginia L. Warfield, died July 12, 1983 at Manila, single. Native of Howard County, Maryland. Reported as a niece of Louise Warfield of Baltimore, and niece of Rose Warfield of Rockville. Miss Rose Warfield was born October 22, 1906 in Howard County, and died December 18, 1988, daughter of Frank Warfield and Nancy Ann Driver; buried at Howard Chapel cemetery, Long Corner, Howard County. Her surviving sister as of that date was Louise Warfield of Woodbine, which gives us some reference to the parentage of Virginia L. and her siblings for further study. The obituary of Rose mentiones all of these other children as nieces and nephews.
2. Helen Warfield, married Jordan; lived Sorrento, Florida.
3. Guinevere M. Warfield, of Woodbine, Maryland.
4. Miriam Warfield, married Reed, of Woodbine.
5. Rose Marie Warfield, married Glenn, of Woodbine.
6. Frank Hammond Warfield, of Hagerstown.
7. William Carr Warfield, of Mt. Airy; and see following two individuals bearing the name William C. Warfield, either of whom (or neither) could be this individual.

William C. Warfield

Married to Bettie E., who died August 28, 1962 at the home of her daughter in Comus, Maryland. They had children:

1. Edna Warfield, married to Spowers.
2. Mildred Warfield, married to Austin.
3. Ethel Warfield, married to Kefauver.

4. Edith Warfield, married to Roberson.
5. Louise Warfield, married to Evans.
6. Doris Warfield, married to Hough.
7. Betty Warfield, married to Luhn.
8. Theodore Warfield.
9. Edward Warfield.
10. Charles Warfield.
11. Warren Warfield.
12. Harding Warfield.

William C. Warfield

References to this William C. Warfield (of several bearing the name), were found in the obituary of the first listed child. The name of his wife was not given; the brothers and sisters were, with place of residence as of 1968:
1. Chauncey P. Warfield, of Silver Spring, Maryland, died October 19, 1968 at Winchester, Virginia, husband of Marjorie A. Warfield.
2. Violet Warfield, married Cotter.
3. Thomas O. Warfield. Probably the same whose middle name was Owings, and was married December 8, 1897 at St. Lukes Episcopal Church, Brighton, Maryland, to Ruth L. Clark, born August 14, 1878, daughter of John O. Clark and Margaret Ann Clagett (1856). They had children:
   a. John O. Warfield, born October 17, 1898
   b. Laura M. Warfield, born September 14, 1901. Married January 14, 1922 Allen Scrivnor and had three children.
   c. Thomas O. Warfield, born August 24, 1904
   d. Gertrude Warfield, born July 12, 1906
   e. Kennard Warfield, born March 8, 1911
4. David N. Warfield.
5. Robert A. Warfield.

Clagett Warfield

From the obituary of his wife, Clagett was married to Mabel Glascock, born October 2, 1913 in West Virginia, died September

30, 1987 at their home in Gaithersburg, daughter of George and Beulah Glascock. Buried Goshen Cemetery leaving one daughter:
1. Caroline Warfield, married Winchester. Lived in Nebraska.

Samuel Dorsey Warfield
1873-1942

Samuel was born 1873 and died 1942. Married October 24, 1894 at Providence Church to Alice Roberta Baker, born March 20, 1873, died 1945, daughter of William H. Baker (1826) and Jemima King Purdum (1832). Both are buried at Montgomery Chapel, Claggettsville, Montgomery County. The couple appear in the 1900 census for Damascus, with their son, there called simply Deets, a name by which he was known throughout his life. Samuel is shown there as being born c.1850, which is apparently an error. It also states that he has been married five years, which is roughly correct. They appear again in the 1920 census for Damascus, with his attained age correct, and again with the one son, who was:
1. Hamilton Deets Warfield, born December 21, 1897 near Browningsville, and died March 29, 1974. Married September 28, 1921 to Fairy Elizabeth Burdette, born February 14, 1902, daughter of William Hubert Burdette (1872) and Beda Cassandra King (1873). He owned and operated Damascus Chevrolet for 56 years; member of the board of Farmers and Mechanics Bank; director emeritus of Citizens Savings and Loan Association, and numerous other civic postions. Children:
    a. Hamilton Deets Warfield, Jr., born September 19, 1931. Married October 24, 1953 Juanita Louise Seboda, born April 6, 1932, and had children:
        (1) Teresa Ann Warfield, born August 29, 1954. Married June 22, 1977 to Gordon Miles Cooley, born February 9, 1953, son of George Wilson Cooley (1930) and Doris Louise Miles (1929). Children:
            (a) Adam Warfield Cooley: March 4, 1981.
            (b) Allison Leigh Cooley: May 2, 1984
        (2) Hamilton David Warfield; October 29, 1957.

b.   Joyce Elaine Warfield, born April 18, 1937. Married February 13, 1959 to Edmond Hamilton Rhodes, Jr., and had children:
    (1)   Mark Hamilton Rhodes, born November 19, 1960. Married to Sharon Lynn Hilton, born April 21, 1961, and had a son:
        (a)   Matthew Hamilton Rhodes: February 5, 1987
    (2)   Kenneth David Rhodes, born November 23, 1963. Married Kimberly Joyce Gartner, born May 11, 1964.
    (3)   Wayne Patrick Rhodes, born February 10, 1968. Married Kimberly Ann Hairfield, born April 15, 1966, and had children:
        (a)   Ashley Elizabeth Rhodes: February 25, 1985.
        (b)   Timothy Wayne Rhodes; August 31, 1990

Elizabeth A. Warfield
1841-1919

Her parents have not yet been identified, but Elizabeth was born August 14, 1841, died December 22, 1919. Buried Damascus Methodist Church. Married to William Harrison Hilton, born March 13, 1836, died July 1, 1919, son of Lloyd Hilton (1798) and Rachel Watkins (1804). Served as a private in Co. B, 5th Maryland Regt, and in Co. C, 13th Maryland. For further reference, the family of Lloyd Hilton and Rachel Watkins is found in the 1860 census of the First District of Montgomery County. William (Harrison) Hilton is then living at home with a number of brothers and sisters.

William G. Warfield
1883-1940

William G. was born February 25, 1883 and died March 10, 1940. Buried at Monocacy cemetery. Married to Bettie E., born March 15, 1891, died August 28, 1962, and had children:
1.   David D. Warfield, born September 28, 1928, drowned in the Dickerson Quarry, February 25, 1945. Buried with parents.

2. Shirley Ann Warfield, born November 23, 1934, died December 27, 1939. Buried with her parents.

Nathan Oliver Warfield
1845-1925

Nathan was born December 7, 1845 near Lisbon and died April 18, 1925. Buried at Morgan Chapel, Carroll County with his wife. He was a farmer, owning part of *Warfield's Range*. Married December 7, 1869 to Laura V. Day, born February 5, 1846 in Carroll County and died May 3, 1927, daughter of John Day (1811) and Emily McKnew. They had children, whose descendants are well discussed in *James Day of Browningsville and his Descendants, A Maryland Family*, by James Harvey Day, 1976. This family does not appear to be closely related to those primarily found in Montgomery and Frederick Counties, with whom we are principally concerned. For those interested in further generations of the family, please refer to the Day book. Suffice to say here that the children were:

1. Dalton Eugene Warfield, born November 8, 1870, died March 24, 1944. Married November 7, 1895 to Margaret Norwood, born January 26, 1871 at Baltimore. Three children.
2. Wilbur Newton Warfield, born February 25, 1874 at Baltimore, died December 23, 1955. Married November 16, 1904 to Julia Brayshaw. Five children.
3. Ernest Carroll Warfield, a twin, born February 11, 1876, died August 7, 1876. Buried at Morgan Chapel, Carroll County.
4. Edgar Howard Warfield, a twin, born February 11, 1876, died June 4, 1876. Buried at Morgan Chapel, Carroll County.
5. Emily Eliza Warfield, born October 31, 1878 in Howard County, died November 12, 1949. Married January 15, 1903 to Daniel J. Longenecker. Two children.
6. Oliver Stanley Warfield, born February 17, 1887 in Carroll County, Maryland; died September 23, 1945. A minister in Maramec, Oklahoma; married August 10, 1907 to Margaret Marr, born August 21, 1882 at Baltimore. Five children.

George Thomas Warfield
1924-

His parents are not yet identified, but George Thomas was born June, 1924, either in Frederick or Montgomery County, and married to Mary Orlean Stull, born March 17, 1925, daughter of Arnold Raymond Stull (1901) and Mary Columbia Kinsey (1906). They had children:
1. Thomas William Warfield, born January 28, 1947. Married December 3, 1968 to Norma Jean Reffitt, born December 28, 1946. Lived in Gaithersburg and had at least one son:
   a. Richard Bryan Warfield, born February 9, 1973
2. Katherine Mary Warfield, born July 11, 1951 at Bethesda.

Joseph Haddaway Warfield
1921-

Joseph Haddaway was born July 8, 1921 and married to Hazel Margaret Stanley, born June 23, 1922, died January 10, 1996 at Frederick, daughter of Grover Mount Stanley (1892) and Rosa Lena Boyer (1891) of Damascus. They had children:
1. Margaret JoAnn Warfield, born October 15, 1942 and died there July 22, 1980, single. She taught art to the Pueblo Indians at the University of New Mexico, and at the Acoma, Zia, Liguna and Jemez reservations.
2. Terrence Wayne Warfield, born June 6, 1946 and married October 14, 1972 Tana Kaye Denn, born June 19, 1944. Two children:
   a. Shelley Warfield.
   b. Justin Warfield.

Sarah E. Warfield
1886-1957

Not identified as yet within a family group, Sarah E. was married to Charles F. Layton and had at least one daughter:
1. Susan Elizabeth Layton, born October 28, 1886, died April 6, 1957 at her home in Damascus. Married to Emory Whitehead

Burdette, born July 30, 1890, and died July 30, 1953, son of Abraham Lincoln Burdette (1864) and Georgia Ellen Waters King (1867). Emory and Susan are buried at the Bethesda United Methodist Church cemetery near Browningsville. The will of Susan E. (Warfield) Layton was dated January 30, 1954 and probated April 23, 1957, recorded in liber EA 75 at folio 480, Montgomery County wills. She named all ten of her children in the will. They had children:

a. Roger Franklin Burdette, born May 20, 1909, died July or August, 1989. Married August 5, 1933 to Isla Lorraine Baker, born April 4, 1909, daughter of William Andrew Baker (1880). Children:
    (1) Natalie Ann Burdette, born September 9, 1938 at Takoma Park, Maryland. A school teacher, she died August 20, 1966, single.
    (2) Carol Baker Burdette, born January 5, 1942 at Takoma Park. Married February 19, 1960 to George Edgar Calahan, born December 21, 1937 at Miami, Arizona, a mining superinten-dent. Children, born at Tucson, Arizona:
        (a) Kenneth Roger Calahan; December 9, 1960
        (b) Rebecca Lynn Calahan; September 9, 1962

b. George Robert Burdette, born March 11, 1913 and died September, 1968; buried Parklawn Cemetery, Baltimore. Married Gladys Markley, born 1913, died July, 1964. They had one child:
    (1) Robert Burdette.

c. Sarah Evelyn Burdette, born July 31, 1915, and married September 2, 1933 at the Methodist parsonage in Ridgeville, Silas Cronin Beall, born September 10, 1906, son of Cronin Beall and Sally Lawson. Children:
    (1) Shirley Ann Beall, born April 27, 1937; Married the Reverend Raymond Bryant.
    (2) Sally Louise Beall, born December 24, 1940. Married Robert Runkles.
    (3) David Emory Beall, born May 20, 1946. Married Barbara Buxton.
    (4) Daniel Beall, married Joyce.

d.   Nellie Laura Burdette, born May 14, 1917. Married to William M. Browning, born January 22, 1914, and had children:
  (1)   William M. Browning, Jr., born July 15, 1948; married Paula Yoft.
  (2)   Susan Browning: April 29, 1950
  (3)   Brenda Kay Browning: October 11, 1951
e.   Emory Warfield Burdette, born July 19, 1919. Married Dorothy Linton, born December 25, 1915 and had children. Married second to Pauline Seir; no children. His children from first marriage were:
  (1)   Betty Lou Burdette, born November 2, 1936. Married Rex Keesee, born March 13, 1937, and had children:
    (a)   Rex Keesee, Jr., born December 9, 1957
    (b)   Dale Keesee, born March 26, 1959
    (c)   Lisa Lynn Keesee, born July 9, 1968
    (d)   Betty Ann Keesee, born July 13, 1969
  (2)   Robert Emory Burdette, born January 31, 1938. Married to Libby Griffith and had a child. He married second Mary and had two more children. He married third Bonnie Myler and had two more children. The first five children are from the three marriages of Robert Emory Burdette; the last two are children of Bonnie Myler by prior marriage, whom he adopted:
    (a)   Randy Burdette, born November 6, 1960
    (b)   Sheryl Burdette: December 26, 1962
    (c)   Robert Burdette: May 8, 1964
    (d)   Kelly Burdette, born November 7, 1973
    (e)   Shane Marie Burdette, born December 20, 1974
    (f)   Kaye Burdette, born December 31, 1963
    (g)   Sherry Burdette: September 18, 1967.
  (3)   Nancy Elizabeth Burdette, a twin, born March 12, 1945. Married to Richard Myers, and had children:
    (a)   Thomas Emory Myers: July 11, 1961
    (b)   Judy Ann Myers: November 3, 1964

(4) Florence Patricia Burdette, a twin, born March 12, 1945. Married Charles Diller, Jr., born April 4, 1945. Children:
  (a) Patty Ann Diller, born June 1, 1965
  (b) Charles Diller, born April 13, 1968
(5) James Richard Burdette, born April 20, 1947. Married to Dorothy Louise Deihl. Children:
  (a) Richard E. Burdette: February 22, 1971
  (b) James Jeffry Burdette: March 16, 1972
(6) Jo Ann Burdette, born August 10, 1958, died September 10, 1958. Buried Pine Grove Cemetery at Mt. Airy, Maryland

f. Betty Jane Burdette, born October 2, 1922. Married to Charles Elon Reed, born September 9, 1919, and had children:
  (1) Allen Elon Reed, born December 17, 1939. Married to Marie Ventresca.
  (2) William Lloyd Reed, born December 10, 1940. Married Barbara Woodfield.
  (3) Charles Francis Reed, born July 13, 1942, and married to Lillian Holt.
  (4) James Edward Reed, born April 5, 1944
  (5) Betty Jane Reed, born December 10, 1946, and married Harold Louis Jones.

g. Georgetta Burdette, born May 22, 1924. Married Paul Kelly, who died in 1967. One daughter:
  (1) Kathleen Kelly.

h. Ira Layton Burdette, born April 28, 1926 in Schaueffersville, Maryland, and died June 14, 1984 of a heart attack at his home in Selbyville, Delaware. Buried at the Howard Chapel United Methodist Church, Long Corner Road, Mt. Airy. The place of his birth is as it was reported in his obituary, although it is not to be found in the Postal Zip Code nor in the Rand McNally maps. Married to Mildred M. Gue, born January 29, 1926, and had children. The place of their residence is as reported in their father's obituary in 1984:

     (1)   Ira Layton Burdette, Jr., born July 25, 1945, of Union Bridge, Carroll County, Maryland. Married Clem Darr, born June 25, 1944 and had children:
          (a) Kimberly Burdette: November 30, 1968
          (b) Brenda Burdette: September 4, 1971
     (2)   Mildred Ann Burdette, of Silver Run (state ?); married James Fritz.
     (3)   David L. Burdette, of Walkersville, Maryland
     (4)   Kevin E. Burdette, of Seaford, Delaware
     (5)   Joyce A. Burdette of Bishopville, in Worcester County, Maryland; married Tubbs.

i.   John Nathan Burdette, born November 28, 1927. Married to Velma Martin; no children.

j.   Margaret Enolia Burdette, born August 22, 1929. Married Eldon Sylvanes Dayhoff, born November 11, 1926. Children:
     (1)   Margaret Ann Dayhoff, born July 16, 1949
     (2)   Allen Milton Dayhoff, born April 4, 1951

Henry Clark Warfield
1942-

Henry was the son of John O. Warfield and Louise Hoffman, and was born October 5, 1942. He was married September 23, 1973 to Cathie May Glaze, born March 23, 1952, daughter of John Russell Glaze (1922) and Constance Marie Brandenburg (1924). They had a daughter:

1.   Julie Marie Warfield, born September 2, 1981.

Ruth Anne Warfield
1931-

Her parents are not yet identified, but Ruth Anne was born June 15, 1931 at Glenelg, Howard County, Maryland. Married December 5, 1948 to Sterling Addison Mullinix, born August 27, 1925, son of Asbury Mullinix (1895) and Lillian Nataline Thomas (1897). At least one daughter:

1. Hilary Allison Mullinix, born March 14, 1960 at Baltimore; married to Scott Darren Sauer.

Clarence O. Warfield
1870-

Clarence is listed as head of household in the 1900 census for the Barnesville District of Montgomery County, born c.1870 in Pennsylvania, where his parents were also born. His mother, Annie E. is living with them, born c.1834 in Pennsylvania. His wife is shown as Lizzie M., born c.1872 in Virginia, where her parents were also born. They have been married three years, and have had two children:
1. Edna Warfield, born 1898
2. Mary E. Warfield, born 1899

Louis A. Warfield
1849-1915

This individual was found listed as head of household in the 1900 census for Damascus, born December, 1849. Birth report of his eldest daughter lists his name as Lewis rather than Louis, which appears to be correct. The census states that he has been married for fifteen years. His wife is Frances L, born January, 1857, and they have had four children, three living. He appears to be the same Lewis A. Warfield who was born December 11, 1849, died February 16, 1915, and is buried in Damascus Cemetery; same stone as Ella May Runkles. Married October 6, 1885 to Frances L. Hopwood, born January 18, 1858, died March 18, 1939. In the 1920 census, Frances is listed as a widow, with her son William M. living at home with his wife. Also in the household are three young children, listed as grandchildren (all named Runkles), the children of their eldest daughter.

In the 1860 census for Clarksburg District, one Lewis A. Warfield, then aged 10, was found living in the household of Mareen Duvall (1808) and his wife Elizabeth Duvall (1812). The household included seven Duvall children, as well as Lewis A. Warfield; Eliza J. Simpson (1824) and Lewis Wyville (1826), a farm laborer. There are relationships between the Duvall, Warfield and Wyville families. Four of the seven Duvall children living in the household of Mareen Duvall were children of his deceased brother, Lewis H. Duvall (1814) and wife Catharine Warfield (1816), which see earlier herein, with Mareen having been appointed their guardian. The parents of Lewis and Mareen Duvall were Lewis W. Duvall (1775) and Sarah Wyville. We do not now know the Simpson relationship in the families. The children of Lewis as found in the 1900 census were:

1. Ella May Warfield, born December 6, 1886 near Damascus. Married to Runkles, and had children:
    a. Stella L. Runkles, born 1910
    b. Norman W. Runkles, born 1913
    c. Lester R. Runkles, born 1916
2. Grace V. Warfield, born April, 1888
3. William M. Warfield, born August, 1890. Probably the same who died 1941 and is buried at Damascus Methodist cemetery with his wife wife Estella B., born 1898.

Frances E. Warfield
1832-

We do not now know the maiden name of Frances, nor the name of her husband. She was found in the 1900 census for the Barnesville area of Montgomery County, born c.1832 and a widow. She is listed as having had six children, all still living, with two of them still at home. Also in her household was a farm laborer, and one Mary E. Umstead, born August, 1829, listed as sister-in-law. Although it does not seem to help with identification of Frances, the 1850 census of Berry District carries the household of Jacob Umpstaddt, born c.1790. One of his daughters is Mary E. Umpstaddt, born c.1830, which could be the same individual living with Frances. The two children were:

1. Frances E. Warfield, born August, 1869
2. John J. Warfield, born January, 1872

There are several miscellaneous entries relative to members of the Warfield that require further research. Each name in the left column bears the Warfield surname, by birth or marriage. Each event occurred in Montgomery County, Maryland, unless otherwise noted.

Individual	Information
Adeline A.	Born 1833 Montgomery Co., died 02/15/1898 at Fort Scott, Kansas. Widow of Captain L. A. Warfield, died 1862 in Union Army. Mother of Mrs. George T. Webb, Mrs. Maggie Gaither, and Mrs. E. D. Marr of Forst Scott; and L. A. Warfield of Kansas City.
Albert	Born in Howard County, one of seven children. Md to Catherine Farrell of Poolesville.
Albert W.	Md 03/11/1939 to Mary Frances Miller.
Alexander	Died 11/07/1825, Zion Episcopal, Urbana, Md.
Alexander W.	Md 05/07/1827 Eliza Ann Burgess. Frederick.
Andrew	Md 08/26/1882 to Jane Dorsey.
Anna	Md 09/03/1812 to Robert Warfield.
Anna	Md 02/23/1796 to John Tucker, Frederick.
Anne	Md 01/23/1883 to Thomas Brown.
Anne	Md 08/17/1802 to Caleb Burgess; Frederick.
Annie	Md 08/19/1880 to Isaac White.
Annie M.	Md 05/25/1893 to Francis M. Hopkins.
Benjamin	Born 09/01/1918, died 06/23/1975.
Bernard	Born 11/02/1892, s/o Joshua Warfield and Margaret Cook of Baltimore.
Bradley Winfield	Born 1879, died 01/04/1961. Laytonsville cemetery. Md 06/20/1908 at Rockville, Georgia Eleanor King of Clarksburg, born c.1886.
Caleb N.	Born 04/15/1839, died 03/20/1895. Husband of Eliza Ellen, born 01/05/1841, died 06/03/1914. Colesville Methodist Church cemetery. He was a native of Howard Co.; lived in the Wheaton District of Montgomery about last 20 years of his life.

Caroline	Born 1827, died 05/24/1827. Sam's Creek cem. Frederick Co.
Cecelia	Md 08/04/1834 to Francis A. Davis; Frederick.
Charles	Of Howard Co., md 11/17/1885 Mary Snowden of Sandy Spring, Montgomery Co.
Charles G.	Born 1866, died 1959. Damascus Methodist.
Charles H.	Born 1795, died May 24, 1823, Frederick.
Charles L.	Md 01/16/1823 to Ruth H. Dorsey. Frederick.
Charlotte	Md 10/16/1820 to Thomas Nicholson.
David A.	Born 1829, died 03/04/1871; buried at Sams Creek Methodist, Frederick Co.
Deborah	Born c.1838; living in household of Bushrod Gartrell (1797); 1860 census, Unity Post Office. Personal property valued at $2,300.
Deborah J.	Of Montgomery County; md St. Bartholomew's Episcopal 12/11/1860 to Alexander N. Crowder of St. Louis, Missouri; moved to live there.
Dennis	Born 1810, died 08/07/1835; buried at Sam's Creek Methodist cemetery, Frederick Co.
Edmund W.	Md 11/16/1883 to Rosa B. Hilton.
Edna R.	Of Damascus, md 12/20/1888 to William J. Grimes of Carroll Co.
Edward	Md 09/12/1831 Elizabeth Norwood. Frederick
Edwin W.	Born 09/10/1888, died 10/06/1918. Buried Mt. Olivet, Frederick
Eleanor D.	Born 1908, died 1976. Mutual Memorial Cem.
Eliza	Md 12/07/1816 to Joshua Mercier. Frederick.
Elizabeth	Md 12/01/1809 to Samuel Burgess; Frederick.
Elizabeth	Md 04/25/1827 to Upton Higgins; Frederick.
Elizabeth Anne	Md to Thomas Coke Watkins (1800); one of his three wives. He had fourteen children from his marriages; some probably by Elizabeth.
Ella B.	Born c.1861, died 01/17/1919; buried Hyattstown Methodist Church.
Elsie M.	Md 02/01/1910 to William Franklin Purdum (1880) at the Kemptown Methodist parsonage. He was the son of Benjamin Franklin Purdum

	(1851) and Sybelle M. Browning (1856). No children.
Elsie W.	Born c.1889, md William T. Purdum, born 1881. Census 1920 Damascus. Also in household is Mary E. Warfield, born 1859, mother.
Evelina	Born c.1830, died 03/24/1877, aged 46-11-18. Buried at the Sams Creek ME Church, Frederick County.
Evelina H.	Born c.1804, died 11/18/1833, aed 29-9-0. Also buried at Sams Creek; perhaps mother of Evelina above.
Fannie E.	Born 01/09/1865, died 06/21/1927. Buried at Mt. Olivet cemetery, Frederick.
Fanny A.	Md 01/01/1862 to George V. Feitz: Frederick.
Frances	Md 04/26/1869 to John Lee.
Francis H.	Infant death, 01/29/1830; buried at Sams Creek in Frederick County.
George	Md 07/11/1818 to Sarah Swomley; Frederick.
George E.	Md 02/07/1896 to Susie Clagett.
George W.	Md 09/09/1845 to Hester Ann Riner; Frederick
Gertrude B.	Born c.1886, died 11/04/1891, d/o William and Laura J. Warfield. Salem United Methodist at Cedar Grove.
Grace Lee	Died 02/26/1937, buried Darnestown Presbyterian Church cemetery. Will dated 08/10/1936 probated 04/06/1937, HGC-17, folio 219, Montgomery Co. Only heir: nephew, James A. Broome.
Greenbury	Md 03/13/1817 to Elizabeth Alder.
Hannah Y.	Born c.1806, died 02/12/1835. Buried at Sams Creek, Frederick County.
Harriet S.	Born 1869, died 1944. Laytonsville cemetery.
Harry E.	Husband of Blanche M., who died 09/17/1969 at Bethesda; father of Mrs. Mason Hopwood.
Harry P.	Born 09/21/1868, died 09/22/1920; buried at Mt. Oliver in Frederick with wife. She was R. Katherine, born 02/20/1877, died 11/19/1937.

Helen E.	Born 12/18/1859, died 02/11/1894. Rockville cemetery.
Helen E.	Md 09/20/1872 to Hanson Bond (see above).
Henry	Md 04/05/1871 to Laura Mitchell.
Horatio	Born 1824, died 1877. Buried at Sams Creek Methodist Church, Frederick County. His wife Eleanor C. is buried there, born 1845, and died 1919. There is also a daughter, Lula C., born 1875, died 1911.
Ida E.	Md 11/18/1886 to Robert H. Mason.
Ignatius V.	Born 1861, died 1937; buried at Mt. Olivet in Frederick.
James A.	Md 12/01/1881 to Mary Bowie. Perhaps parents of Anna Ray Warfield, born 10/06/1882, died 03/16/1884. Mt. Olivet cem., Frederick.
James H. B.	A doctor; md 09/11/1856 to Ann M. Wynkoop in Frederick County
James R.	Md 05/25/1880 to Mollie K. Weltz; Frederick.
Jeffrey	Md 07/22/1878 to Martha Bond.
Joan B.	Born 07/03/1888, d/o James D. Warfield and Emma Margaret Cook.
John	Md 03/07/1804 to Fanny James; Frederick.
John	Md 05/10/1833 Harriet Merryman; Frederick.
John G.	Md 12/20/1853 to Drusy Ann Warthen.
John R.	Md 07/--/1882 to Lucy Holland.
John W.	Md 01/03/1889 to Lucy Dunley.
Josephine	Md 01/--/1880 to Higgison B. Penn, born 1828, s/o William G. Penn (1781).
Joshua	Born c.1800, died 04/01/1880 aged 79-7-18. Buried at Sams Creek, Frederick County.
Larkin	Md 03/14/1827 to Lethea Blackburn.
Laura A.	Md 11/21/1882 to Charles F. Davis of New Market District, in Frederick County, born 10/03/1848. He was son of Eli Davis (1809) and Rachel Morsel (1809).
L. Elizabeth	Md 07/14/1859 to William H. Baker; Frederick
Laura L.	Md 02/03/1876 to John Cooper.
Lemuel A.	Md 12/10/1852 to Ada A. Miller.

Lewis	Md 09/23/1823 Juliet Hodgkiss; Frederick.
Loretta	Born 1835; 1900 census for Damascus, widow, mother of four children, three still living.
Lucretia	Born c.1851; living in household of Horace W. Beall (1825); 1870 census of Damascus.
Lula E.	Born 1875, died 1938; buried at Mt. Olivet in Frederick.
Lycurgus L.	Baptized 05/25/1905 at Park Mills by Isaac G. Warfield. Husband of Nettie Warfield and father of Milton Theodore Warfield. Clarksburg Methodist Church.
Lydia A.	Born 1810, died 03/20/1896, Goshen Methodist cemetery; stone marked mother.
Mabel Poole	Born 04/11/1895, died 03/11/1941. Buried Monocacy cemetery in plot of William Thomas Poole, next to Algernon Poole.
Margaret M.	Born 1918, died 1932. Buried at the Monrovia Brethren Church, Frederick County.
Margaret W.	Born 12/27/1809, died 05/15/1842, single; buried Israel Creek cemetery, Walkersville, in Frederick County. D/o Alexander Warfield.
Marian	Md 03/14/1812 to William Clarke; Frederick.
Martha Ann	Md 10/21/1835 to William G. Knowles.
Mary	Md 05/25/1818 in Frederick to Mordecai Purdum, born 05/01/1794, died 11/12/1847 Ross County, Ohio. s/o Walter Purdum (1765) and Priscilla Browning (1762).
Mary	Born c.1783, died 07/06/1844; buried at Israel Creek cemetery near Walkersville, in Frederick County.
Mary	Md 12/03/1799 to Rezin Darby.
Mary	Md 06/01/1880 to Jesse Harity.
Mary	Md 12/23/1896 to Richard Powell.
Mary E.	Md 10/27/1864 to Levi Evans; Frederick.
Mary E.	Born 1835, died 09/04/1854 at age 19, married to R. Dorsey Warfield.
Mary Ellen	Md 09/21/1880 to Charles W. Sage.
Mary G.	Md 11/11/1903 at Damascus to John F. Young.

Mary Susie	Born 1850, died 1940. Buried at Mt. Olivet in Frederick.
Minerva A.	Md 10/20/1845 Francis E. Shreves; Frederick.
Mollie L.	Md 12/02/1878 to Alexander Broome.
Nathan	Md 09/10/1828 Catherine W. Burgess; Frederick County.
Nelly	Md 05/19/1876 to Miles Smith.
Nettie	Of Montg. Co., born c.1859, md 05/19/1880 to Asa Hepner, born c.1855 of Carroll County. She could be Hettie Warfield.
Nora V.	Md 07/09/1895 to Lot B. Duvall.
Philip	Md 04/28/1801 to Sarah Davis.
R. O. D.	A doctor, born 07/29/1844, died 06/21/1918. Buried at Taylorsville Methodist Church with his wife. She was Fannie Bell Crawford, born 04/10/1854, died 12/09/1905.
Rachel	Md 04/05/1803 to West Burgess; Frederick.
Rebecca	Md 01/19/1886 to Charles Nelson.
Richard	Md 07/07/1780 to Anne Delashmutt; Frederick.
Robert	Md 08/05/1820 to Elizabeth Kinney; Frederick.
Robert Edward	Born 12/10/1909, died 12/04/1980. Mutual Memorial cemetery.
Rosalie Hilton	Born c.1862, died 05/09/1906. Buried at the Damascus Methodist Church.
Ruth	Md 11/26/1802 to Edward Dorsey; Frederick.
Samuel Harwood	Born 10/07/1824, s/o Alexander and Mary Warfield.
Sarah	Md 05/10/1792 to James Perry.
Sarah	Md 11/04/1816 to Lamack Duvall; Frederick.
Sarah A.	Died 02/06/1885, w/o Edward Warfield. Record of Darnestown Presbyterian Church.
Sarah Ann	Md 05/06/1833 to Rev. Thomas H. W. Monroe Frederick County.
Sarah L.	Died 05/04/1962 at Takoma Park; d/o Augustus Warfield; s/o Irma W. Warfield Fenwick.
Sarah T.	Md 07/10/1867 to Isaiah Dent.
Susanna	Md 01/11/1806 to Greenbury Murphy.

T. W.	Born 1849, died 1936; wife A. C., born 1848, died 1929. Montgomery Chapel, Claggettsville cemetery. Headstone reads Warfield-Gue.
Viola V.	Born 06/04/1916, died 08/30/1984. Buried at Darnestown Presbyterian Church.
William	Of Frederick; the *Sentinel* reported that he was killed 12/25/1877 in Barnesville by Nathan Jamison.
William H.	Md 03/24/1892 to Hattie Tyler.
Zadock	Md 12/23/1801 to Rachael Chambers.

Clarksburg United Methodist Church
Clarksburg, Montgomery County, Maryland

BIBLIOGRAPHY

Adams, Katharine Beall. *Maryland Heritage-A Family History.* Hillsboro, NC Privately printed 1983

American Genealogical Research Institute. *Walker Family History,* Washington, D. C. 1972.

Andrews, Mathew Page. *Tercentary History of Maryland.* Three volumes. Chicago & Baltimore. S. J. Clarke Publishing Co. 1925.

Baltz, Shirley Vlasak. *A Chronicle of Belair.* Bowie, Md. Bowie Heritage Committee.

Baltz, Shirley V. & George E. *Prince George's County, Maryland, Marriages and Deaths in Nineteenth Century Newspapers. Volumes 1 and 2.* Bowie, Md. 1995. Heritage Books, Inc.

Barnes, Robert. *Maryland Marriages, 1634-1777*
_____. *Maryland Marriages, 1778-1800*
_____. *Marriages and Deaths From the Maryland Gazette 1727-1839.* Baltimore. Genealogical Publishing Co. 1973
_____. *Colonial Families of Anne Arundel County, Maryland.* Westminster, Maryland: Family Lines Publications, 1996.
_____. *Marriages and Deaths from Baltimore Newspapers.* Three volumes. Baltimore. Genealogical Publishing Co. 1978

Barnes, Robert W. and F. Edward Wright. *Colonial Families of the Eastern Shore of Maryland, Volumes 1 and 2.* Westminster, Md. Family Line Publications. 1996

Beall, Frederick Carroll. *Robert Beall, the Scotsman, Immigrant.* Privately printed booklet. 1976. Copy at Montgomery County Historical Society Library, Rockville, Md.

Boggs, Ardith Gunderman. *Goshen, Maryland, A History & Its People.* Bowie, Md. Heritage Books, Inc. 1994

Bowie, Effie Gwynn. *Across The Years in Prince George's County.* Baltimore, Md. Genealogical Publishing Company. Original 1947. Reprint 1996.

Bowman, Tressie Nash. *Montgomery County Marriages, 1796-1850*

Broderbund Software, Inc. *Family Tree Maker, Deluxe Edition III.* Social Security Death Index, Volumes 1 and 2; and World Family Tree, Volumes 1 thru 5. Redwood, California. 1997

Brown, Ann Paxton. Personal collection of genealogical notes and abstracts; major families of Montgomery County, Maryland.

Brown, Helen W. *Index of Marriage Licenses, Prince George's County, Maryland 1777-1886.* Baltimore, Md. Genealogical Publishing Co. Reprint. 1995

_____. *Prince George's County Maryland Indexes of Church Registers 1686-1885, Volume 2.* Westminster, Md. Family Line Publications. 1994

Brumbaugh. *Maryland Records.* 1915 and 1928 issues; Washington County Marriages.

_____. *Maryland Records, Colonial, Revolutionary, County and Church.*

Burke, Sir Bernard, Ulster King of Arms. *The General Armory of England, Scotland, Ireland and Wales, Volumes 1, 2 & 3..* Bowie, Md. Heritage Books, Inc. 1878, Reprint 1996

Bussard, Ruthella. *The Genealogy of Peter Bossert-Bussard, 1761-1802.* Frederick, Maryland. Jeanne Bussard Workshop. 1970-1974.

Buxton, Allie May. *Family of Harry and Rosa Hurley.* Manuscript; Montgomery County Historical Society, Rockville, Maryland.

_____. *The Family of Isaac Moxley.* Damascus, Md. 1984

_____. *Nehemiah Moxley, His Clagettsville Sons and Their Descendants.* Chelsea, Michigan. BookCrafters. 1989

Carothers, Bettie Sterling. *1776 Census of Maryland.* Westminster, Md. Family Line Publications. 1992

Carr, Lois Green; Menard, Russell R.; Peddicord, Louis. *Maryland at the Beginning.*

Carroll County Genealogy Society, Md. *Carroll County Cemeteries, Volume Three: Southwest.* Westminster, Maryland 1992.

Cavey, Kathleen Tull-Burton. *Tombstones and Beyond, Prospect U. M. Church Cemetery and Marvin Chapel Church Cemetery.* Westminster, Maryland: Family Lines Publications, 1995

Chapman. *Portrait and Biographical Record of the Sixth Congressional District, Maryland.* Chapman Publishing Company, New York. 1898

Church of Jesus Christ of Latter Day Saints. *Family group sheets, computerized ancestral files, International Genealogical In-*

dex, and other pertinent records. Family History Center, Silver Spring, Maryland.

Clark, Edythe Maxey. *William Pumphrey of Prince George's County, Maryland, and his Descendants.* Anundsen Publishing Company. 1992.

Coldham, Peter Wilson. *The Bristol Register of Servants Sent to Foreign Plantations 1654-1686,* Genealogical Publishing Company, Baltimore. 1988

_____. *The Complete Book of Emigrants, 1607-1660,* Genealogical Publishing Co., Baltimore, 1987

Cook, Eleanor M. V. *Guide to the Records of Montgomery County, Maryland, Genealogical and Historical.* Westminster, Md. Family Line Publications. 1997

Daughters of the American Revolution, Youghiogheny Glades Chapter. *Maryland's Garrett County Graves.* Parsons, West Virginia. McClain Printing Company. 1987. Corrigendum, 1995, Garrett County Historical Society.

Daughters of the American Revolution, Conococheague Chapter. *Washington County Cemetery Records, Volumes I thru VII.* Westminster, Md. Family Line Publications. 1992 to 1994

Day, Jackson H. *The Story of the Maryland Walker Family, Including the Descendants of George Bryan Walker and Elizabeth Walker Beall.* 1957, privately printed manuscript.

_____. *James Day of Browningsville, and his descendants, A Maryland Family.* Columbia, Md, private printing, 1976.

Delaware Hall of Records, Dover. Wills, estates, inventories, births, deaths, marriages, deeds and other reference works relative to counties of Delaware.

Dern, John P. and Grace L. Tracey. *Pioneers of Old Monocacy, The Early Settlement of Frederick County, Maryland 1721 to 1743.* Baltimore. Genealogical Publishing Co. 1987

Dern, John P. and Mary Fitzhugh Hitselberger. *Bridge in Time, The Complete 1850 Census of Frederick County, Maryland.* Redwood City, CA. Monocacy Book Company. 1978

Doliante, Sharon J. *Maryland and Virginia Colonials: Genealogies of Some Colonial Families.* Genealogical Publishing Co. Baltimore, Md. 1991

Drake, Paul. *Now in Our Fourth Century: Some American Families.* Bowie, Md. Heritage Books, Inc. 1994

Dunlap, Wilma Walker. *Along Came Joe*

Eader, Edith Oliver & Trudie Davis-Long. *The Jacob Engelbrecht Marriage Ledger of Frederick County, Maryland 1820-1890.* Monrovia, Md. Paw Prints, Inc. 1994.

_____. *The Jacob Engelbrecht Death Ledger of Frederick County, Maryland 1820-1890.* Monrovia, Md. Paw Prints, Inc. 1995.

_____. *The Jacob Engelbrecht Property and Almshouse Ledgers of Frederick County, Maryland.* Monrovia, Md. Paw Prints, Inc. 1996.

Ferrill, Matthew & Gilchrist, Robert. *Maryland Probate Records 1635-1777.* Volume 9.

Filby. *Passenger and Immigration Lists Index.*

Fleming, Bertha Ann. *The Brandenburg Family in America.* Not published; private compilation deposited with the Frederick County, Maryland, Historical Society.

Flowers, Susanne Files & Edith Olivia Eader. *The Frederick County, Maryland Will Index 1744-1946.* Monrovia, Md. Paw Prints, Inc. 1997

Frain, Elizabeth R. *Monocacy Cemetery, Beallsville, Montgomery County, Maryland.* Lovettsville, Va. 1997, Willow Bend Books.

Fry, Joshua & Jefferson, Peter. *Map of Virginia, North Carolina, Pennsylvania, Maryland, New Jersey 1751.* Montgomery County, Md Library, Atlas Archives.

Gaithersburg, Maryland, City. *Gaithersburg, The Heart of Montgomery County.* Privately printed. 1978

Gannett, Henry. *The Origin of Certain Place Names in the United States.* Bowie, Md. Heritage Books, Inc. 1996

Garrett County Bicentennial Committee, with Stephen Schlosnagle. *Garrett County, A History of Maryland's Tableland.* Parsons, West Virginia. McClain Printing Company. Second Edition, 1989.

Garrett County Historical Society. *Hoye's Pioneer Families of Garrett County.* Parsons, West Virginia. McClain Printing Company. 1988

_____. *The Glades Star.* Quarterly. Marriage Record Issues, October, 1993 & October, 1995. Civil War Issue, June, 1961.

Gilland, Steve. *Frederick County Backgrounds.* Westminster, Maryland: Family Lines Publications, 1995.

_____. *Early Families of Frederick County, Maryland and Adams County, Pennsylvania.* Westminster, Maryland: Family Lines Publications, 1997.

Goldsborough. *Maryland Line in the Confederacy.*

Government, United States. *Guide to Genealogical Research in the National Archives.* Washington, D. C. 1982

Green, Karen Mauer. *The Maryland Gazette, Genealogical and Historical Abstracts, 1727-1761.* Galveston, TX The Frontier Press. 1989

Gurney, John Thomas, III. *Cemetery Inscriptions of Anne Arundel County, Maryland. Volume 1 .* Pasadena, Md. Anne Arundel Genealogical Society. 1982, 1994.

_____. *Cemetery Inscriptions of Anne Arundel County, Maryland. Volume 2.* Chelsea, MI. BookCrafters. 1987

Haney, Ritchie Lee. *1920 Census for Damascus, Montgomery County, Maryland.* From personal notes of his father, Ritchie E. Haney, census-taker. Damascus, Md. Private. 1997

Hartzler, Daniel D. *Marylanders in the Confederacy.* Westminster, Maryland: Family Lines Publications, 1994.

Hinke and Reinecke. *Evangelical Reformed Church, Frederick, Maryland*

Holdcraft, Jacob Mehrling. *Names in Stone; 75,000 Cemetery Inscriptions From Frederick County, Maryland.* Ann Arbor, Michigan. 1966. Reprinted with "More Names in Stone" in two volumes, Genealogical Publishing Co., Baltimore, 1985

Hopkins, G. M. *Atlas of Fifteen Miles Around Washington, Including the County of Montgomery, Maryland.* Baltimore, Md. Garamond/Pridemark Press, Inc. for the Montgomery County Historical Society. Original 1879. Reprint, 1975

Jacobs, Elizabeth Jeanne King. *Personal papers and records.*

Jones, Elias. *New Revised History of Dorchester County, Maryland,* Centreville, Maryland: Tidewater Publishers, 1966

Jourdan, Elise Greenup. *The Land Records of Prince George's County, Maryland, 1710-1717*

_____. *Early Families of Southern Maryland. Volumes 1 through 5.* Westminster, Md. Family Line Publications. 1993 to 1996

Lebherz, Margaret Biser Green. *Biser Family Journals, Volumes 1, 2 and 3.* Privately printed. 1991. Frederick County Library Collection.

_____. *Jacob Beyser and Family 1746-1986.* Private printing. Frederick County Historical Society Collection.

Lloyd, Richard H. *Some Descendants of Leonard Wayman, Maryland Planter, 1670 to 1721.* Privately printed pamphlet. October, 1993. Copy at Montgomery County Historical Society Library. Rockville, Md.

Lord, Elizabeth M. *Burtonsville, Maryland Heritage, Genealogically Speaking*

Malloy, Mary Gordon; Sween, Jane C.; Manuel, Janet D. *Abstract of Wills, Montgomery County, Maryland 1776-1825*

Malloy, Mary Gordon; Jacobs, Marian W. *Genealogical Abstracts, Montgomery County Sentinel, 1855-1899.* Rockville, Md. Montgomery County Historical Society. 1986.

Malone, Johnita P. *Land Records of Sussex County, Delaware, 1722-1731, Deed Book F, No 6.* Bowie, Md. Heritage Books, Inc. 1997

Manuel, Janet Thompson. *Montgomery County, Maryland Marriage Licenses, 1798-1898*

Maryland State. *Archives of Maryland,* all volumes.

Maryland Hall of Records. *Wills, estates, inventories, births, deaths, marriages, deeds and other reference works relative to counties of Maryland.*

_____. *Maryland Calendar of Wills.* All volumes.

_____. *Maryland Historical Society Magazine.*

_____. *Vestry Book of St. John's Episcopal Parish Church, 1689-1810.* Original.

Maryland Bicentennial Commission. *Maryland at the Beginning.* Compiled by Lois Green Carr, Russell R. Menard, and Louis Peddicord. Not dated.

Maryland Historical Society. *St. Mary's City Commission, Special Issue, Vol. 69, No. 2.* Baltimore, Md. 1974

McFarland, Robert H. and Twilah M. Seefeld. *McFarland Collections.* Ann Arbor, Michigan. Privately printed by Braun-Brumfield, Inc. 1985

Meyer, Mary Keysor. *Divorces and Names Changed in Maryland By Act of the Legislature 1634-1867.* Mt. Airy, Md. Pipe Creek Publications, Inc. 1991

Montgomery County Court Records. *Wills, inventories of estate, deeds.* Rockville, Maryland.

Montgomery County Historical Society, Rockville, Maryland. *Folder files; census, church, correspondence, newspaper, manuscripts, library, and family records.*

_____. *Queen Anne Parish Records, 1686-1777*

_____. *King George Parish Records 1689 - 1801*

_____. *King George Parish Records 1797-1878*

_____. *St. Paul's at Baden, Parish Records*

_____. *Frederick County Maryland Marriage Licenses*

_____. *Montgomery County Marriages*

_____. *1850 Census, Montgomery County, Maryland*

_____. *1860 Census, Montgomery County, Maryland*

_____. *1850 Census, Prince George's County, Maryland*

_____. *1850 Census, Frederick County, Maryland*

_____. *Pioneers of Old Monocacy*

_____. *Mt. Olivet Cemetery, Frederick, Md.* Computer printout of burial records.

Morrow and Morrow. *Marriages of Washington County, Maryland, An Index, 1799-1866.* DAR library, Washington, D. C.

Myers, Margaret Elizabeth. *Marriage Licenses of Frederick County, Maryland 1778-1810.* Westminster, Md. Family Line Publications. Second Edition, 1994

_____. *Marriage Licenses of Frederick County, Maryland 1811-1840.* Family Line Publications. 1987

_____. *Marriage Licenses of Frederick County, Maryland 1841-1865.* Family Line Publications. 1988

_____. *George Zimmerman and Descendants of Frederick County, Maryland 1714-1987.* Family Line Publications. 1987.

Newman, Harry Wright. *Anne Arundel Gentry, A Genealogical History of Some Early Families of Anne Arundel County,*

Maryland. Volumes One, Two and Three. Annapolis, Md. Privately printed. 1979

_____. *Charles County Gentry.* Baltimore, Md. Genealogical Publishing Co. 1971 and 1990 reprints from 1940 original publication.

_____. *Mareen Duvall of Middle Plantation.* Private printing 1952. Baltimore, Md. Port City Press, Inc. Reprint 1984

Omans, Donald James and Nancy West. *Montgomery County (Maryland) Marriages 1798-1875.* Compiled by Potomack River Chapter, National Society of Colonial Dames. Athens, Georgia. 1987. Iberian Publishing Co.

Peden, Henry C., Jr. *Revolutionary Patriots of Prince George's County 1775-1783.* Westminster, Md. Family Line Publications. 1997

_____. *Revolutionary Patriots of Montgomery County 1776-1783.* Westminster, Md. Family Line Publications. 1996

_____. *Quaker Records of Southern Maryland, Births, Deaths, Marriages and Abstracts from the Minutes, 1658-1800.* Westminster, Md. Family Line Publications. 1992

Powell, John W. *Anne Arundel County, Maryland Marriage Records 1777-1877.* Pasadena, Md. Anne Arundel Genealogical Society. 1991

Preston, Dickson J. *Talbott County, A History,* Centreville, Md., Tidewater Publishers, 1983

Prince George's County, Md Genealogical Society. *Index to the Probate Records of Prince George's County, Maryland, 1696-1900.* Bowie, Md. 1989.

_____. *Prince George's County Land Records, Volume A, 1696-1702.* Bowie, Maryland, 1976

_____. *1850 Census, Prince George's County, Maryland.* Bowie, Maryland, 1978

_____. *1828 Tax List Prince George's County, Maryland.* Bowie, Maryland, 1985.

Reinton, Louise Joyner. *Prince George's County, Md. Piscataway or St. John's Parish (now called King George's Parish. Index to Register, 1689-1878.*

Remsberg, Reverend W. L. *Genealogy of the Remsberg Family in America.* The Valley Register, Middletown, Md. 1912

Richardson, Hester Dorsey. *Side-lights on Maryland History, with Sketches of Early Maryland Families.* Cambridge, Md. Tidewater Publishers. 1967

Ridgely. *Historic Graves of Maryland and the District of Columbia*

Riggs, John Beverley. *The Riggs Family of Maryland.* Baltimore, Maryland. 1989

Russell, Donna Valley. *Western Maryland Genealogy.* Volumes 1 thru 12. Catoctin Press, Middletown, Md. 1985-1996

Sargent. *Stones and Bones, Cemetery Records of Prince George's County, Maryland.*

Scharff, J. Thomas. *History of Maryland.* Three Volumes. Hatboro, Pennsylvania. Tradition Press. 1967

_____. *History of Western Maryland, Volume 1.* Baltimore, Md. Genealogical Publishing Co., Inc. 1995

_____. *History of Western Maryland, Volume II.* Baltimore, Md. Genealogical Publishing Co., Inc. 1995

_____. *History of Western Maryland, Index to Volumes I and II.* By Helen Long (which see). Baltimore, Md. Genealogical Publishing Co., Inc. 1995

_____. *History of Delaware 1609-1888,Volume II.* Westminster, Md. Family Line Publications. Reprint. Original Philadelphia. L. J. Richards & Co. 1888

_____. *History of Delaware 1609-1888 Index.* Westminster, Md. Family Line Publications. Reprint. Original Philadelphia. L. J. Richards & Co. 1888

Schildknecht, Calvin E. *Monocacy and Catoctin, Volumes 1 thru 111.* Gettysburg, Pa. 1994

Schlosnagle, Stephen. *Garrett County, A History of Maryland's Tableland.* Second Edition. Parsons, West Virginia. McClain Printing Company. 1989

Schweitzer, George K. *Revolutionary War Genealogy.* Knoxville, Tennessee. Private printing. 1982

_____. *Maryland Genealogical Research.* Private Printing. For sale by Family Line Publications, Westminster, Md. 1997

Skinner, V. L., Jr. *Abstracts of the Prerogative Court of Maryland, 1726-1729*

Skordas, Gust. *Early Settlers of Maryland*

Stein, Charles Francis, Jr. *Origin and History of Howard County, Maryland.* Baltimore. Howard County Historical Society. 1972

Tombstone Records. *Bethesda United Methodist Church, Browningsville, Maryland. Forest Oak Cemetery, Gaithersburg, Maryland. Goshen United Methodist Church (now Goshen Mennonite Church), Laytonsville, Maryland. St. Paul's Methodist Church, Laytonsville, Maryland.*

Tracey, Grace L. and Dern, John P. *Pioneers of Old Monocacy, The Early Settlement of Frederick County, Maryland 1721 to 1743.* Baltimore. Genealogical Publishing Co. 1987

VanHorn, R. Lee. *Out of the Past.*

Warfield, J. D. *The Founders of Anne Arundel and Howard Counties, Maryland.* Baltimore. Kohn & Pollock. 1905. Reprinted 1995, Heritage Books, Bowie, Md.

Warfield, Thomas Ord. *Warfield Records,* By Evelyn Ballenger. Annapolis, Md 1970.

Washington County, Maryland. Folder files of the County Historical Society; correspondence and family records; courthouse records of wills, estates, deeds, births, deaths and marriages.

Washington County Historical Society. *Bible Records of Washington County, Maryland.* Westminster, Md. Family Line Publications. 1992

Washington County, Maryland Library. *Church Records, Zion Reformed Church at Hagerstown.*

Weeks, Thekla Fundenberg. *Oakland Centennial History, 1849 to 1949.* Oakland, Maryland. Sincell Printing Company. 1949

Weiser, Frederick Sheely. *Records of Marriages and Burials in the Monocacy Church in Frederick County, Maryland, and in the Evangelical Lutheran Congregation in the City of Frederick, 1743-1811.* National Genealogical Society. 4th Printing, 1993
_____. *Frederick, Maryland Lutheran Marriages and Burials 1743-1811.* Washington, D. C. National Genealogical Society. Fourth printing, 1993

Welsh, Luther W., A.M., M.D. *Ancestral Colonial Families, Genealogy of The Welsh and Hyatt Families of Maryland and Their Kin.* Lambert Moon Printing Co., Independence, Missouri. 1928.

162

Western Maryland Genealogy. *Frederick County (Md) Wills, Unprobated Wills, Will Book A1, 1744-1777*. Middletown, Md.

Wilcox, Shirley Langdon. *1828 Tax List Prince George's County, Maryland.* Prince George's County Genealogical Society. Special Publication No. 6. 1985

———. *1850 Census Prince George's County, Maryland.* Prince George's County Genealogical Society. Special Publication No. 4. 1978

———. *Prince George's County Land Records Volume A, 1696-1702.* . Prince George's County Genealogical Society Special Publication No. 3. 1976

———. *Index to the Probate Records of Prince George's County, Maryland 1696-1900.* . Prince George's County Genealogical Society. 1988

Williams, T. J. C. & Folger McKinsey. *History of Frederick County, Maryland, Volume 1.* Baltimore, Md. Genealogical Publishing Co., Inc. 1997

———. *History of Frederick County, Maryland, Volume 2.* Baltimore, Md. Genealogical Publishing Co., Inc. 1997

Williams, Thomas J. C. *History of Washington County, Maryland, Volume 1.* Baltimore, Md. Genealogical Publishing Co., Inc. 1992

———. *History of Washington County, Maryland, Volume 2.* Baltimore, Md. Genealogical Publishing Co., Inc. 1992

Williams, Ruth Smith; Griffin, Margarette Glenn. *Bible Records of Early Edgecombe, North Carolina*

Wright, F. Edward. *History of Washington County, Maryland, Index to Volumes 1 and 2.* Westminster, Md. Family Line Publications. 1992, 1995

———. *Anne Arundel County Church Records of the 17th and 18th Centuries.* Westminster, Md. Family Line Publications. 1989, 1994

———. *Marriages and Deaths in the Newspapers of Frederick and Montgomery Counties, Maryland. 1820-1830.* Westminster, Maryland: Family Lines Publications, 1992.

———. *Marriages and Deaths From the Newspapers of Allegany and Washington Counties, Maryland.* Westminster, Md. Family Line Publications. 1993

_____. *Newspaper Abstracts of Frederick County 1811-1815.* Westminster, Md. Family Line Publications. 1992

_____. *Newspaper Abstracts of Frederick County, 1816 to 1819.* Westminster, Maryland: Family Lines Publications, 1993.

_____. *Newspaper Abstracts of Allegany and Washington Counties 1811-1815.* Westminster, Md. Family Line Publications. 1993

_____. *Maryland Eastern Shore Vital Records, Book 1, 1648-1725.* Westminster, Md. Family Line Publications. 1993

_____. *Maryland Eastern Shore Vital Records, Book 2, 1726-1750.* Westminster, Md. Family Line Publications. 1993

_____. *Maryland Eastern Shore Vital Records, Book 3, 1751-1775.* Westminster, Md. Family Line Publications. 1993

_____. *Maryland Eastern Shore Vital Records, Book 4, 1776-1800.* Westminster, Md. Family Line Publications. 1994

_____. *Maryland Eastern Shore Vital Records, Book 5, 1801-1825.* Westminster, Md. Family Line Publications. 1994

_____. *Washington County, Maryland Church Records of the 18th Century, 1768-1800.* Westminster, Md. Family Line Publications. 1988

_____. *Bible Records of Washington County, Maryland.* Westminster, Md. Family Line Publications. 1992

_____. *Frederick County Militia in the War of 1812.* Westminster, Md. Family Line Publications.

INDEX

All names appearing in the text have been indexed, with reference to each page on which they appear. Most names are accompanied by a date, generally indicating date of birth, in order to differentiate between individuals having the same given name. In some cases where birth dates are not available, dates of marriage or death will appear, such as m/1825 or d/1876. In the case of common names such as John or Mary, where no date is specified, the references are without question to more than one individual.

Bantz, Mary W. 1846, 123
Bantz, William A. 1843, 123
Bantz, William S. 1818, 123
Barfield, Eliza J., 103
Barr, Mary, 51, 52
Barr, Nancy, 52
Barr, Robert, 51
Barrie, Annette, 21
Beale, John, 10
Beale, Mosely, Reverend, 54
Beall, Barry, 78
Beall, Cassandra 1769, 20
Beall, Clement 1734, 20
Beall, Cronin, 139
Beall, Daniel, 139
Beall, David Emory 1946, 139
Beall, Elisha 1800, 89
Beall, Elvira M. 1811, 34
Beall, Evelina, 109
Beall, Horace W. 1825, 89, 149
Beall, Joyce, 139
Beall, Lindy N., 78
Beall, Mary Elizabeth, 109
Beall, Sally Louise 1940, 139
Beall, Sarah Ann 1824, 89
Beall, Shirley Ann 1937, 139
Beall, Silas Cronin 1906, 139
Bear Garden, 97
Beasley, Anna Grace, 40
Beck, Candace, 37
Beckwith, Margaret Cecelia, 37
Bell, Bell, 94
Bell, Caroline, 14
Bell, Ethel, 94
Bell, Garrison, 94
Bell, Lewis, 94
Bell, Maud, 94
Bell, William D., 94
Belmont, 10
Bennett, Elisha, 108
Benson, Nancy, 6, 8
Bentley, Caleb, 104
Bentley, Sarah Brooke, 104
Berry, Ruth 1762, 67
Billanger, Jane, 21
Bite the Skinner, 46

Blackburn, Lethea, 148
Blake, Ellen Percy 1892, 42
Blakely, Mary, 27
Boddie, Chloe E., 32
Boggs, Jane, 102
Bond, Anne Marie, 107
Bond, Hanson, 148
Bond, Martha, 148
Bordley's Choice, 48
Bosley, Nancy, 22
Boules, Sandra Dee 1947, 37
Bourne, Eleanor, 68
Bowie, Mary, 148
Bowlos, Alexander, 24
Bowlos, Henry, 24
Bowlos, Sarah, 24
Bowman, William Asbury, 41
Boyeau, Adeliz, 60
Boyer, Basil Edward d/1920, 84
Boyer, Carolyn Sue 1946, 84
Boyer, Catherine Elizabeth 1909, 84
Boyer, Elizabeth A. 1827, 84
Boyer, Elsie 1890, 84
Boyer, George Milton 1872, 81
Boyer, George Milton, II, 81
Boyer, Harold R. 1923, 85
Boyer, Helen Elizabeth 1923, 85
Boyer, James Lee 1944, 84
Boyer, James William 1921, 84
Boyer, John Wesley 1854, 91
Boyer, Louana T. 1854, 95
Boyer, Mary Luana 1870, 88
Boyer, McKendree Warfield, 81
Boyer, Milton McKendree 1907, Dr.,
   81
Boyer, Muller W. 1888, 84
Boyer, Muller W. 1921, 84
Boyer, Nellie Day 1914, 84
Boyer, Norman Day 1885, 84
Boyer, Raymond 1884, 84
Boyer, Rosa Lena 1891, 138
Boyer, Rudy W. 1931, 85
Boyer, Rudy Wendell 1895, 84
Boyer, Sally Ann, 81
Boyer, William 1821, 95
Boyer, William C. 1897, 85

Bramwell, Ezra, 103
Bramwell, Jesse V., 103
Brand, Elizabeth, 52
Brandenburg, Constance Marie 1924, 142
Brandenburg, Lucinda 1832, 76
Brandy, 4, 6, 106
Brayshaw, Julia, 137
Breckenridge, Mary, 52
Broadhurst, Alfred Davis 1921, 90
Broadhurst, Alfred Wayne 1943, 90
Broadhurst, Brian Eugene 1955, 91
Broadhurst, Claudia Marlene 1948, 91
Broadhurst, Jeffrey Scott 1961, 91
Broadhurst, Joyce Ann 1958, 91
Broadhurst, Justin Marshall 1973, 91
Broadhurst, Lisa Christine 1963, 91
Broadhurst, Matthew Dwane 1970, 90
Broadhurst, Preston Wade 1977, 91
Broome, Alexander, 150
Broome, James A., 147
Browder, George R., 60
Browder, Thomas E., 60
Brown, Abel, 104
Brown, Elinor, 6, 8, 10, 11, 97
Brown, Elizabeth 1792, 63
Brown, Melody, 78
Brown, No given name, 62
Brown, Paul Wesley, 83
Brown, Rebecca 1774, 104
Brown, Thomas, 145
Brown, William, Colonel, 52
Browne, Catherine 1807, 63
Browne, Elinor 1649, 4
Browne, John, Captain, 4
Browning, Alfred 1815, 13, 15, 17
Browning, Benjamin 1786, 13
Browning, Brenda Kay 1951, 140
Browning, Charles Edward 1882, 19
Browning, Daniel 1779, 68
Browning, Dorothy May, 18
Browning, Ethel 1906, 18
Browning, Frances G. 1880, 90
Browning, Frances Lucretia 1923, 90

Browning, Gladys Ann, 18
Browning, Goldie, 18
Browning, Grace Ursula 1877, 18
Browning, Greenberry 1814, 68
Browning, Hannorah 1873, 18
Browning, Jacob Marion 1879, 18
Browning, Jacob Maynard 1924, 18
Browning, Jane E. 1819, 95
Browning, John 1871, 18
Browning, John William 1832, 76
Browning, Jonathan, Jr. 1750, 13, 14
Browning, Laurena 1884, 19
Browning, Mahlon 1821, 90
Browning, Margaret 1779, 14
Browning, Mary Ann, 121
Browning, Mary E. 1858, 76
Browning, Mary Elizabeth 1866, 18
Browning, Maydecker 1869, 18
Browning, No given name, 63, 121
Browning, Priscilla 1762, 149
Browning, Sarah Elizabeth 1866, 18
Browning, Sarah F. 1826, 90
Browning, Sarah Jane 1875, 90
Browning, Silas Young 1870, 90
Browning, Surratt Dickerson Warfield 1834, 13, 15, 17
Browning, Susan 1950, 140
Browning, Susannah Warfield 1886, 19
Browning, Sybelle M. 1856, 147
Browning, Thomas Morris, 18
Browning, Thomas Morris, Jr., 18
Browning, Wesley 1820, 68
Browning, William Ellsworth 1864, 18
Browning, William M. 1914, 140
Browning, William M., Jr. 1948, 140
Bryant, Raymond, Reverend, 139
Buck, Caherine, 5
Buckingham, Ephraim, 27
Bullen, Candace Marie 1956, 115
Bullen, Nancy Lynn 1967, 115
Bullen, Oliver E., Jr. 1919, 115
Bullen, Randy Oliver 1951, 115
Burbank, Elmira, 52
Burdette, Benjamin d/1833, 63

Burdette, Betty Jane 1922, 141
Burdette, Betty Lou 1936, 140
Burdette, Brenda 1971, 142
Burdette, Carol Baker 1942, 139
Burdette, Columbia 1862, 79
Burdette, David L., 142
Burdette, Emma C. 1870, 86, 113
Burdette, Emma F. 1862, 35
Burdette, Emory Warfield 1919, 140
Burdette, Emory Whitehead 1890, 139
Burdette, Fairy Elizabeth 1902, 135
Burdette, Florence Patricia 1945, 141
Burdette, Franklin 1854, 79
Burdette, George Robert 1913, 139
Burdette, Georgetta 1924, 141
Burdette, Hazel, 82
Burdette, Ida E. 1872, 64
Burdette, Ira Layton 1926, 141
Burdette, Ira Layton, Jr. 1945, 142
Burdette, James Jeffry 1972, 141
Burdette, James Richard 1947, 141
Burdette, Jo Ann 1958, 141
Burdette, John 1927, 117
Burdette, John Nathan 1929, 142
Burdette, Joyce A., 142
Burdette, Kay 1963, 140
Burdette, Kelly 1973, 140
Burdette, Kevin E., 142
Burdette, Kimberly 1968, 142
Burdette, Lucetta 1829, 82
Burdette, Margaret Enolia 1929, 142
Burdette, Martha Pauline 1893, 78
Burdette, Mary, 140
Burdette, Mildred Ann, 142
Burdette, Nancy Elizabeth 1945, 140
Burdette, Natalie Ann 1938, 139
Burdette, Nathan J. 1827, 63
Burdette, Nathan James 1842, 86
Burdette, Nellie Laura 1917, 140
Burdette, Nettie Estelle 1882, 80
Burdette, Olea 1882, 79
Burdette, Randy 1960, 140
Burdette, Richard E. 1971, 141
Burdette, Richard Souder, 81
Burdette, Robert, 139

Burdette, Robert 1964, 140
Burdette, Robert Emory 1938, 140
Burdette, Roger Franklin 1909, 139
Burdette, Roger William 1909, 81
Burdette, Roger William, Jr., 81
Burdette, Sarah Evelyn 1915, 139
Burdette, Shane Marie 1974, 140
Burdette, Sherry 1967, 140
Burdette, Sheryl 1962, 140
Burdette, William Hubert 1872, 81, 135
Burgess, Basil, Captain, 62
Burgess, Caleb, 12, 145
Burgess, Carter, Doctor, 46
Burgess, Catherine W., 150
Burgess, Eliza Ann, 145
Burgess, Joseph, 105
Burgess, Joseph, Captain, 51
Burgess, Michael, 105
Burgess, Rebecca, 28
Burgess, Ruth, 51
Burgess, Samuel, 146
Burgess, Vachel, 28
Burgess, Vallie, 46
Burgess, West, 12, 150
Burrell, Jesse M., 117
Bushy Park, 28, 101
Bussard, Eliza 1822, 122
Button, Charles W., 94
Button, Mary E., 94
Butzer, Ephraim, 65
Buxton, Barbara, 139
Buzi, Lawrence 1920, 117
Buzi, Lawrence Martin, 117
Buzi, Tanya Lee, 117
Bye, Martha, 21

—C—

Calahan, George Edgar 1937, 139
Calahan, Kenneth Roger 1960, 139
Calahan, Rebecca Lynn 1962, 139
Caldwell, Marian, 23, 27
Caldwell, Sallie, 52
Campbell, Robert Eugene, 35
Cannoni, Maxine Alexis 1947, 118

Canter, Mary Augusta 1859, 107
Carothers, No given name, 30
Carroll, Charles, 7
Cecil, Nancy 1780, 105
Cecil, Philip, 105
Chambers, Rachael, 151
Chaney, Mary, 6
Chapman, Frances, 30
Chapman, Hannah, 53
Chase, Dudley, Reverend, 102
Chase, J., 103
Chase, Philander, 102
Cherry Grove, 46, 49, 50, 132
Chew, Henrietta Maria, 10
Chew, Samuel, 10
Childs, Mary A. E. 1814, 38, 99
Christian, Sarah Winston, 104
Clagett, Eleanor Bowie 1782, 54, 55
Clagett, Margaret Ann 1856, 134
Clagett, Mary E. 1864, 130
Clagett, Susie, 147
Clagett, Zachariah T. 1839, 130
Claggett, Sarah Jane, 95
Clark, Bazaleel 1816, 101
Clark, Beverly Eugene 1927, 39
Clark, Dorothy Garland 1923, 39
Clark, Florence, 129
Clark, Hezekiah 1802, 101
Clark, Isabel, 103
Clark, James Thomas 1917, 39
Clark, Jane, 115
Clark, John 1807, 101
Clark, John O., 134
Clark, Jonas, 101
Clark, Katherine 1798, 101
Clark, Lydia 1814, 101
Clark, Mary 1812, 101
Clark, Robert 1809, 101
Clark, Ruth L. 1878, 134
Clark, Sarah 1804, 101
Clark, Wallace Jones, 39
Clark, Wallace Jones, Jr. 1919, 39
Clarke, Abraham, 120
Clarke, Ann, 121
Clarke, Ariana, 121
Clarke, Drady, 121

Clarke, Elizabeth, 120, 121
Clarke, George, 120
Clarke, Henry, 120
Clarke, Mary A., 22
Clarke, Rachel, 3
Clarke, Samuel, 120
Clarke, Tilghman, 121
Clarke, William, 120, 149
Clarke, William d/1783, 120
Clary, Bonnie Marlene 1955, 114
Clary, Dennis Blaine 1951, 114
Clary, Kay Lorraine 1963, 114
Clary, Nathan Monroe 1888, 114
Clary, Robert 1925, 114
Clary, Robert Wade 1946, 114
Cleveland, Grover, President, 77
Clough, Elizabeth, 81
Clough, Eunice, 81
Clough, Hobart, 81
Clough, Noah C., Reverend, 81
Coale, Julia, 34
Cole, Richard, 98
Coleman, James, General, 52
Collins, Kathleen A. 1954, 114
Colston, Elizabeth, 65
Condon, Lorraine 1926, 114
Cook, Emma Margaret, 148
Cook, Margaret, 145
Cooke, Margaret E., 48
Cooke, Septimus J., Doctor, 48
Cooley, Adam Warfield 1981, 135
Cooley, Allison Leigh 1984, 135
Cooley, George Wilson 1930, 135
Cooley, Gordon Miles 1953, 135
Cooper, J. Edgar, 41
Cooper, John, 148
Cooper, Mildred, 41
Cooper, No given name, 14
Cooper, Volney S., 21
Cotter, No given name, 134
Craig, Russell Lee, Jr. 1920, 85
Craig, Terry Lee 1953, 85
Crapster, Alice, 55
Crapster, Bowie, 55
Crapster, Eleanor, 55
Crapster, Emma, 54, 55

169

Crapster, Ernest, 55
Crapster, Florence, 54
Crapster, John G., 46
Crapster, Mary Blanche, 55
Crapster, Mortimer Dorsey, 55
Crapster, Mortimer Dorsey, Jr., 55
Crapster, Rhodolphus, 54, 55
Crapster, Robert Gordon, 55
Crapster, Thaddeus, 55
Crapster, William Channing, 54
Crapster, William, Reverend, 54
Crawford, Fannie Bell 1854, 150
Creager, Alcinda H. 1841, 122
Creager, Caroline E. 1847, 122
Creager, Daniel 1779, 122
Creager, Daniel Alexander 1834, 122
Creager, Ephraim 1808, 122
Creager, Francis Asbury W. 1835,
    122
Creager, George E. 1839, 122
Creager, Lancetta V. 1845, 122
Creager, Manelia S. 1837, 122
Creager, Mary Elizabeth 1851, 123
Creager, Noble H. 1843, 122
Creager, Octavia1853, 123
Crites, Annette, 115
Cromwell, No given name, 7
Crowder, Alexander N., 146
Crutchley, Ruth 1683, 97
Crutchley, Thomas, 97
Culler, David, 124
Culler, Henry, Jr. 1817, 124
Culler, William C. 1846, 124
Cummings, Adaline, 47
Currier, Minnie, 84

—D—

Dalrymple, Mary, 48
Darby, Rezin, 149
Darby, Sarah Ann 1826, 111
Darr, Clem 1944, 142
Davay, Nancy, 81
Davidge, Dinah, 63, 97, 99, 100, 105,
    106
Davidge, John, 98

Davidge, Robert, 98, 99
Davis, Arthur, 132
Davis, Caleb, 14
Davis, Charles F. 1848, 148
Davis, Eli 1809, 148
Davis, Elizabeth, 15
Davis, Elizabeth 1768, 46
Davis, Francis A., 146
Davis, Frederick A., 107
Davis, G. Wallace, 95
Davis, George 1775, 24
Davis, George W. 1837, 95
Davis, Henrietta 1838, 132
Davis, Ira Lynnwood, 94
Davis, John, 14
Davis, Juliet, 110
Davis, Kathleen, 95
Davis, Malcolm, 95
Davis, Mary, 59
Davis, No given name, 89
Davis, Richard, 14, 24
Davis, Richard, Jr., Captain, 14
Davis, Ruth, 9, 15
Davis, Samuel Greenberry, 47
Davis, Sarah, 150
Davis, Stanley, 95
Davis, Thomas, 9, 14
Dawley, Elizabeth, 47
Dawley, John, 47
Dawley, Tonny, 48
Day, Bradley J. Day, 128
Day, Effie Madeline 1912, 89
Day, Elizabeth 1769, 20
Day, Eunice Ann 1845, 95
Day, Fannie E., 128
Day, Frances Mary 1872, 114
Day, Franklin B. 1836, 75
Day, Hamilton 1836, 95
Day, Hester Ann 1809, 21
Day, Jackson 1831, 91
Day, Jackson Harvey, 20, 95
Day, James, 14
Day, James 1762, 20, 76, 95
Day, James Edward 1838, 95
Day, Jefferson 1807, 21, 95
Day, John 1720, 20

Day, John 1811, 137
Day, John Fletcher 1849, 114
Day, Laura V. 1846, 137
Day, Lorenzo 1805, 20
Day, Luther 1803, 20
Day, Luther 1832, 95
Day, Mary 1801, 20
Day, Sarah Ann 1814, 21
Day, Sarah Warfield 1848, 96
Day, Survila Augusta Webster 1842, 95
Day, Urban 1798, 20
Day, Washington Lafayette 1840, 95
Day, Wellington 1834, 95
Day, Zeru Clarke 1855, 91
Dayhoff, Allen Milton 1951, 142
Dayhoff, Eldon Sylvanes 1926, 142
Dayhoff, Margaret Ann 1949, 142
Debnam, Audra, 36
Debnam, Drew, 36
Debnam, George, 36
Debnam, Mark, 36
Debnam, Raney, 36
Decker, Keith, 41
Deihl, Dorothy Louise, 141
Delashmutt, Anne, 150
Denn, Tana Kaye 1944, 138
Denson, James H., 121
Dent, Isaiah, 150
Dent, Patricia, 116
Diamond, Eleanor 1915, 35
Diamond, Herbert Laurence, 35
Dickerson, John, 12
Dickerson, Susanna, 12, 15, 23
Dicus, Mary 1790, 121
Diller, Charles 1968, 141
Diller, Charles, Jr. 1945, 141
Diller, Patty Ann 1965, 141
Dillon, Raymond J., 42
Dillon, Tracey Leigh 1967, 42
Dischinger, Bernard, 116
Discovery, 21
Disney, No given name, 7
Disney, Sarah, 22
Dixon, Emery, 18
Dixon, Florence, 93

Dixon, John T., 93
Dixon, Lillian, 93
Dixon, Thomas 1818, 93
Donaldson, Susanna, 7
Dorsey, Achsah, 29
Dorsey, Achsah 1705, 10
Dorsey, Alexander Warfield 1828, 107
Dorsey, Ann, 9, 63
Dorsey, Ann 1730, 100
Dorsey, Ann 1740, 12
Dorsey, Ann 1741, 105
Dorsey, Ariana 1755, 28
Dorsey, Basil, 9, 46
Dorsey, Basil 1705, 10
Dorsey, Benedict 1768, 53
Dorsey, Caleb, 99
Dorsey, Caleb 1685, 10
Dorsey, Caleb, Jr. 1710, 10
Dorsey, Carrie, 46
Dorsey, Catherine, 12, 53
Dorsey, Catherine 1745, 45
Dorsey, Catherine 1746, 9
Dorsey, Deborah, 5
Dorsey, Deborah 1722, 10, 99
Dorsey, Edward, 150
Dorsey, Edward 1718, 10
Dorsey, Eleanor 1715, 10
Dorsey, Elijah 1865, 18
Dorsey, Elizabeth, 10, 19, 51, 53, 55, 109
Dorsey, Elizabeth 1735, 105
Dorsey, Elizabeth 1743, 51
Dorsey, Elizabeth 1761, 109, 110
Dorsey, Elizabeth Ann 1795, 53
Dorsey, Ely, 10, 99
Dorsey, Frances, 30
Dorsey, Henry, 28, 51
Dorsey, Henry 1712, 28, 51, 53, 105
Dorsey, Hester, 42
Dorsey, Hester 1834, 39
Dorsey, Humphrey, 50, 132
Dorsey, Jane, 145
Dorsey, Jemima 1775, 106
Dorsey, John 1708, 10
Dorsey, John 1734, 12

Dorsey, John A., 50
Dorsey, John of Patuxent, 10
Dorsey, John, Honorable, 10
Dorsey, Joshua, 9, 10
Dorsey, Joshua 1686, 11
Dorsey, Joshua 1720, 10
Dorsey, Joshua Warfield 1783, 38, 99
Dorsey, Lancelot 1747, 22
Dorsey, Lloyd 1772, 107
Dorsey, Lloyd 1856, 107
Dorsey, Lucretia, 48
Dorsey, Mary 1725, 10
Dorsey, Mary A. E. 1815, 38
Dorsey, Matilda S., 50
Dorsey, Michael, 22, 51, 106
Dorsey, Nicholas, 109
Dorsey, Nicholas 1712, 29, 30
Dorsey, Nicholas W., Lieutenant, 99
Dorsey, No given name, 23, 29
Dorsey, Philemon 1714, 45, 50
Dorsey, Philemon, Colonel, 9
Dorsey, R., 28
Dorsey, Rachel, 19, 53
Dorsey, Rachel 1717, 11
Dorsey, Rachel Virginia 1845, 38
Dorsey, Ralph, 20
Dorsey, Richard, 98
Dorsey, Richard 1714, 10
Dorsey, Richard Green 1799, 107
Dorsey, Richard Green, Jr., 107
Dorsey, Ruth H., 146
Dorsey, Ruth Virginia 1845, 99
Dorsey, Samuel 1712, 10
Dorsey, Sarah, 98
Dorsey, Sarah 1715, 99
Dorsey, Sarah 1747, 50
Dorsey, Sarah Elizabeth 1873, 132
Dorsey, Sophia 1707, 10
Dorsey, Susannah 1717, 98
Dorsey, Thomas, 19, 53
Dorsey, Thomas 1737, 53
Dorsey, Thomas Beale 1727, 10
Dorsey, Thomas, Colonel, 9
Dorsey, Warren, 29
Dorsey, Washington, 53
Draggo, Ann, 30

Draggo, Jacob, 30
Draggo, Jeannette, 30
Draggo, Peter, 30
Draggo, William, 30
Driver, Nancy Ann, 133
Drodiowski, Hania M. 1906, 70
Dugan, Mary, 50
Dunley, Lucy, 148
Duperu, Celina, 56
Dutrow, Amos W., 69
Dutrow, Susan Natalie 1872, 69
Duvall, Alfred Ward 1906, 37
Duvall, Catharine S. 1844, 130
Duvall, Charlotte 1835, 19, 54
Duvall, Delilah H., 128
Duvall, Elizabeth, 143
Duvall, Elizabeth 1687, 8
Duvall, Flavilla, 7
Duvall, Jeremiah, 22
Duvall, John, Captain, 8
Duvall, Lamack, 150
Duvall, Lewis Dorsey 1851, 130
Duvall, Lewis H. 1814, 129, 144
Duvall, Lewis W. 1775, 128, 129,
   144
Duvall, Lot B., 150
Duvall, Mareen, 130
Duvall, Mareen 1808, 143
Duvall, Mareen Merriken 1807, Dr.,
   19, 54
Duvall, Mary F. 1849, 130
Duvall, No given name, 68
Duvall, Patricia Carol 1931, 37
Duvall, Sally Elizabeth 1846, 130
Dyson, Vernon Hilleary, Dr., 72

—E—

Easterday, William W. 1935, 84
Easterday, William Willard 1912, 84
Easton, No given name, 130
Edgehill, 49
Edwards, Benjamin, 104
Edwards, Rachel, 104
Ellinghaus, Maryanne, 43
Ellis, Catherine Elizabeth 1951, 71

Ellis, Pierce S., Jr., 71
Ellis, Robert, 116
Ellis, Robert P. 1948, 71
Ely, Charles, 18
Ely, Dorothy May, 18
Ely, Pleasance, 10
England, Abram, 54
England, Cordelia, 55
England, Cordelia R. 1839, 54
England, Elizabeth, 55
England, George, 54
England, Ruth Davis, 39
Engle, No given name, 31
English, Katie Ann 1983, 37
English, Mathew Charles 1982, 37
English, Sara Kendall 1984, 37
Errors Corrected, 45
Etchison, Eunice, 73
Etchison, F., 33
Etchison, Janet, 36
Etchison, John, 68
Etchison, William, 68
Evans, Harriet, 19, 54
Evans, Levi, 149
Evans, No given name, 134
Exchange, 50

—F—

Fairbanks, James, 100
Falcone, Bryan, 80
Farrall, Jane Marie 1946, 118
Farrell, Catherine, 145
Farver, Ruth 1927, 115
Feitz, George V., 147
Fenton, Ann, 30
Fenton, Emmaette, 30
Fenton, Sufrona, 30
Fenton, William, 30
Fenwick, No given name, 150
Ferguson, Claibourne, 41
Fetter, Daniel 1807, 102
Fetter, George, 102
Fetter, George, Jr. 1809, 102
Fetter, Hezekiah 1811, 102
Fetter, Roderick 1814, 102

Fields, Katherine Rebecca 1868, 131
Fields, R. G., 131
Fisher, John 1797, 31
Fisher, Lemuel, 31, 35
Fisher, Mary Catherine 1855, 31, 35
Fitez, George V., 121
Fitzgerald, Benjamin, 14
Flook, Joanna R., 24
Flook, Susan, 24
Ford, Charles, 51
Ford, Eliza P., 51
Ford, George Wilmer, 53
Ford, James C., 51
Ford, John, 53
Ford, William, 51
Forsythe, Thomas, 7
Fotterell, No given name, 10
Fox, Elizabeth E. 1920, 78
Francis, Cornelia A., 32
Franklin, Hanson, 28
Franklin, Thomas, 19
Fredericksburg, 46, 58
Frence, Hannah, 21
Fritz, James, 142
Fritz, Mary E., 121

—G—

Gaither, Beal, 29
Gaither, Caroline Riggs 1848, 63
Gaither, Deborah, 29
Gaither, Edward, 63
Gaither, Elizabeth, 40, 62
Gaither, Elizabeth 1805, 69
Gaither, Evan, 63
Gaither, Frederick, 40
Gaither, Greenberry 1792, 62
Gaither, Hezekiah, 62
Gaither, James, 62
Gaither, John, 8, 61, 63
Gaither, John 1646, 11
Gaither, John 1713, 27
Gaither, John, II, 8
Gaither, Kate A., 47
Gaither, Lucretia D., 62
Gaither, Lucy, 63

173

Gaither, Maggie, 145
Gaither, Mary, 27, 29
Gaither, Matilda Riggs, 62
Gaither, Millicent, 62
Gaither, Perry, 47
Gaither, Rachel, 62
Gaither, Ruth, 21
Gaither, Ruth 1679, 11, 45, 59
Gaither, Samuel 1806, 62
Gaither, Samuel R., 29
Gaither, Sarah, 8, 62, 106
Gaither, Sarah Warfield, 63
Gaither, Thomas B. 1827, Major, 62
Gaither, William, 62
Gaither, Zachariah, 61
Gaither, Zachariah, Jr., 62
Gambrill, Sarah, 23
Gardner's Warfield, 4
Gardner, Edward, 4
Garnkirk, 35
Garret, No given name, 62
Garrett, Ashley, 36
Garrett, Ashton Montgomery, 36
Garrett, Carolyn, 36
Garrett, Jeffrey Moore, 36
Garrett, Laura Elizabeth, 36
Garrett, Laurie, 36
Garrett, Miles, 36
Garrett, Molly, 36
Garrett, No given name, 127
Garrett, Paige, 36
Garrett, Sharon, 36
Garrett, Sharon Ann, 36
Garrett, Thomas Ashton, 36
Gartner, Kimberly Joyce 1964, 136
Gartrall, Pearl, 79
Gartrell, Bushrod 1797, 146
Gartrell, Jane, 40
Garver, Elizabeth 1786, 62
Garver, Samuel, 62
Gassaway, Ann, 59
Gassaway, Brice John, 59, 101
Gassaway, Nancy, 8, 32
Geriking, No given name, 30
Gibbins, John, 22
Gibson, Mary Ann Hinkle, 63

Gill, Howard, 57
Gill, M. Gillet, 57
Gill, M. Gillett, Jr., 57
Gill, Mildred, 57
Gill, Royal, 57
Glascock, Beulah, 135
Glascock, George, 135
Glascock, Mabel 1913, 134
Glass, Leroy, 18
Glaze, Cathie May 1952, 142
Glaze, John Russell 1922, 142
Glaze, W. F., 130
Glenn, No given name, 133
Glenwood, 100
Godey, Mary, 66
Godfrey, No given name, 30
Golden, Flora, 66
Goltha, Elizabeth, 103
Good Range, 50
Gordon, No given name, 92
Gore, Clarissa Jane 1820, 16
Gorsuch, No given name, 107
Gosnell, Betty 1923, 115
Gosnell, Doris Marie 1929, 115
Gosnell, Ethel Mary 1916, 114
Gosnell, Herbert Monroe 1886, 114
Gosnell, Leo Monroe 1918, 115
Gosnell, Peggy Webb 1932, 115
Gott, Louise Warfield 1903, 41
Gott, Marianna Virginia, 41
Gott, Muriel Virginia 1898, 41
Gott, Nathan Elwood, 41
Gough, Thomas, 10
Gramkow, David, 57
Gramkow, Edwin, 57
Gramkow, Frank, 57
Gravelly Hill, 13
Gray, James 1825, 31
Green, Anna, 107
Greenberry, Katherine, 5
Greenberry, Katherine 1674, 9
Greenberry, Nicholas, 5
Gregory, Julia, 54
Griffith, Alexander W. 1835, 103
Griffith, Allen, 11
Griffith, Ann 1776, 101

Griffith, Anna 1828, 103
Griffith, Anne E. 1815, 103
Griffith, Catherine 1829, 103
Griffith, Charles, 42, 100
Griffith, Charles Greenberry 1792, 103
Griffith, Charles Greenberry, Colonel, 10
Griffith, Charles Greenberry, Jr. 1830, 104
Griffith, Charles Harrison 1840, Judge, 39
Griffith, Charles, Jr., 7
Griffith, Clarence 1863, 33
Griffith, Columbia Magruder 1870, 65
Griffith, Cordelia Elizabeth 1867, 65
Griffith, Eleanor, 7
Griffith, Elisha Riggs 1805, 40, 69
Griffith, Elizabeth, 49
Griffith, Festus Farmer, Captain 1838, 49
Griffith, Florence, 33
Griffith, Florence May 1862, 65
Griffith, Forest India, 33, 94
Griffith, Franklin 1840, 47
Griffith, Greenbury 1727, 101
Griffith, Greenbury Gaither 1874, 42
Griffith, Henry, 12
Griffith, Henry, Colonel, 11
Griffith, Hezekiah 1752, 101
Griffith, Hezekiah 1824, 103
Griffith, Hezekiah, 3rd 1832, 103
Griffith, Hezekiah, Jr. 1790, 103
Griffith, Howard 1757, 32
Griffith, Ida May 1858, 33
Griffith, James J. 1819, 103
Griffith, Jane 1794, 104
Griffith, Jefferson, 65
Griffith, Jennie 1833, 104
Griffith, John 1814, 103
Griffith, John Belford 1780, 102
Griffith, John Jefferson 1865, 65
Griffith, Lebbeus, Sr. 1804, 32, 94
Griffith, Leonidas Magruder 1835, 65

Griffith, Leonidas Magruder, Jr. 1876, 66
Griffith, Libby, 140
Griffith, Lillian C. 1871, 39
Griffith, Lloyd, 11
Griffith, Lyde, Colonel, 11
Griffith, Lydia 1785, 102
Griffith, Lydia 1837, 103
Griffith, Margaret 1820, 103
Griffith, Maria Gaither 1838, 69
Griffith, Mary 1828, 103
Griffith, Mary 1837, 47
Griffith, Mary Warfield 1861, 65
Griffith, Nancy, 129
Griffith, Orlando, 10
Griffith, Rachel, 48
Griffith, Rachel 1827, 103
Griffith, Rachel 1832, 104
Griffith, Randolph, 103
Griffith, Rebecca 1827, 103
Griffith, Robert Lee 1862, 33, 94
Griffith, Roderick 1787, 102
Griffith, Roderick R. 1816, 103
Griffith, Rosalie 1869, 65
Griffith, Ruth 1794, 28
Griffith, Samuel 1752, 67
Griffith, Samuel 1752, Captain, 12
Griffith, Samuel 1822, 103
Griffith, Sarah, 100
Griffith, Sarah 1718, 29, 30
Griffith, Sarah 1778, 102
Griffith, Sarah 1792, 67, 69
Griffith, Sarah 1817, 103
Griffith, Seth Warfield 1860, 33
Griffith, Thomas, 49
Griffith, Varena, 33
Griffith, Walter 1783, 102
Griffith, Wiley Gaither 1914, 42
Grimes, No given name, 130
Grimes, Priscilla Elizabeth 1862, 18
Grimes, William J., 146
Groveland, 104
Gue, Edgar B. 1879, 83
Gue, Irving, 81
Gue, John, 81
Gue, Mabel Elizabeth 1915, 83

Gue, Mildred M. 1926, 141
Gue, Susie, 79
Guinney, Michael, 5
Gun, Barbara, 61

—H—

Haddaway, Angela, 18
Hairfield, Kimberly Ann 1966, 136
Hall, Elisha G. 1818, 131
Hall, Helga Leister, 115
Hall, John, 15, 36
Hall, Joseph, 59, 99
Hall, Kada, 36
Hall, Mary B. 1810, 131
Hall, Nicholas, Captain, 68
Hall, Tagart, 36
Hamilton, Charles, 19
Hamilton, Elizabeth Ann, 66
Hamilton, No given name, 107
Hamm, James, 87, 113
Hamm, Jennifer Lynn 1954, 86, 113
Hammond, Anne, 105
Hammond, Helen, 10
Hammond, No given name, 106
Hammond, Ruth 1782, 12
Hammond, Vachel, 105
Hansen, Charles, 18
Hansen, John, 18
Hanshaw, Eugenia Waite 1873, 40
Hanson, Mary, 98
Harden, Emily, 28
Hardy, No given name, 128
Hargett, Harold, 41
Harity, Jesse, 149
Harris, Barbara, 57
Harris, E. G., 26
Harris, Eliza, 101
Harris, Ephraim G., 26
Harris, Louise, 57
Harris, Rosalind, 57
Harris, Virginia, 57
Harris, William Hugh, 57
Harris, William Hugh, Jr., 57
Harrison, Archibald Carlyle, Doctor, 47

Harwood, Mary, 14, 19
Harwood, Samuel, 14
Hasson, Sara Nell, 82
Hatfield, Thomas P., 18
Hawkins, Caroline, 7
Hawkins, Elizabeth 1816, 112
Hawkins, James, Jr. 1798, 111
Hawkins, No given name, 111
Helm, David, 116
Henderson, James, 31
Henderson, Margaret, 129
Henderson, No given name, 29
Hendrick, David, 60
Henley, Samuel, 116
Henry, Patrick, 104
Hentish, Daria Nadja, 82
Hentz, J. P., Reverend, 107
Hepner, Asa 1855, 150
Higgins, Annie Lucille 1894, 39
Higgins, Charles Austin 1918, 39
Higgins, Charles Edwin 1892, 39
Higgins, Charles Prather, 39
Higgins, Daisy Cornelia 1898, 39
Higgins, Elizabeth, 61
Higgins, Emma Catherine 1921, 39
Higgins, Eugene Staley 1900, 39
Higgins, Jeanne Dorsey 1926, 39
Higgins, Jesse Thomas 1903, 39
Higgins, Joseph, 22
Higgins, Kenneth Crawford 1802, 39
Higgins, Thomas Warfield, 39
Higgins, Upton, 107, 146
Hill, Priscilla, 10
Hillard, Bernard, 93
Hilton, Lloyd 1798, 136
Hilton, Rosa B., 146
Hilton, Sharon Lynn 1961, 136
Hilton, William Harrison 1836, 136
Hines, Julia Ann 1820, 68
Hinkle, Mary Ann, 63
Hobbs, Amos, 61
Hobbs, Anna, 61, 67, 73
Hobbs, Aseneth, 22
Hobbs, Caleb, 61
Hobbs, Corilla Elizabeth 1806, 64
Hobbs, Dennis, 61

Hobbs, Eliza, 22
Hobbs, Elizabeth, 61
Hobbs, Ephraim, 61
Hobbs, George W. 1856, 77
Hobbs, Gerard, 64
Hobbs, Gustavus Warfield, Reverend, 61
Hobbs, Hannah, 61
Hobbs, Henry Macken, 61
Hobbs, Jared, 64
Hobbs, Joseph, 61
Hobbs, Noah, 61
Hobbs, Rachel, 61
Hobbs, Remus Riggs, 61
Hobbs, Rezin Thomas, 61
Hobbs, Ruth, 61
Hobbs, Samuel Adams, 61
Hobbs, Sarah Jane, 61
Hobbs, Susannah, 21
Hobbs, Thomas, 61
Hobbs, Warfield 1794, 61
Hobbs, William, 21, 67
Hobbs, William, Jr., 22
Hockley, 10
Hodgkiss, Juliet, 149
Hoffman, Louise, 142
Holland, Amos, 129
Holland, Ann 1871, 129
Holland, Charles, 129
Holland, Charles Griffith 1867, 129
Holland, Hester L., 129
Holland, James Philip 1874, 129
Holland, James Thomas 1833, 129
Holland, Lloyd Walter 1869, 129
Holland, Lucy, 148
Holland, Mary, 20
Holland, Susanna, 13
Holland, Thomas Henderson, 129
Holland, William, 13
Hollingsworth, Ann, 106
Holloway, Lindlay, 21
Holloway, No given name, 21
Holloway, William, 21
Holmes, Richard, 105
Holsten, Ethel Maree 1939, 115
Holsten, John Henry 1916, 114

Holsten, John Henry, Jr. 1943, 115
Holsten, Leo Gosnell 1946, 115
Holt, Lillian, 141
Hood, Charles Wayman, Major, 48
Hood, Naomi 1898, 115
Hoopes, Albert W., 58
Hoopes, Edward, 58
Hoopes, Herman, 57
Hoopes, Marian, 57
Hopkins, Eliza, 31, 33, 35
Hopkins, Francis M., 145
Hopkins, Thomasin, 6
Hopwood, Frances L. 1858, 143
Hopwood, Mason, 147
Hopwood, No given name, 128
Hopwood, William Mareen, 128
Horine, Adelaide, 71
Hough, No given name, 134
Hovens, Samuel, 103
Howard, Absolute, 5
Howard, Benjamin, 5
Howard, Cornelius, 4
Howard, Dowell Jennings, 41
Howard, Dowell Jennings, Jr. 1924, 41
Howard, Henry, 41, 98
Howard, Henry 1710, Sir, 99
Howard, Honour, 106
Howard, Honour Elder 1740, 98
Howard, Jemima, 108
Howard, John, 108
Howard, John, Jr., Captain, 4
Howard, Joshua, 106, 108
Howard, Rachel, 5, 109
Howard, Rachel 1832, 99
Howard, Rebecca, 46
Howell, Malvina, 21
Howell, Sarah, 69
Hugus, Lydia, 62
Hugus, Michael, 62
Hutchings, Mary C., 61
Hutton, Enoch B., 56
Hutton, Lucy W., 56
Hyatt, Asa 1787, 24
Hyatt, Asa 1848, 24
Hyatt, Charlotte 1796, 26

177

Hyatt, Eleanor Ann 1816, 25
Hyatt, Eli, 24
Hyatt, Eli 1754, 23
Hyatt, Eli, Jr. 1798, 26
Hyatt, Elizabeth, 24
Hyatt, Elizabeth 1785, 24
Hyatt, Elizabeth 1825, 24
Hyatt, Ella 1846, 24
Hyatt, Isabella 1818, 26
Hyatt, James D., 24
Hyatt, John 1781, 24
Hyatt, John William, 24
Hyatt, Leah Ann Willson 1826, 26
Hyatt, Levi Thomas 1815, 24
Hyatt, Lloyd 1803, 26
Hyatt, Lucinda Mariah 1830, 26
Hyatt, Margaret, 24
Hyatt, Mary Ann, 24
Hyatt, Mary Ann 1800, 26
Hyatt, Mary Ann 1824, 26
Hyatt, Meshach, 23
Hyatt, Philip, 24
Hyatt, Polly 1794, 26
Hyatt, Rebecca, 24
Hyatt, Samuel 1792, 26
Hyatt, Sarah Elizabeth 1828, 26
Hyatt, Sary Ann S. 1823, 26
Hyatt, Susannah 1790, 26
Hyatt, Theophilus 1820, 26
Hyatt, Theophilus 1849, 25
Hyatt, William 1783, 24
Hyatt, Wilson Lee 1833, 26
Hyland, Millicent, 53

—J—

Jacob, E., 121
Jacobs, Jemima, 32
Jaeger, Edna Sophia 1903, 85
James, Fanny, 148
James, William, 106
Jamison, Nathan, 151
Jenkins, Henry, 20, 54
Jensen, Teri, 38
Johnson, Amelia Lee, 66
Johnson, Dorothy Lillian 1928, 78

Johnson, Elizabeth J., 60
Johnson, Guy, 77
Johnson, James V., 77
Johnson, Jane, 103
Johnson, Larry E., 78
Johnson, No given name, 103, 128
Johnson, Ruth, 78
Johnson, Samuel, 108
Johnson, Sarah, 68
Johnson, Vernon, 78
Johnson, Walter, 78
Johnson, William, 77
Jones, Catherine, 78
Jones, Clara Louise, 115
Jones, Elizabeth, 8, 22
Jones, Evan Aquila, 49
Jones, Florence, 41
Jones, Harold Louis, 141
Jones, Isaac, 19, 53
Jones, Joshua, 108
Jones, Marie Lyddane, 35
Jones, Mary Ann, 19, 53
Jones, No given name, 79
Jones, William H., 16
Jordan, No given name, 133
Junkin, No given name, 79

—K—

Keefer, Albert W. 1843, 124
Keefer, Ellen C. V. 1846, 124
Keefer, Michael 1821, 123
Keefer, Michael C. 1849, 124
Keesee, Betty Ann 1969, 140
Keesee, Dale 1959, 140
Keesee, Lisa Lynn 1968, 140
Keesee, Rex 1937, 140
Keesee, Rex, Jr. 1957, 140
Kefauver, No given name, 133
Kelley, Truman Leo 1927, 89
Kellogg, Ezra, Reverend, 102
Kelly, Kathleen, 141
Kelly, Leslie Norris 1895, 89
Kelly, Paul, 141
Kelly, Sarah, 7
Kemp, James Raymond 1898, 86, 113

Kemp, Julia Louise 1920, 86, 113
Kemp, Sarah, 64
Kempel, Jill Marie, 80
Kempel, Matthew James, 80
Kempel, Matthew James, Jr. 1989, 80
Kempel, Megan Ann 1987, 80
Kenley, Edna, 54
Kenley, John R., 54
Kenley, Nelly, 54
Kervick, No given name, 23
Kilb, Clifford Francis 1960, 72
Kilb, Deborah Sue 1958, 72
Kilb, James Noble, 72
King, Ardella Mae 1882, 35
King, Ascenah S. 1825, 85
King, Beda Cassandra 1873, 81, 135
King, Bryan MacDonald 1965, 82
King, Christine Anne 1968, 82
King, Clark Fout 1910, 82
King, Daniel Clark 1939, 82
King, Donald John 1989, 80
King, Dorothy Ann 1949, 78
King, Eileen M., 78, 79
King, Eva Lee 1864, 92
King, Filmore Clark 1890, 82
King, Frances Lucille 1914, 79
King, Frank Robert 1951, 78
King, Franklin Webster 1927, 78
King, Georgia Eleanor 1886, 145
King, Haller Howard 1912, 79
King, Harvey Webster 1890, 78
King, Holady Hix 1857, 78
King, James Rufus 1871, 80
King, John Duckett 1778, 75
King, John Lewis 1905, 80
King, John Lewis, Jr. 1942, 80
King, John MacDonald 1942, 82
King, Karl Lewis 1969, 80
King, Kenneth Stanley 1965, 80
King, Kimberly Ann 1963, 80
King, Lucille M., 79
King, Mark Sheridan 1962, 82
King, Mary Frances 1900, 86, 113
King, Michael Andrew 1966, 82
King, Pamela Beth 1988, 80
King, Patricia Lucille, 78, 79

King, Robert M., 78, 79
King, Rufus Kent 1850, 35
King, Sandra Lee 1940, 80
King, Sarah Rebecca 1818, 75, 77
King, Shirley, 117
King, Singleton Lewis 1843, 93
King, William Haller 1893, 78
Kinna, Peggy, 24
Kinney, Elizabeth, 150
Kinsey, Mary Columbia 1906, 138
Kirchgessner, Joan Marie, 71
Kirk, 19
Klapp, Purnell, 116
Knickerbocker, William T., 65
Knight, Kathryn, 70
Knowles, William G., 149
Kulp, No given name, 70

—L—

Lakins, Gaither, 132
Lamar, Archibald, 108
Lambden, James D., 34
Lansdale, John, 53
Lansdale, William, 28
Larimore, Caroline, 30
Larimore, Rosine, 30
Larimore, Woodville, 30
Larrimore, Aldine, 30
Larrimore, John, 30
Lawrence, John, Jr. Colonel, 19, 54
Lawrence, Josephine E., 19, 54
Lawrence, Levin, 98
Lawrence, Nicholas Otho 1825, 110
Lawrence, Richard, 110
Lawrence, Richard 1757, 98
Lawrence, Richard Joseph 1827, 110
Lawrence, Warfield 1831, 110
Lawson, Claudia Olivia 1883, 90
Lawson, Josiah Wolf 1849, 89
Lawson, Ola Blanche 1887, 91
Lawson, Sally, 139
Layton, Charles F., 138
Layton, Susan Elizabeth 1886, 138
Leach, No given name, 61
Leatherwood, Elizabeth 1851, 114

Ledochowski, Stanislaus, 57
Ledochowski, Therese, 57
Ledochowski, Vladimir, Count, 57
Ledochowski, Yadwiga, 57
Lee, John, 147
Lee, Katherine Lawrence, 57
Leek, Samuel, 22
Leeke, Obed, 105
Leishear Miller, 88
Leishear, Lucretia, 88
Leishear, Mary Elizabeth 1895, 88
Leishear, Thomas, 88
Lewis, Aleathea Ann 1806, 89
Lewis, Angeline 1828, 74
Lewis, Ann Eliza 1848, 95
Lewis, Annie Elizabeth, 93
Lewis, Caroline 1835, 33, 93
Lewis, Charles H. 1860, 85
Lewis, Edith S. 1889, 93
Lewis, Elizabeth 1840, 74
Lewis, Frances Fielding, 5
Lewis, Jane, 121
Lewis, Jane 1776, 74
Lewis, Jeremiah 1781, 74, 93
Lewis, Jeremiah of Levi, 95
Lewis, John A. 1832, 93
Lewis, Rispah Ann 1844, 86
Lilley, Zack, 34
Linthicum, Gassaway W., 45
Linthicum, Lancelot, 50
Linthicum, Lloyd W., 51
Linthicum, Mary, 51
Linthicum, Sarah, 51
Linthicum, Vachel W., 50
Linton, Dorothy 1915, 140
Lloyd, Mark Kenneth, 71
Locust Grove, 46
Locust Park, 120
Locust Thicket, 120
Lodge, James L., 112
Longenecker, Daniel J., 137
Longwood, 101
Lucas, Elizabeth, 6, 7
Lucas, Isabel, 6
Luhn, No given name, 134
Lupari, Brooklyn Leigh 1986, 38

Lupari, Emerald 1994, 38
Lupari, Henry 1992, 38
Lupari, Kierianne 1992, 38
Lupari, Miles 1995, 38
Lush, Stephen, Major, 99
Lydard, Emma Jane 1890, 82
Lyddane, Nannie 1858, 131
Lyddane, Stephen M., 131
Lynch, William, 10
Lyon, Benjamin, 67
Lyon, Sarah 1794, 69

—M—

Macgill, Sarah, 9
Mactier, Nancy, 28
Madiera, Oscar, 19
Magee, No given name, 52
Magruder, Cordelia, 65
Magruder, Ellen Bowie 1800, 31
Magruder, Jeffery P. T. 1805, 31
Magruder, Jeffry, Doctor, 31
Magruder, Susanna, 100
Magruder, Zachariah L., 33
Manaca, Reuben, 27
Mark, Sarah 1799, 20, 76
Markey, Frederick A., Sr., 122
Markley, Gladys 1913, 139
Marr, E. D., 145
Marr, Margaret 1882, 137
Marriott, Achsah, 15
Marriott, Augustine, 15
Marriott, John, 8, 15, 98
Marriott, Mary, 15
Marsh, Ann, 6
Marshall, Martha, 5
Martin, Alton M., 117
Martin, Gloria Eileen 1927, 117
Martin, Helen, 116
Martin, James S., Doctor, 48
Martin, Jeffrey, 133
Martin, Jeffrey, Jr., 133
Martin, Joyce Denore 1929, 117
Martin, Phyllis Ann 1933, 117
Martin, Roger Holmes 1903, 117
Martin, Shirley Marie 1935, 117

Martin, Velma, 142
Martin, Velma Mae 1928, 117
Martin, William Tobias, 117
Martin, William Warfield, 117
Mason, Robert H., 148
Maynard, M. C., 103
McCaslin, Rolland, 66
McCauley, Christine Margaret 1973, 91
McCauley, Erica Marlene 1975, 91
McCauley, James Irvin, Jr. 1947, 91
McCubbin, Charles 1807, 110
McCubbin, Elizabeth Achsah, 110
McCubbin, Joseph Nicholas 1839, 110
McDonough, No given name, 92
McDonough, Wesley Joseph, 92
McDowell, John W., 102
McGill, Lloyd Thomas, Doctor, 49
McKeehan, No given name, 103, 104
McKnew, Emily, 137
McLaughlin, Brendan Kent 1987, 37
McLaughlin, Brian Patrick 1983, 37
McLaughlin, Kara Megan 1990, 37
McLaughlin, Kevin Michael 1983, 37
McLemore, Mary D., 32
McMillan, Alice, 64
McMillan, Hugh, 64, 65
McMillan, James, 65
Mercier, Joshua, 146
Meredith, Lydia A. 1810, 32, 38, 99
Meredith, Ruth, 32
Meredith, Thomas, 32
Meriweather, Mack, 60
Meriweather, Sarah, 28
Merryman, Harriet, 148
Mershaw, No given name, 7
Messenger, Mildred, 65
Messer, Roberta Ann 1941, 80
Metcalf, Huldah, 60
Michael, John T., 24
Michael, Lydia, 24
Miederlehner, Leonard, 41
Miles, Alexandra 1991, 38
Miles, Doris Louise 1929, 135
Miles, Eleanor, 37

Miles, Elizabeth 1795, 82
Miles, Hanson Thomas 1850, 32, 34
Miles, Henry Kent, 37
Miles, Howard Montgomery 1879, 35
Miles, Howard Montgomery, Jr., 35
Miles, James Hanson 1810, 34
Miles, Janet Marian 1943, 36
Miles, Jemima 1782, 75
Miles, Karen Anne 1956, 37
Miles, Kathryn Patricia 1963, 38
Miles, Kendall Mae 1960, 38
Miles, Kent Montgomery 1965, 38
Miles, Kim Ardell 1958, 37
Miles, Laura Virginia, 36
Miles, Mary Catherine, Major, 36
Miles, Richard Henry 1848, 35
Miles, Sandra Diamond, 35
Miles, Thomas Etchison 1947, 36
Miles, Thomas Hanson 1911, 36
Millar, Eliza, 52
Miller, Ada M., 148
Miller, George Ellsworth, 65
Miller, Mary A. 1803, 86
Miller, No given name, 7
Mitchell's Range, 13
Mitchell, Laura, 148
Mobley, Lydia, 103
Mogenson, Allen O., 71
Mogenson, James, 71
Mogenson, Jean, 71
Molesworth, Annie C. 1857, 83
Molesworth, Elizabeth A. 1823, 76
Molesworth, Joshua 1818, 85
Molesworth, Josiah 1819, 76
Molesworth, Mary E. 1847, 76
Molesworth, Mary F., 88
Molesworth, No given name, 128
Monee, Linda, 79
Monroe, Ellen, 76
Monroe, Thomas H. W., Reverend, 150
Montandon, Mary J., 56
Moore, Luther James, 86
Moore, Thomas H. W., 107
Morgan, Charles D., 57
Morley, Ruth, 11

—P—

Riggs, Mary 1776, 49
Riggs, Mary Olivia 1834, 49
Riggs, Nicholas Ridgely Warfield
    1849, 50
Riggs, Rachel 1724, 59, 67, 105
Riggs, Rachel Griffith 1836, 49
Riggs, Ruth 1730, 101
Rine, Lucy A., 93
Riner, Hester Ann, 147
Roberson, No given name, 134
Rockland, 49
Roe, Dorothy, 116
Rogers, Agnes, 27, 62
Rogers, Nancy, 22
Rose Hill, 66
Rout, Margaret, 117
Rowling, Thomas 1698, 27
Roxbury Hall, 101
Runkles, Ella May, 143
Runkles, Lester R. 1916, 144
Runkles, No given name, 144
Runkles, Norman W. 1913, 144
Runkles, Robert, 139
Runkles, Stella L. 1910, 144
Ryan, Susanna, 7

—S—

Sadler, Ann, 61
Saffell, John, 120
Sage, Charles W., 149
Sanders, Gail, 91
Sappington, Harriet Lucy, 101
Sargent, Harriet Sophia, 70
Sauer, Scott Darren, 143
Schwartz, Loretta Kathryn, 39
Scrivener, Elizabeth, 97
Scrivnor, Allen, 134
Seboda, Juanita Louise 1932, 135
Second Addition to Snowden's Manor,
    100
Seir, Pauline, 140
Selby, Ginny, 19
Sellman, Sarah, 19, 53
Sewell, John, 15
Sharp, Nannie Louise 1919, 84

Sharretts, Samuel, 55
Shaw, Julia Ann 1832, 93
Shaw, Kate L. 1870, 72
Sheeran, Kerie, 37
Sherman, Audrey, 116
Shields, No given name, 54
Shillenburg, Dominick, 6
Shipley, Eliza, 27
Shipley, Elizabeth, 27
Shipley, Ellen, 64
Shipley, Emeline, 27
Shipley, Lethia, 27
Shipley, Rebekah 1815, 17
Shreves, Francis E., 150
Sigsbee, Charles 1908, 84
Sigsbee, Charles Norman 1940, 84
Simmons, Nannie, 94
Simmons, Nannie 1870, 119
Simpson, Anne, 99
Simpson, Delilah 1759, 105
Simpson, Eliza J. 1824, 143
Simpson, Francis, 12
Simpson, Joshua, 105
Simpson, Richard, 99
Singleton, Leslie Edward, 115
Sisson, John, 1, 3
Slave, Becky, 67
Slave, Bett, 104
Slave, Dinah, 68
Slave, Frank, 67
Slave, George, 104
Slave, Harry, 67
Slave, Hen, 67
Slave, Isaac, 14
Slave, Sam, 67
Slave, Tuase, 67
Small Purchase, 111
Smith, Cora, 116
Smith, Edward, 7
Smith, Gregory Thomas, 35
Smith, James 1822, 101
Smith, John Sylvester, 116
Smith, Lydia E., 21
Smith, Mary Ann 1823, 101
Smith, Miles, 150
Smith, Murray Baker, 91

Smith, No given name, 34
Smith, Ola Blanche, 90
Smith, Sarah F. 1826, 90
Smith, Sharon Lee 1951, 89
Smith, Wesley R., 78
Snapp, Carol, 81
Snapp, Hubert, 81
Snapp, James, 81
Snapp, John, 81
Snell, George, 98
Snowden's Manor, 105
Snowden, Edward, Colonel, 100
Snowden, Mary, 146
Snowden, Richard N., Major, 100
Sollers, No given name, 55
Soper, W. C., 104
Souder, Archie W. 1884, 81
Souder, Dorothy Laurene 1912, 81
Souder, Grace Wilson 1913, 82
Souder, Helen, 81
Souder, Jane, 81
Souder, Ruth, 81
Speace, Brandon King 1972, 80
Speace, Stanley Coulson 1968, 80
Speace, Willard Coulson 1937, 80
Spear, Elizabeth Ann 1825, 34
Spowers, No given name, 133
Spragins, Louyse Duvall 1869, 66
Spragins, Stith Bolling, 66
Spring Garden, 98
Spurrier, Henrietta, 19
Spurrier, Matilda 1785, 15
Spurrier, Rebecca, 7
St. John, Jack Visscher, 71
St. John, Richard William 1961, 72
St. John, Robert Warfield 1954, 71
St. John, Susan Elizabeth 1956, 71
Standiford, H. Webster, 115
Stanley, Estelle, 80
Stanley, Esther, 80
Stanley, Grover Mount 1892, 138
Stanley, Hazel Margaret 1922, 138
Stanley, Jeanne, 80
Stanley, Louise, 80
Stanley, Mary, 77
Stanley, Mary Lee, 80

Stanley, Robert L. 1874, 80
Stanley, Roland, 80
Starrett, Brandon 1994, 38
Starrett, Breelyn Nicole 1992, 38
Starrett, Mathew, 38
Stauffer, Elizabeth, 66
Stephenson, Daniel, 100
Stevens, Mary Ann, 103
Stevens, Thomas, 14
Stinchcomb, No given name, 121
Stockett, Ann 1792, 19
Stockett, Mary Elizabeth, 14
Stockett, Thomas Nobel 1747, Doctor, 19
Stringer's Chance, 97, 106
Stringer, Lucy, 9
Stringer, Rachel, 99
Stringer, Samuel, 99
Stringer, Samuel 1734, Dr., 99
Strong, Achsah, 102
Stull, Arnold Raymond 1901, 138
Stull, Mary Orlean 1925, 138
Stup, Dwayne Vernon, 117
Stup, Suzanne Joyce, 117
Stup, Vernon, 117
Susannah, 111, 112
Swartz, Catherine C., 84
Swomley, Sarah, 147
Sypert, D. P., 60

—T—

Tabler, Bernice, 93
Tabler, Ella B. 1860, 94
Tabler, Harold, 94
Tabler, Oscar, 93
Tabler, Roger William, 118
Tabler, Roger William, Jr. 1975, 118
Taylor, No given name, 54
Tew, Doris Lee, 115
The Addition, 4
The Cedars, 71
The Gap Filled Up, 13
The Resurvey on William and John, 111, 112

187

Warfield, Albert Gallatin 1817, 50, 55
Warfield, Albert Gallatin, III, 56
Warfield, Albert Gallatin, Jr. 1843, 55
Warfield, Albert W., 145
Warfield, Alberta Clay, 55
Warfield, Alexander, 8, 12, 14, 15, 63, 97, 99, 100, 105, 106, 149, 150
Warfield, Alexander 1678, 4, 6
Warfield, Alexander 1737, 12
Warfield, Alexander 1764, 106
Warfield, Alexander 1805, 121
Warfield, Alexander 1815, 16
Warfield, Alexander 1837, 16
Warfield, Alexander d/1825, 145
Warfield, Alexander Guen, 60
Warfield, Alexander S. D. 1836, 16, 17
Warfield, Alexander W. m/1827, 145
Warfield, Alfred, 29
Warfield, Alfred 1825, 28
Warfield, Alfred Griffith 1867, 72
Warfield, Algetha May, 127
Warfield, Alice, 54
Warfield, Alice 1841, 129
Warfield, Alice 1849, 57
Warfield, Alice Virginia 1848, 112
Warfield, Allen, 7, 50
Warfield, Allen, Jr., 50
Warfield, Alverta, 54
Warfield, Amanda, 60
Warfield, Amanda 1821, 46
Warfield, Amanda 1849, 76, 77
Warfield, Amelia, 20, 22, 27, 28
Warfield, Amelia 1755, 12
Warfield, Amos, 8, 32
Warfield, Amos Wiley 1829, 32
Warfield, Amos Wiley 1883, 42
Warfield, Amos Wiley, Jr. 1860, 32
Warfield, Amy Cornelia 1866, 32
Warfield, Amy Louise 1900, 116
Warfield, Andrea, 42
Warfield, Andrew, 21, 145
Warfield, Ann, 28, 52, 98, 101, 105
Warfield, Ann 1736, 98

Warfield, Ann 1762, 104
Warfield, Ann 1824, 130
Warfield, Ann E., 105
Warfield, Ann M. 1832, 16
Warfield, Ann Maria 1825, 123
Warfield, Anna, 21, 68
Warfield, Anna 1795, 63
Warfield, Anna 1844, 16
Warfield, Anna Belle 1917, 41
Warfield, Anna Elizabeth, 47
Warfield, Anna m/1796, 145
Warfield, Anna m/1812, 145
Warfield, Anna Ray 1882, 148
Warfield, Anne, 20, 98, 108
Warfield, Anne 1741, 11
Warfield, Anne Eliza, 51
Warfield, Anne Elizabeth, 60
Warfield, Anne Henry, 104
Warfield, Anne m/1802, 145
Warfield, Anne m/1883, 145
Warfield, Annie E. 1834, 143
Warfield, Annie M. m/1893, 145
Warfield, Annie m/1880, 145
Warfield, Araminta, 14
Warfield, Arnold 1776, 13
Warfield, Asbury 1827, 74
Warfield, Asbury O., 107
Warfield, Augustus, 133, 150
Warfield, Augustus 1830, 47
Warfield, Augustus L. 1862, 132
Warfield, Avolina 1813, 48
Warfield, Avolina 1833, 48
Warfield, Azel, 31
Warfield, Azel 1728, 97, 100
Warfield, Azel, Jr., 31
Warfield, Ballinger D., 116
Warfield, Basil, 98
Warfield, Basil 1780, 105
Warfield, Basil Hanson, 98
Warfield, Basil T. 1859, 86, 87
Warfield, Basil Thomas 1917, 88
Warfield, Beale, 19, 98
Warfield, Beale A. 1834, 54
Warfield, Beale d/1815, 46, 53
Warfield, Bela, 29
Warfield, Beni, 28, 29

Warfield, Benjamin, 7, 9, 27, 42, 46, 48, 52, 53
Warfield, Benjamin 1680, 4, 8
Warfield, Benjamin 1702, 9, 12, 45
Warfield, Benjamin 1892, 145
Warfield, Benjamin Benson, 6
Warfield, Benjamin Dorsey, 47
Warfield, Benjamin Worthington 1734, Captain, 9, 45
Warfield, Benjamin, Jr., 9, 52
Warfield, Bernard 1892, 145
Warfield, Bernard Dalrymple, 48
Warfield, Bertha 1876, 72
Warfield, Bessie 1885, 76
Warfield, Bessie C., 88
Warfield, Bessie Frances 1892, 114
Warfield, Betsy, 7
Warfield, Bettie E., 133
Warfield, Bettie E. 1891, 136
Warfield, Betty, 134
Warfield, Blanche M., 147
Warfield, Bowie, 132
Warfield, Bowie Clagett, 54
Warfield, Bradley 1854, 76
Warfield, Bradley Winfield 1879, 92, 145
Warfield, Brice 1742, 12, 15, 23
Warfield, Burgess Barr, 52
Warfield, Byrtle 1903, 117
Warfield, C. Holmes, 116
Warfield, Caleb, 7, 9, 53
Warfield, Caleb 1806, 73, 74
Warfield, Caleb N. 1839, 145
Warfield, Camsadel, 54
Warfield, Caroline, 27, 51, 95, 135
Warfield, Caroline 1818, 123
Warfield, Caroline 1827, 146
Warfield, Caroline Barr, 51
Warfield, Carrie 1888, 57
Warfield, Carrie Olivia, 94
Warfield, Carroll 1919, 115
Warfield, Catharine 1816, 129
Warfield, Catherine, 8, 34, 50, 56
Warfield, Catherine 1757, 101
Warfield, Catherine 1758, 61
Warfield, Catherine A. 1783, 123

Warfield, Catherine A. 1826, 123
Warfield, Catherine Dorsey, 19, 50, 53
Warfield, Catherine Dorsey 1825, 47
Warfield, Cecelia m/1834, 146
Warfield, Cecilia, 107
Warfield, Cecilius Edwin 1841, 66
Warfield, Cecilius Edwin, Jr. 1880, 66
Warfield, Charles, 22, 27, 72, 98, 108, 134
Warfield, Charles 1738, 98, 106
Warfield, Charles 1752, 12
Warfield, Charles 1867, 114
Warfield, Charles A., 27, 31
Warfield, Charles A. Hamilton, 107
Warfield, Charles Alexander, 101, 106
Warfield, Charles Alexander 1751, Doctor, 100
Warfield, Charles Alexander, Doctor, 104
Warfield, Charles Alexander, Jr., 101
Warfield, Charles Carroll 1898, 116
Warfield, Charles Chase, 52
Warfield, Charles Dorsey, 28
Warfield, Charles Edwin 1884, 93
Warfield, Charles G. 1851, 146
Warfield, Charles H. 1795, 146
Warfield, Charles L. 1875, 17
Warfield, Charles L. m/1823, 146
Warfield, Charles m/1885, 146
Warfield, Charles Milton, 61
Warfield, Charles P., 60
Warfield, Charles Preston 1920, 41
Warfield, Charlotte 1793, 110
Warfield, Charlotte m/1820, 146
Warfield, Chauncey P., 134
Warfield, Cheryl Ann, 92
Warfield, Chloe Anne 1873, 41
Warfield, Clagett, 134
Warfield, Clarence 1855, 57
Warfield, Clarence Griffith, Admiral, 70
Warfield, Clarence O. 1870, 143
Warfield, Clyde Gardiner 1925, 88

Warfield, Connie L., 92
Warfield, Cornelia Isabella 1877, 42
Warfield, Cost J. 1851, 128
Warfield, Courtney, 72
Warfield, Dana Rudelle, 116
Warfield, Daniel, 28
Warfield, David, 108
Warfield, David A. 1838, 146
Warfield, David D. 1928, 136
Warfield, David H. 1857, 131
Warfield, David N., 134
Warfield, Davidge 1729, 63, 97, 105
Warfield, Deborah, 12
Warfield, Deborah 1792, 13
Warfield, Deborah 1838, 146
Warfield, Deborah J., 146
Warfield, Deborah Jane, 29
Warfield, Della Elizabeth 1887, 83
Warfield, Dennis, 7, 107
Warfield, Dennis 1784, 108
Warfield, Dennis 1810, 146
Warfield, Dennis T. 1843, 16
Warfield, Diane Louise 1948, 87, 114
Warfield, Dinah, 59, 99, 106
Warfield, Dinah 1742, 98
Warfield, Dinah 1753, 101
Warfield, Donald Elisha 1918, 86, 113
Warfield, Donald Eugene 1870, 137
Warfield, Donald M., 116
Warfield, Doris, 134
Warfield, Dorothy Elizabeth 1934, 88
Warfield, Douglas C., 116
Warfield, Drusilla 1832, 132
Warfield, Earnest W. 1849, 122
Warfield, Edgar 1901, 117
Warfield, Edgar Howard 1876, 137
Warfield, Edith, 134
Warfield, Edith L. 1889, 93
Warfield, Edmond, 21
Warfield, Edmund, 31
Warfield, Edmund W. m/1883, 146
Warfield, Edna, 133
Warfield, Edna 1862, 112
Warfield, Edna 1898, 143
Warfield, Edna G. 1868, 85

Warfield, Edna James, 74
Warfield, Edna R. m/1888, 146
Warfield, Edward, 34, 67, 134, 150
Warfield, Edward 1710, 15, 59, 67, 105
Warfield, Edward D. 1853, 77
Warfield, Edward d/1836, 67, 73, 74, 75, 82, 85, 89, 93, 95
Warfield, Edward Dorsey 1858, 91
Warfield, Edward m/1831, 146
Warfield, Edward R., 52
Warfield, Edward Ray 1894, 92
Warfield, Edward Stansbury, 74
Warfield, Edward, Jr. 1745, 59
Warfield, Edward, the Younger 1769, 63, 105
Warfield, Edwin, 80
Warfield, Edwin 1818, 111
Warfield, Edwin 1848, Governor, 9, 56
Warfield, Edwin Alonzo 1859, 94
Warfield, Edwin W. 1888, 146
Warfield, Edwin, III, 57
Warfield, Edwin, Jr. 1891, 57
Warfield, Effie A. 1887, 128
Warfield, Eldred Dudley, Captain, 48
Warfield, Eleanor, 6, 31, 48
Warfield, Eleanor Amelia, 54
Warfield, Eleanor C. 1845, 148
Warfield, Eleanor D. 1908, 146
Warfield, Eleanor m/1804, 22
Warfield, Eletheer, 41
Warfield, Eli Gaither, 31
Warfield, Elie, 30, 48
Warfield, Elijah, 108
Warfield, Elinor, 9, 14
Warfield, Elinor 1683, 5, 10
Warfield, Elisha, 51, 52
Warfield, Elisha G. 1893, 86
Warfield, Elisha Griffith 1863, 70
Warfield, Elisha Nicholas, 52
Warfield, Elisha S. 1893, 86, 113
Warfield, Elisha, Jr., 51
Warfield, Eliza, 32, 33, 52, 94
Warfield, Eliza 1811, 121
Warfield, Eliza Ellen 1841, 145

Warfield, Eliza m/1816, 146
Warfield, Elizabeth, 7, 9, 12, 22, 29, 31, 73, 106, 107, 108, 120
Warfield, Elizabeth 1764, 63
Warfield, Elizabeth 1782, 109
Warfield, Elizabeth 1798, 131
Warfield, Elizabeth 1810, 75
Warfield, Elizabeth 1812, 73
Warfield, Elizabeth 1818, 16
Warfield, Elizabeth 1826, 112
Warfield, Elizabeth A. 1841, 136
Warfield, Elizabeth Ann, 27
Warfield, Elizabeth Ann 1816, 46
Warfield, Elizabeth Ann 1817, 124
Warfield, Elizabeth Anne, 146
Warfield, Elizabeth Anne 1817, 111
Warfield, Elizabeth Chase, 52
Warfield, Elizabeth Dorsey 1791, 110
Warfield, Elizabeth H., 118
Warfield, Elizabeth J. 1862, 84
Warfield, Elizabeth m/1809, 146
Warfield, Elizabeth m/1827, 146
Warfield, Elizabeth May 1905, 117
Warfield, Elizabeth R., 100
Warfield, Elizabeth Wallace, 28
Warfield, Elizabeth Walter, 61
Warfield, Elizabeth Worthington 1865, 71
Warfield, Ella, 128
Warfield, Ella B. 1861, 146
Warfield, Ella May 1886, 144
Warfield, Ellis King 1942, 88
Warfield, Eloise, 94
Warfield, Elsie E., 129
Warfield, Elsie M. m/1910, 146
Warfield, Elsie W. 1889, 147
Warfield, Emily Eliza 1878, 137
Warfield, Emma, 21, 54, 131
Warfield, Emma 1864, 131
Warfield, Emma 1899, 57
Warfield, Enoch 1821, 7
Warfield, Ephraim, 22
Warfield, Ephraim 1742, 59
Warfield, Ephraim 1797, Reverend, 63
Warfield, Ernest 1917, 115

Warfield, Ernest Carroll 1876, 137
Warfield, Estella B. 1898, 144
Warfield, Esther Gertrude, 87
Warfield, Ethel, 133
Warfield, Ethel P. V. 1894, 86, 113
Warfield, Eugenia Elizabeth 1907, 41
Warfield, Eunice Etchison 1891, 114
Warfield, Evelina 1830, 147
Warfield, Evelina H. 1804, 147
Warfield, Eveline 1859, 76
Warfield, Exeline 1859, 76
Warfield, Fannie, 31
Warfield, Fanny A. m/1862, 147
Warfield, Florence Evelyn, 127
Warfield, Frances, 48, 56
Warfield, Frances Ann 1836, 74
Warfield, Frances E. 1832, 144
Warfield, Frances E. 1869, 144
Warfield, Frances L. 1849, 93
Warfield, Frances m/1869, 147
Warfield, Frances Mae, 116
Warfield, Francina H., 107
Warfield, Francis, 57
Warfield, Francis H. 1829, 147
Warfield, Frank, 133
Warfield, Frank 1854, 57
Warfield, Frank Hammond, 133
Warfield, Freda, 127
Warfield, Frederick Gaither 1879, 72
Warfield, Frederick Howard 1874, 66
Warfield, G. Thomas, 129
Warfield, Gaither Postley 1896, Reverend, 70
Warfield, Garrettson 1822, 93
Warfield, Garrison 1822, 33, 73, 93
Warfield, Gassaway Watkins, 54
Warfield, Gassaway Watkins 1846, 56
Warfield, George, 30, 40
Warfield, George E. m/1896, 147
Warfield, George Fraser 1769, 104
Warfield, George Hanson, 60
Warfield, George m/1718, 147
Warfield, George Thomas 1924, 138
Warfield, George W., 31
Warfield, George W. 1817, 122

Warfield, George W. 1864, 86, 113
Warfield, George W. Dorsey, 54
Warfield, George W. m/1845, 147
Warfield, George Waters, 60
Warfield, Georgetta 1854, 128
Warfield, Georgianna 1847, 122
Warfield, Georgietta, 55
Warfield, Gerard, 7
Warfield, Gertrude 1906, 134
Warfield, Gertrude B. 1886, 147
Warfield, Gladys Marie 1915, 118
Warfield, Grace Lee d/1937, 147
Warfield, Grace V. 1888, 144
Warfield, Gracie L. 1864, 112
Warfield, Green, 132
Warfield, Greenberry, 50
Warfield, Greenbury, 67
Warfield, Greenbury m/1817, 147
Warfield, Guinevere M., 133
Warfield, Gustavus, 27, 28
Warfield, Gustavus, Doctor, 101
Warfield, Guy Trevelyn, 46
Warfield, Hamilton David 1957, 135
Warfield, Hamilton Deets 1897, 135
Warfield, Hamilton Deets, Jr. 1931, 135
Warfield, Hamilton G. 1817, 73, 75, 85, 87
Warfield, Hannah Holland Virginia 1879, 42
Warfield, Hannah Y. 1806, 147
Warfield, Harding, 134
Warfield, Harriet, 20, 28
Warfield, Harriet 1787, 110
Warfield, Harriet Burgess, 52
Warfield, Harriet S. 1869, 147
Warfield, Harry E., 147
Warfield, Harry P. 1868, 147
Warfield, Hazel Eveline 1907, 117
Warfield, Helen, 133
Warfield, Helen E. 1859, 148
Warfield, Helen E. m/1872, 148
Warfield, Helen Elizabeth, 71
Warfield, Helen Elizabeth 1889, 70
Warfield, Helen Virginia 1922, 41
Warfield, Henrietta, 107

Warfield, Henrietta 1818, 16, 17
Warfield, Henry, 9, 31, 52, 60, 105
Warfield, Henry 1748, 12
Warfield, Henry Clark 1942, 142
Warfield, Henry Clay, 61
Warfield, Henry m/1871, 148
Warfield, Henry N., 52
Warfield, Henry Ridgely, 100
Warfield, Henry, Jr., 52
Warfield, Hester Ann 1824, 122
Warfield, Hettie, 29, 150
Warfield, Honor, 107
Warfield, Horace 1814, 73, 75, 77, 85
Warfield, Horatio 1824, 148
Warfield, Ida E. m/1886, 148
Warfield, Ida Fidelia 1861, 94
Warfield, Ida V. 1853, 83
Warfield, Ignatius 1861, 148
Warfield, Irma W., 150
Warfield, Isabella 1833, 17
Warfield, Isabella D. 1843, 33
Warfield, Isabella Josephine, 127
Warfield, Israel Griffith 1832, 68, 69
Warfield, Israel Griffith 1869, 72
Warfield, J. M., 39
Warfield, Jack 1904, 40
Warfield, Jacob Holloway, 22
Warfield, James, 132
Warfield, James 1751, 59
Warfield, James A. m/1881, 148
Warfield, James Albert, 127
Warfield, James Albert, Jr., 127
Warfield, James D., 148
Warfield, James Earl 1923, 92
Warfield, James H. 1835, 17
Warfield, James H. B., Doctor, 148
Warfield, James Harvey, 60
Warfield, James Harvey 1947, 86, 113
Warfield, James Harvey, Major, 60
Warfield, James Henry Harrison 1841, Doctor, 33
Warfield, James Latimer 1850, 93
Warfield, James Meredith 1880, 42
Warfield, James Paul 1900, 92
Warfield, James R., 120

Warfield, James R. m/1880, 148
Warfield, James Stuart 1952, 118
Warfield, Jane, 92
Warfield, Jane 1820, 16
Warfield, Jane R. 1848, 131
Warfield, Janet V. 1905, 120
Warfield, Jared, 7
Warfield, Jason Edward 1979, 89
Warfield, Jeffrey m/1878, 148
Warfield, Jemima A. 1841, 121
Warfield, Jennifer Lynn 1987, 87, 113
Warfield, Jesse Lee 1801, Doctor, 107
Warfield, Joan B. 1888, 148
Warfield, Joanna R. 1843, 121
Warfield, Jodi, 92
Warfield, John, 7, 19, 20, 21, 22, 27, 53, 98, 120
Warfield, John 1613, 3
Warfield, John 1673, 4, 11, 45, 59
Warfield, John 1700, 11
Warfield, John 1722, 23
Warfield, John 1730, 6
Warfield, John 1744, 11
Warfield, John 1850, 57
Warfield, John A., 107
Warfield, John A. 1813, 16, 17
Warfield, John A. T. 1846, 16
Warfield, John Alexander 1855, 112
Warfield, John Breckinridge, 48
Warfield, John Clark, 70
Warfield, John Davidge 1799, 64
Warfield, John Davidge 1880, 65
Warfield, John E. 1846, 76
Warfield, John F. d/1957, 127
Warfield, John Francis 1854, 32
Warfield, John G. m/1853, 148
Warfield, John Gordon 1920, 42
Warfield, John Gordon, Jr. 1950, 42
Warfield, John Hardy 1915, 118
Warfield, John Hebb, 118
Warfield, John Hood Owings, 46
Warfield, John J. 1872, 144
Warfield, John M. 1816, 73, 82
Warfield, John m/1804, 148

Warfield, John m/1833, 148
Warfield, John O., 142
Warfield, John O. 1898, 134
Warfield, John Ogle 1871, 66
Warfield, John P., 92
Warfield, John R. m/1882, 148
Warfield, John Rhodes 1916, 41
Warfield, John T. 1904, 40
Warfield, John T., Jr., 41
Warfield, John Thomas 1835, 33, 38, 99
Warfield, John Thomas 1857, 17
Warfield, John Thomas, Jr. 1875, 41
Warfield, John W., 129
Warfield, John W. m/1889, 148
Warfield, John Worthington 1749, 13, 20
Warfield, John, Jr., 23
Warfield, Jonathan S., 6
Warfield, Joseph, 23
Warfield, Joseph 1758, 99, 109, 110
Warfield, Joseph E., 116
Warfield, Joseph Gassaway, 60
Warfield, Joseph Haddaway 1921, 138
Warfield, Joseph m/1880, 148
Warfield, Joseph Watkins 1941, 92
Warfield, Josephine 1846, 131
Warfield, Joshua, 7, 9, 29, 31, 43, 50, 98, 145
Warfield, Joshua 1761, 11, 12, 19, 53
Warfield, Joshua 1779, 9
Warfield, Joshua 1781, 48, 55
Warfield, Joshua 1800, 148
Warfield, Joshua D. 1822, 128
Warfield, Joshua D. 1823, 112, 114
Warfield, Joshua Dorsey, 132
Warfield, Joshua Dorsey 1838, Professor, 48
Warfield, Joshua M., 97, 99, 109
Warfield, Joshua Nicholas 1845, 56
Warfield, Joshua Nicholas, Jr. 1885, 56
Warfield, Joy Marie, 92
Warfield, Joyce Elaine 1937, 136
Warfield, Julia Genevive, 51

Warfield, Julie Marie 1981, 142
Warfield, Juliet, 30, 108
Warfield, Juliet 1785, 110
Warfield, Justin, 138
Warfield, Katherine, 57
Warfield, Katherine M., 129
Warfield, Katherine Mary 1951, 138
Warfield, Kathryn D., 70
Warfield, Kennard 1911, 134
Warfield, Kitty, 46
Warfield, Kristin Leanne 1984, 89
Warfield, L. A., 145
Warfield, L. A. d/1862, Captain, 145
Warfield, L. Elizabeth m/1859, 148
Warfield, Laban, 60
Warfield, Lancelot, 8
Warfield, Lancelot, Jr., 98
Warfield, Lancelot, Reverend, 108
Warfield, Larkin m/1827, 148
Warfield, Launcelot, 7
Warfield, Laura, 128
Warfield, Laura A. m/1882, 148
Warfield, Laura E. 1858, 83
Warfield, Laura L. m/1876, 148
Warfield, Laura M. 1901, 134
Warfield, Laura Ruth, 51
Warfield, Lavinia, 120
Warfield, Lavinia Leishear 1926, 89
Warfield, Learnard E. 1836, 121
Warfield, Lee Clagett 1886, 42
Warfield, Lee Clagett, Jr. 1916, 42
Warfield, Lemuel, 132
Warfield, Lemuel 1819, 46
Warfield, Lemuel A. m/1852, 148
Warfield, Lemuel, Jr., 46
Warfield, Lena Matthews 1872, 72
Warfield, Levin, 67
Warfield, Levin 1753, 61, 67, 73
Warfield, Lewis, 14
Warfield, Lewis A. 1849, 143
Warfield, Lewis M. 1837, 131
Warfield, Lewis m/1823, 149
Warfield, Lilly Belle 1876, 17
Warfield, Linda Virginia 1908, 92
Warfield, Lizzie M. 1872, 143
Warfield, Lloyd, 45, 50

Warfield, Lloyd A. 1847, 122
Warfield, Lloyd, Doctor, 52
Warfield, Lloyd, Jr., 52
Warfield, Lorenzo, 27
Warfield, Loretta 1835, 149
Warfield, Louis, 29
Warfield, Louis A. 1849, 143
Warfield, Louis Edwin 1864, 64
Warfield, Louisa, 31
Warfield, Louisa A., 128
Warfield, Louise, 127, 128, 133, 134
Warfield, Louise 1889, 57
Warfield, Lucille, 94
Warfield, Lucretia, 29, 30
Warfield, Lucretia 1851, 89, 149
Warfield, Lucretia Griffith 1832, 48
Warfield, Luke, 23
Warfield, Lula C. 1875, 148
Warfield, Lula E. 1875, 149
Warfield, Lusetta 1829, 82
Warfield, Luther, 61
Warfield, Luther Day 1853, 94
Warfield, Luther Laban, 60
Warfield, Lycurgus L., 149
Warfield, Lydia, 21, 22, 99
Warfield, Lydia 1799, 33
Warfield, Lydia A. 1810, 149
Warfield, Lydia Augusta 1839, 75
Warfield, Lydia E. 1861, 86
Warfield, Lydia Hammond, 27, 28
Warfield, Mabel L., 40
Warfield, Mabel Poole 1895, 149
Warfield, Magruder 1834, 31
Warfield, Mahlon H. 1819, 73, 89
Warfield, Malcolm White 1954, 43
Warfield, Mamie E., 88
Warfield, Mamie E. 1888, 76
Warfield, Manelia E. S., 20, 54
Warfield, Marcellus, 19, 54
Warfield, Margaret, 29, 56, 106
Warfield, Margaret A. 1832, 121
Warfield, Margaret Ann, 116
Warfield, Margaret Ann 1837, 63
Warfield, Margaret Clare, 48
Warfield, Margaret Gassaway, 20

Warfield, Margaret Gassaway 1858, 57
Warfield, Margaret JoAnn 1942, 138
Warfield, Margaret M. 1918, 149
Warfield, Margaret Rachel, 133
Warfield, Margaret W. 1809, 149
Warfield, Maria, 29
Warfield, Maria 1807, 21
Warfield, Maria G. 1838, 69
Warfield, Marian m/1812, 149
Warfield, Marian Serenah, 48
Warfield, Marjorie A., 134
Warfield, Marshall T. 1861, 58
Warfield, Martha, 107
Warfield, Martha 1845, 64, 75
Warfield, Martha A. 1855, 91
Warfield, Martha Ann m/1835, 149
Warfield, Martha H., 60
Warfield, Martha Jane 1874, 72
Warfield, Martin, 116
Warfield, Mary, 6, 9, 15, 19, 20, 21, 22, 28, 33, 68, 98, 105, 108, 150
Warfield, Mary 1679, 4
Warfield, Mary 1754, 8
Warfield, Mary 1783, 149
Warfield, Mary 1786, 110
Warfield, Mary 1797, 31
Warfield, Mary 1805, 21
Warfield, Mary 1841, 64
Warfield, Mary Adams, 71
Warfield, Mary Ann, 21, 63
Warfield, Mary Ann 1788, 29
Warfield, Mary Ann 1809, 73, 95
Warfield, Mary Anne 1761, 23
Warfield, Mary C., 120
Warfield, Mary C. 1834, 121
Warfield, Mary Catherine, 107, 133
Warfield, Mary Cornelia 1905, 40
Warfield, Mary E. 1835, 149
Warfield, Mary E. 1850, 112
Warfield, Mary E. 1852, 122, 131
Warfield, Mary E. 1855, 91
Warfield, Mary E. 1856, 76
Warfield, Mary E. 1859, 147
Warfield, Mary E. 1869, 113
Warfield, Mary E. 1899, 143

Warfield, Mary E. m/1864, 149
Warfield, Mary Eliza 1820, 112
Warfield, Mary Elizabeth 1808, 122
Warfield, Mary Ellen, 51
Warfield, Mary Ellen 1827, 64
Warfield, Mary Ellen m/1880, 149
Warfield, Mary Eunice, 94
Warfield, Mary G., 30
Warfield, Mary G. m/1903, 149
Warfield, Mary Hollingsworth, 106
Warfield, Mary Jane, 51, 52
Warfield, Mary Josephine 1877, 65
Warfield, Mary Lee 1947, 42
Warfield, Mary m/1799, 149
Warfield, Mary m/1818, 149
Warfield, Mary m/1880, 149
Warfield, Mary m/1896, 149
Warfield, Mary Meredith 1862, 32
Warfield, Mary Octavia, 48
Warfield, Mary Olive 1884, 128
Warfield, Mary R., 53
Warfield, Mary Susy 1850, 150
Warfield, Mary Washington 1863, 39
Warfield, Matilda, 32
Warfield, Merhle Basil 1898, 88
Warfield, Merhle Basil, Jr. 1927, 88
Warfield, Merhle Wayne 1950, 89
Warfield, Mildred, 133
Warfield, Milton Theodore, 149
Warfield, Milton Welsh 1827, 47
Warfield, Minerva A. m/1845, 150
Warfield, Miranda 1835, 124
Warfield, Miriam, 133
Warfield, Mollie L. m/1878, 150
Warfield, Molly, 17
Warfield, Monica 1937, 70
Warfield, Nancy, 7, 14, 22, 32, 61
Warfield, Nancy 1805, 6
Warfield, Nancy Ann, 105
Warfield, Nancy Dorsey, 52
Warfield, Nannie M., 60
Warfield, Natalie Jo 1937, 87
Warfield, Nathan, 22
Warfield, Nathan C. 1849, 16
Warfield, Nathan m/1828, 150
Warfield, Nathan Oliver 1845, 137

Warfield, Nelly, 7
Warfield, Nelly Louisa 1863, 17
Warfield, Nelly m/1876, 150
Warfield, Nettie, 149
Warfield, Nettie 1859, 150
Warfield, Nicholas, 51
Warfield, Nicholas Dorsey, 28, 29
Warfield, Nicholas Dorsey 1789, 110, 112
Warfield, Nicholas R., 31, 48
Warfield, Nicholas Ridgely, Captain, 45, 50
Warfield, Nicholas, Doctor, 51
Warfield, Nina Clarke, 23
Warfield, Nina Harding 1866, 64
Warfield, Noel N. P. 1864, 39
Warfield, Nora V. m/1895, 150
Warfield, Norcisa E. 1842, 16
Warfield, Norman, 56
Warfield, Oliver Stanley 1887, 137
Warfield, Opray O., 127
Warfield, Owen B. 1838, 121
Warfield, Paul M., 116
Warfield, Peregrine, Doctor, 101
Warfield, Perry Gould 1813, 14
Warfield, Philemon 1744, 98
Warfield, Philemon D., 47
Warfield, Philemon Dorsey, 45, 46, 50
Warfield, Philemon Dorsey 1776, 46
Warfield, Philip, 15, 21
Warfield, Philip 1751, 21
Warfield, Philip m/1801, 150
Warfield, Phyllis, 41
Warfield, Polly, 7
Warfield, Polly 1772, 51
Warfield, R. Dorsey, 149
Warfield, R. Katherine 1877, 147
Warfield, R. O. D. 1844, Dr., 150
Warfield, Rachael, 68
Warfield, Rachael C. 1837, 17
Warfield, Rachel, 6, 8, 20, 22, 23, 30, 98, 99
Warfield, Rachel 1681, 5
Warfield, Rachel 1731, 97
Warfield, Rachel 1760, 61

Warfield, Rachel 1761, 12
Warfield, Rachel m/1803, 150
Warfield, Rachel Virginia 1912, 41
Warfield, Randolph Ridgely, 33
Warfield, Raymond C., 128
Warfield, Raymond C. 1896, 116
Warfield, Raymond Curtis 1952, 89
Warfield, Raymond Lafayette 1890, 87
Warfield, Raymond Lafayette, Jr. 1937, 88
Warfield, Rebecca, 7, 51, 105
Warfield, Rebecca Elizabeth 1868, 65
Warfield, Rebecca m/1886, 150
Warfield, Rebecca Pollock, 52
Warfield, Rebecca Ridgely, 52
Warfield, Rebecca Tilton, 51
Warfield, Reuben, 30, 31, 34
Warfield, Reuben Dorsey 1871, 41
Warfield, Rezin, 31, 108
Warfield, Rezin 1740, 98
Warfield, Richard, 6, 7, 8, 11, 23, 27, 31, 106
Warfield, Richard 1646, 1, 6, 8, 10, 11, 17, 97
Warfield, Richard Benson, 6
Warfield, Richard Bryan 1973, 138
Warfield, Richard D. 1830, 16
Warfield, Richard Hardy 1946, 118
Warfield, Richard m/1780, 150
Warfield, Richard m/1803, 22
Warfield, Richard, Jr., 8, 32
Warfield, Richard, Jr. 1677, 4, 97
Warfield, Ridgely Brown, 47
Warfield, Rispah, 68
Warfield, Robert, 52, 67, 70, 132, 133, 145
Warfield, Robert 1749, 59
Warfield, Robert 1790, 67, 69
Warfield, Robert A., 134
Warfield, Robert Clarence 1861, 69
Warfield, Robert E. 1940, 87
Warfield, Robert Edward 1909, 150
Warfield, Robert H. 1835, 68
Warfield, Robert Leroy 1889, 70
Warfield, Robert m/1820, 150

Warfield, Robert Meredith 1898, 120
Warfield, Roderick, 19
Warfield, Roland M., 116
Warfield, Rosalba, 54
Warfield, Rosalie, 128
Warfield, Rosalie Hilton 1824, 150
Warfield, Rose 1906, 133
Warfield, Rose Marie, 133
Warfield, Roy Day 1893, 115
Warfield, Roy Day, Jr. 1923, 116
Warfield, Rufus, 31
Warfield, Russell S. 1899, 119
Warfield, Ruth, 13, 14, 22, 28, 51, 52, 89, 99
Warfield, Ruth 1756, 61
Warfield, Ruth 1789, 6, 8
Warfield, Ruth Ann 1931, 142
Warfield, Ruth Elizabeth Gaither 1836, 65
Warfield, Ruth Ethel 1895, 116
Warfield, Ruth m/1802, 150
Warfield, Ruth S., 32, 94
Warfield, Sally, 51
Warfield, Samuel, 7, 27
Warfield, Samuel Dorsey 1873, 135
Warfield, Samuel Harwood 1824, 150
Warfield, Samuel J., 60
Warfield, Samuel m/1727, 6
Warfield, Sarah, 6, 8, 20, 22, 29, 32, 52, 68, 98, 99, 105, 107, 108
Warfield, Sarah 1734, 98
Warfield, Sarah 1762, 61
Warfield, Sarah 1797, 124
Warfield, Sarah 1845, 121
Warfield, Sarah A. d/1885, 150
Warfield, Sarah Ann 1843, 130
Warfield, Sarah Ann m/1833, 150
Warfield, Sarah B. 1746, 11
Warfield, Sarah d/1821, 14, 20, 95
Warfield, Sarah E. 1856, 138
Warfield, Sarah Elizabeth 1861, 17
Warfield, Sarah Elizabeth 1981, 87, 113
Warfield, Sarah L. d/1962, 150
Warfield, Sarah Lavinia 1852, 112
Warfield, Sarah m/1783, 105

Warfield, Sarah m/1792, 150
Warfield, Sarah m/1816, 150
Warfield, Sarah T. m/1867, 150
Warfield, Scott Welty 1890, 120
Warfield, Seth, 21, 23, 31
Warfield, Seth 1723, 27
Warfield, Seth H., Jr., 40
Warfield, Seth Henry 1904, 40
Warfield, Seth Leonard, 41
Warfield, Seth Washington 1805, 32, 38, 99
Warfield, Seth Washington 1856, 32
Warfield, Seth Washington 1870, 40
Warfield, Seth, III, 27
Warfield, Seth, IV, 27
Warfield, Seth, Jr., 27
Warfield, Shelley, 138
Warfield, Shirley Ann 1934, 137
Warfield, Sophia, 99
Warfield, Surratt D., 23
Warfield, Surratt Dickerson 1787, 23
Warfield, Surratt Dickerson, Jr. 1820, 16
Warfield, Surratt Dickerson, Sr. 1787, 12, 15
Warfield, Surratt R. 1846, 16
Warfield, Susan 1833, 31
Warfield, Susan Virginia, 60
Warfield, Susanna m/1806, 150
Warfield, Susannah 1796, 105
Warfield, T. W. 1849, 151
Warfield, Tabitha, 7
Warfield, Temperance, 7
Warfield, Terecia 1848, 16
Warfield, Teresa Ann 1954, 135
Warfield, Terrence Wayne 1946, 138
Warfield, Terri, 92
Warfield, Theodore, 134
Warfield, Thomas, 6, 7, 9, 12, 27
Warfield, Thomas 1770, 105
Warfield, Thomas Barr, 51
Warfield, Thomas Beale, 7
Warfield, Thomas Benson, 6
Warfield, Thomas John, 19, 53
Warfield, Thomas O., 134
Warfield, Thomas O. 1904, 134

Warfield, Thomas Owings, 134
Warfield, Thomas Wallace 1833, 64
Warfield, Thomas Wallace, Jr. 1875, 65
Warfield, Thomas William 1947, 138
Warfield, Thomas Worthington, 14
Warfield, Titus W. 1856, 83
Warfield, Truman R., 128
Warfield, Vachel, 7, 29, 50
Warfield, Vera M., 116
Warfield, Viola V. 1895, 151
Warfield, Violet, 134
Warfield, Virginia A., 127
Warfield, Virginia L., 133
Warfield, Walter 1760, 104
Warfield, Walter Hamilton 1865, 114
Warfield, Walter, Doctor, 100
Warfield, Warner Washington 1787, 19, 53
Warfield, Warren, 134
Warfield, Watkins, 132
Warfield, Webb, 70
Warfield, Welsh, 8
Warfield, Wesley G. 1859, 124
Warfield, Wilbur Newton 1874, 137
Warfield, William, 22, 31, 52, 67, 94
Warfield, William 1778, 21
Warfield, William 1851, 76
Warfield, William C., 61, 133, 134
Warfield, William Carr, 133
Warfield, William Christian, Reverend, 104
Warfield, William d/1877, 151
Warfield, William E., 129
Warfield, William Edwin 1909, Colonel, 87
Warfield, William F. 1841, 16
Warfield, William F. 1856, 119
Warfield, William F., Jr. 1902, 120
Warfield, William G. 1883, 136
Warfield, William H. 1868, 86, 113
Warfield, William H. m/1892, 151
Warfield, William Henry, 19, 54
Warfield, William Henry, 1807, Lieutenant, 104
Warfield, William Hinks 1815, 130

Warfield, William Lucas, 6
Warfield, William M. 1890, 144
Warfield, William Pollock, 51
Warfield, William R. 1844, 75
Warfield, William Ridgely 1807, 54
Warfield, William Ridgely, Jr., 55
Warfield, William Smith, 21
Warfield, William Thompson 1866, 39
Warfield, William Wallace, 60
Warfield, William Woodward, 108
Warfield, William Wright 1858, 112
Warfield, Wilson E., 129
Warfield, Zachariah 1765, 104
Warfield, Zadock m/1801, 151
Warner, Henry, 66
Warner, Julia Rogers 1876, 66
Warthen, Brice Thomas Beall, 9
Warthen, Drusy Ann, 148
Warthen, Emma Warfield, 131
Washington, George, 100
Waters, Asenah, 98
Waters, Ignatius, 61, 104
Waters, Jacob, Colonel, 60
Waters, John, 105
Waters, Joseph, 98
Waters, Susan, 60
Waters, Walter Warfield, 61
Watkins, Alonzo Claggett 1867, 88
Watkins, Ariana Worthington 1769, 22
Watkins, Avie C. 1903, 92
Watkins, Dorothy Elizabeth 1900, 88
Watkins, Eleanor C., 54
Watkins, Gassaway 1752, Colonel, 54, 55
Watkins, Janice, 116
Watkins, Jeremiah 1739, 53
Watkins, John Oliver Thomas 1860, 92
Watkins, John R., Jr., 41
Watkins, John W. C. 1859, 83
Watkins, Mamie Cleveland 1884, 84
Watkins, Margaret, 53
Watkins, Margaret Gassaway, 55
Watkins, Nicholas, 22

Watkins, No given name, 41
Watkins, Rachel 1804, 136
Watkins, Richard, Captain, 54
Watkins, Sallie, 22
Watkins, Sarah Ann, 22
Watkins, Thomas 1736, 22
Watkins, Thomas Coke 1800, 146
Watkins, Tobias C. 1859, 84
Watson, Julia, 65
Wayman, Amelia, 11
Wayman, John, 11
Webb, Constance Ann 1926, 71
Webb, Ellen, Mrs., 28
Webb, Francis Clarence 1866, 71
Webb, Francis Ignatius Devereaux
    1833, 69, 71
Webb, Francis Warfield 1893, 71
Webb, George T., 145
Webb, Gladys Elizabeth 1891, 71
Webb, Margaret 1861, 69
Webb, Miriam Horine 1930, 72
Webster, Margaret Anna 1821, 121
Webster, Mary R. 1830, 107
Weddle, James, 24
Weeks, Mary, 56
Weismantel, Laura J., 42
Welling, Elizabeth, 31
Wellman, John, 6
Wells, Alexander 1805, 102
Wells, Ann C. 1813, 102
Wells, Bazaleel, 102
Wells, Bazaleel, Jr. 1808, 102
Wells, Catherine 1798, 102
Wells, Elizabeth, 60
Wells, Frank A. 1813, 102
Wells, Hezekiah Griffith 1811, 102
Wells, James Ross 1801, 102
Wells, Mary 1822, 102
Wells, Rebecca 1799, 102
Wells, Samuel D. 1803, 102
Wells, Sarah Griffith 1818, 102
Welsh, Amelia, 28
Welsh, Amos W. 1818, 34
Welsh, Brunette 1829, 34
Welsh, Caroline 1832, 30
Welsh, Charles, 27, 28, 29

Welsh, Charles 1746, 34
Welsh, Charles Stanhope, 28
Welsh, Columbus O'Donnell 1827, 28
Welsh, Cornelia 1822, 30
Welsh, Elizabeth Ann 1826, 34
Welsh, Greenberry 1809, 30
Welsh, Henry, 28
Welsh, Jeanette 1826, 30
Welsh, John, 48
Welsh, John 1672, Colonel, 6
Welsh, John, Captain, 27, 29
Welsh, Lucretia Griffith 1799, 46
Welsh, Lycurgus Gassaway 1820, 34
Welsh, Lydia, 27, 28
Welsh, Lydia Dorsey 1790, 48, 55
Welsh, Mary Ann, 28
Welsh, Mary Ann 1820, 30
Welsh, Mary Elizabeth 1837, 34
Welsh, Middleton 1810, 30
Welsh, Philip 1765, 46
Welsh, Rachel Griffith 1790, 48
Welsh, Rezin 1774, 29
Welsh, Rezin Hammond, 28
Welsh, Rezin, Jr. 1816, 30
Welsh, Ruth, 27, 28
Welsh, Samuel, 48
Welsh, Sarah 1711, 6
Welsh, Thomas, 7
Welsh, Warren 1793, 33
Welsh, Washington Warfield 1823,
    34
Welter, Francis Easby, 35
Welter, Julie Ann, 35
Welter, Kate Frances, 35
Welter, Kelly Maureen, 35
Welter, Tricia Ann, 35
Weltz, Mollie K., 148
West, Martha, 19, 54
Westley, William, 7
Whalen, Clarence, 117
Whitaker, Christopher Thomas, 37
Whitaker, Corrine Dee, 37
Whitaker, David Miles 1953, 37
Whitaker, Ernest Jennet 1916, 36
Whitaker, James Miles 1942, 36
Whitaker, Jamie Michele 1972, 36

Whitaker, Jordan Cahill, 37
Whitaker, Marie Katherine Jennet
    Worlow, 37
Whitaker, Miles Sheeran, 37
Whitaker, Nicholas Miles, 37
Whitaker, Patrick Joseph 1954, 37
Whitaker, Ryland Grant, 37
Whitaker, Stacey Kathryn, 37
Whitaker, Stephanie Catherine, 37
Whitaker, Stephen Jennet 1948, 37
Whitaker, Thomas Michael 1951, 37
Whitaker, William Ernest 1946, 37
White Hall, 15, 98
White, Anne, 45
White, Elizabeth, 108
White, Frank Malcolm 1890, 42
White, Georgina 1848, 47
White, Isaac, 145
White, Mary Maxine 1918, 42
White, No given name, 127
Wiener, No given name, 92
William the Conqueror, 28
Williams, Achsah Elizabeth 1809,
    110
Williams, Alpheus, 110
Williams, Alpheus B. 1818, 110
Williams, Benjamin Joseph 1813, 110
Williams, Eswell, 110
Williams, Harriet C. 1839, 85
Williams, Margaret, 7
Williams, Nicholas 1815, 110
Wilson, Ann Eliza, 102
Wilson, Rebecca A., 21
Wincopen Neck, 8, 97
Windsor, Duchess of, 28
Windsor, Edmund L. 1810, 74
Windsor, Mary 1787, 74, 93
Windsor, Zadock 1781, 74
Winn, John, 115
Wise, Walter Dent, Doctor, 65
Wood, Guy, 129
Wood, Guy Holland, 129
Wood, Sarah, 60
Woodfield, Ann, 6
Woodfield, Barbara, 141
Woodfield, Della Waters 1879, 80

Woodport, 35
Woodward, Amos, 10
Woodward, Elizabeth, 98, 106
Woodward, Maria, 98
Woodward, William, 98, 106
Worthington Range, 45
Worthington, Ann, 10
Worthington, Charles Alexander, 107
Worthington, Elizabeth 1717, 28, 51,
    53, 105
Worthington, John, Jr., 10
Worthington, Sarah, 10
Worthington, Sarah 1696, 45
Worthington, Thomas, 10
Worthington, Thomas 1691, 12
Worthington, Thomas I., 107
Worthington, Thomasine 1724, 12
Wright, Fuller, 132
Wynkoop, Ann M., 148
Wyville, Lewis 1826, 143
Wyville, Sarah, 128, 129, 144

—Y—

Yate's Contrivance, 100
Yates, Benjamin 1707, 5
Yates, Eleanor 1709, 5
Yates, George, 5
Yates, George, III 1701, 5
Yates, George, IV 1727, 5
Yates, George, Jr. 1674, 5
Yates, Joanna, 5
Yates, Joshua 1703, 5
Yates, Mary 1711, 5
Yates, Michael 1722, 5
Yates, Rachel 1713, 5
Yates, Samuel 1704, 5
Yates, William, 5
Yeadhall, Henrietta, 6
Yeadhall, No given name, 7
Yellott, Hannah, 107
Yoft, Paula, 140
Yost, Ann Regina, 27
Young, David W. 1836, 125
Young, Emanuel J. 1844, 125
Young, J. R., 61

200

Young, Jacob 1796, 124
Young, John F., 149
Young, Joseph D. 1845, 125
Young, Mary E. 1844, 125
Young, Mary Evelyn 1842, 91
Young, Sarah A. 1850, 125

—Z—

Zachary, Mary Olivia, 62
Zachary, William, Captain, 62
Zeigler, Airy E. 1846, 25
Zeigler, Alice B. 1862, 26
Zeigler, Alva W. 1866, 26
Zeigler, Arthur E. 1867, 25
Zeigler, Asa H. 1838, 25
Zeigler, Clarence 1869, 25
Zeigler, David A. 1813, 25
Zeigler, David F. 1870, 26

Zeigler, David T. 1847, 26
Zeigler, Eda M. 1866, 25
Zeigler, Francis T. 1840, 25
Zeigler, Herbert E. 1869, 25
Zeigler, Ida J. 1856, 26
Zeigler, Jesse L. 1851, 26
Zeigler, John Wilson 1842, 25
Zeigler, Julia 1844, 25
Zeigler, Laura E. 1869, 26
Zeigler, Levi B. 1836, 25
Zeigler, Lillian L. 1863, 25
Zeigler, Mary E. 1844, 26
Zeigler, Mary F. 1847, 25
Zepp, Ellen, 28
Zepp, Ephraim, 28
Zimmerman, Curtis, 116
Zollikoffer, Mary E., 94